'A must-read book for those concerned with evidence-based truth-telling, which in this book has been shown to discredit the Pascoe thesis of social evolutionism as the "true" basis of Aboriginal economy before and after European colonisation.

Sutton and Walshe show that Pascoe tried, and failed, to overturn over a century of anthropological and archaeological study, analysis and documentation, in addition to Aboriginal oral testimony, of the ways of life, governance, socioeconomic behaviour, material, technological and spiritual accomplishments and preferences of Aboriginal people in classical society and on the cusp of colonisation.

This corpus of research overwhelmingly suggests that ancestors of Aboriginal people before and after European colonisation were predominantly hunters-gatherers-fishers, not agriculturalists. As Sutton points out, the Old People were proud but humble about economic practices of the ancestors, and the Old People still are.

That should give every young Aboriginal person in Australia a reason to also be proud of ancestors as hunters-gatherers-fishers.'

Dr Kellie Pollard, Wiradjuri archaeologist, lecturer
and researcher, Charles Darwin University

'I welcome this deeply thoughtful and scholarly response to *Dark Emu*. Peter Sutton and Keryn Walshe pay Bruce Pascoe's work the respect of a forensic analysis. This richly satisfying study draws on generations of research and cross-cultural dialogues on Country to offer a complex portrait of First Nations cultures, economies and spirituality. *Farmers or Hunter-gatherers?* is infused with a profound esteem for the unique achievements of humanity on this continent over millennia.'

Emeritus Professor Tom Griffiths,
Australian National University

T0285108

FARMERS OR HUNTER-GATHERERS?

THE *DARK EMU* DEBATE

PETER SUTTON and KERYN WALSHE

MELBOURNE
UNIVERSITY
PRESS

MELBOURNE UNIVERSITY PRESS
An imprint of Melbourne University Publishing Limited
Level 1, 715 Swanston Street, Carlton, Victoria 3053, Australia
mup-contact@unimelb.edu.au
www.mup.com.au

f ⓨ ⊙

First published 2021
Text © 2021, Peter Sutton and Keryn Walshe
Design and typography © Melbourne University Publishing Limited, 2021

Every attempt has been made to locate the copyright holders for material quoted in this book. Any person or organisation that may have been overlooked or misattributed may contact the publisher.

Text design and typesetting by Cannon Typesetting
Cover design by Philip Campbell Design
Cover image photo by Jade Stephens on Unsplash

A catalogue record for this book is available from the National Library of Australia

NATIONAL LIBRARY OF AUSTRALIA

9780522877854 (paperback)
9780522877861 (ebook)

For Enkidu and Gilgamesh

About this book

Chapters 12 and 13 and Appendix 1 of this book were written by Keryn Walshe. The remainder of the book was written by Peter Sutton.

In this assessment we mainly use the original 2014 edition of the book *Dark Emu* when referring to its contents, and page references refer to this edition. Minor alterations to that text were made in the 2018 edition, and we reference these accordingly where mentioned.

Note that parts of quotations that are in in italics are to be understood as 'emphasis added', not emphasis in the original, unless the latter is stated.

Aboriginal and Torres Strait Islander peoples are advised that the book contains the names and images of people who have passed away.

Contents

TORRES STRAIT
○ Murray Island

Cape York

Bathurst Island

Darwin

Arnhem Land

Groote
Eylandt   Cape
          Keerweer
Aurukun

Cape
York
Peninsula

Princess Charlotte Bay

Daly River

Careening Bay

Top End

GULF OF
CARPENTARIA

Mornington
Island

Mitchell River

Cooktown

○ Cairns

Kimberley

Broome ○

Townsville

Tanami
Desert

Balgo ○

Charters Towers ○

West Cape

Pilbara

NORTHERN
TERRITORY

Gibson
Desert

Central Australia

Diamantina River

QUEENSLAND

Gascoyne River

Shark Bay

WESTERN
AUSTRALIA

Tomkinson
Ranges

Oodnadatta ○

Simpson
Desert

Brisbane
River

Barwon River

Bunya
Mountains

Brisbane

Murchison River

Great Victoria Desert

SOUTH
AUSTRALIA

Lake Killalpaninna

WA goldfields

Lake Eyre

Lake Torrens

Flinders Ranges

Darling River

NEW
SOUTH WALES

Bogan River

Perth
Rottnest Island ○   Fremantle

Riverina

Adelaide

Murrumbidgee River

Sydney ○ ○ Port Jackson

Fleurieu Peninsula
Kangaroo Island

Gariwerd
(The Grampians)

Murray River

Canberra

ACT

Lake Alexandria

Western
District

VICTORIA

Australian
Alps

0   100 200 300 400km

Glenelg River

Moyjil

Colac ○ ○ Melbourne

Port Philip

Gippsland

SOUTHERN OCEAN

Flinders Island

TASMANIA

Huon River

Bruny Island

1
The *Dark Emu* debate

This book is about a debate over how Australia's First Peoples lived, and made a living economically, before conquest by the British Empire. Were they farmers, hunter-gatherers, or something in between?

The issues have come to be debated by a wider than merely academic public since Bruce Pascoe published his book *Dark Emu: Black Seeds: Agriculture or Accident?* in 2014. Here, Dr Keryn Walshe and I approach the relevant facts and interpretations from a scientific and scholarly point of view, as free as possible from identity politics and racial polemics.

I have described our focus as on Australia 'before conquest', not 'before settlement', for some very good reasons. Australia was not 'settled' in or after 1788 by British, Asian and other non-Aboriginal people, as if the lands were void of human societies. 'Settlement' is accurately applied to the occupation of previously uninhabited lands, such as the Norwegian migration to Ísland (Iceland) and the Māori migration to Aotearoa (New Zealand). It is not an accurate description of the uninvited imperial British invasion of Australian First Nations' territories, followed by the subjugation and displacement of the Indigenous Australians who were the lands' owners. While this usurpation was happening, Aboriginal land tenure systems were ignored—and replaced, in the eyes of the colonials, by property laws imported from England. It was not until 1992 that Australian law recognised that pre-existing Indigenous titles of 1788 could, to varying degrees, have survived these usurpations, and the living native-title holders of certain lands and waters could be acknowledged as such.

The real 'discoverers', 'pioneers' and 'early settlers' of Australia— the people who actually 'opened up the country'—were the people who arrived around 50,000–55,000 years ago (see Appendix 1), when what are now New Guinea, mainland Australia and Tasmania were a single landmass known today as Sahul. They are rightly called the First Australians, and their descendants have in recent years been accurately referred to as First Nations People. For longer, in recent centuries, they have been known as Aborigines or Aboriginal people. These terms also refer to First People, because they derive from the Latin expression *ab origine*, which means 'from the beginning'. There is therefore nothing at all disrespectful about 'Aboriginal' as a term, and we use it here accordingly. It stresses primacy. We also refer to the pre-colonial Aboriginal population as the Old People, because that is what their descendants commonly call them, and because it also is a term of respect.

Our subject is a now-famous book about Australia's First People and their way of life before conquest: *Dark Emu*, by Bruce Pascoe.[1] In *Dark Emu*, Pascoe sets out to overthrow what he regards as the falsities of past accounts of classical (that is, pre-conquest) Aboriginal ways of life. He argues that, in contrast to what most Australians have been told and believe, at the time of European invasion Aboriginal Australians practised agriculture, stored food, built and lived in large numbers in substantial dwellings and permanent villages, and sewed clothes. He argues further that Aboriginal people having lived in this manner constitutes evidence of their 'advancement', of a 'level of development' that has not previously been recognised. He writes to correct these untruths and enlighten his readers.

We contend that Pascoe is broadly wrong, both about what Australians have been told of pre-conquest Aboriginal society and about the nature of that society itself. We also take issue with the notion that recognisably European 'settled' ways of living, focused on material and technical 'development' in food production, are in any way to be valued more than the ways of living that existed in Australia before invasion. In the light of these contentions, and the extensive evidence we present in support of them, we ask how and why *Dark Emu* has become the phenomenon that it has. Is it time for all Australians to take more responsibility for learning about Aboriginal society, and to demand more careful attention to questions of historical and other truths?

Throughout *Dark Emu*, Pascoe puts a high value on technological and economic complexity as a standard of a people's worth, and then seeks out examples of these complexities in classical Aboriginal life.

In his words, such complexities are signs of 'advancement'. He doesn't employ a term for lack of advancement except for the 'social backwardness' he says others have attributed to a perceived lack of pottery and storage among Australians before conquest. He says, 'This attitude prejudices opinion about the level of development of Aboriginal and Torres Strait Islander people' (page 105).

As noted, the key areas in which Pascoe seeks to find corrective examples to false estimates of this 'level of development' are agricultural food production and storage, substantial dwellings, settlement in permanent villages, high numbers of people in the villages, and the sewing of clothes. The evidence he provides for these subjects is selected in such a way as to compensate for what he believes is a falsely assumed simplicity or crudity—even a 'brutishness' (page 100) before conquest by the British Empire—attributed to Aboriginal people by today's Australians.

All of these subjects belong to the world of the material. For that reason, they may be more readily grasped by the average reader than the complexities of Aboriginal mental and aesthetic culture: those highly intricate webs of kinship, mythology, ritual performance, grammars, visual arts and land tenure systems. *Dark Emu* does not enter into the non-physical complexities to any real degree. Like its major sources, Bill Gammage's *The Biggest Estate on Earth*[2] and Rupert Gerritsen's *Australia and the Origins of Agriculture*,[3] it is largely confined to material economic behaviour and often separated from meaning, from intent, from values, from culture, from the spiritual, and from the emotional. This disconnect, we suggest, is the book's biggest gap.

In the present book, Keryn Walshe brings to her chapters (12 and 13) a wealth of scholarship and field site work with Aboriginal collaborators, as an archaeologist.

My own contributions draw on wide reading in the anthropology and linguistics of Aboriginal Australia, but, most importantly, are derived from facts and insights I have been given directly by senior Aboriginal people of knowledge. I am here passing these on, and as such, giving back. Over the past fifty years I have been carrying out collaborative research with Aboriginal people, in many cases in remote regions, including Cape York Peninsula (CYP), western Arnhem Land, Daly River, the Murranji Track, Central Australia, and the corner country of the Lake Eyre basin. I have also worked with people in urban and rural regions. In three cases (eastern Cape York, western Cape York, and north-central Northern Territory), I have been taken as a son by senior men and incorporated into their families (Johnny Flinders, Victor Wolmby, Pharlap Dixon Jalyirri). I have given the names and language groups of my principal teachers in the Acknowledgements. Under the tutorship of those Aboriginal mentors, I have recorded, on site, several thousand places and their cultural and historical significance, including in many cases their botanical and faunal resources and how those resources were garnered and in what seasons. Three men of highly specialised botanical learning stand out: Noel Peemuggina and Ray Wolmby (Wik people, western CYP), and Pompey Raymond (Jingulu, Murranji Track region, Northern Territory).

I have recorded many Aboriginal languages and learned to speak three by month after month sitting at the feet of teachers whose languages were still spoken, yet unwritten. And—I note this as it is relevant to later discussions—I've done my share of hunting and foraging in days gone by, when I was the only non-local person living with Wik people for months in the wetlands country north of the Kendall River in CYP in the 1970s. All of our protein and fat came from hunting.

The positive contribution of *Dark Emu*
Through *Dark Emu*, Pascoe has engendered much interest within Australia in the history of the nation, the traditional ways of life of Australian Aboriginal peoples, and past and present relations between Aboriginal and non-Aboriginal Australians. He builds awareness of the fact that British Empire colonists in Australia assumed their own superiority and justified conquest, slaughter and massive land theft on that basis (pages 12–13, 154). Internationally, the British Empire was the greatest kleptocracy in human history (see opposite).[4]

Pascoe popularises the work of Bill Gammage on the evidence for pre-1788 environmental management, principally through the use of fire, and on related topics (pages 20, 26, 42, 54, 79, 117, 121, 123, 128).

He also brings attention to Gerritsen's *Australia and the Origins of Agriculture*, an amateur but densely scholarly and demanding work that has been controversial among specialists.[5] This is his most frequently used source.

Pascoe also popularises part of the important work by Paul Memmott, who presented the first comprehensive survey of classical-period Aboriginal dwellings.[6]

The British Empire and its 'races' in 1937.

Pascoe contradicts the false belief, perhaps held by some, that all Aboriginal people were naked all of the time. Some Aboriginal people sewed animal skins into cloaks (page 89).

He criticises the uninformed view that classical Aboriginal society consisted of constantly nomadic people who simply lived off nature's bounty, were not ecological agents, did not stay in one place for more than a few days and did not store resources (for example, page 12).

And he gives considerable attention to the storage of foods (pages 105–14), this being a useful corrective to ignorance of Aboriginal storage methods.

Even here, however, the answer to the false belief that Aboriginal people stored nothing is not to assert that they universally amassed major stores of food. Many people stored a few food sources for shorter or longer periods, differing by region, and some stored almost nothing. Different climates set up different challenges for storage. Deserts were more friendly than hot, humid tropics. After long experience with bush-dwelling people in the Mitchell River area of CYP in the 1930s, trained anthropologist Lauriston Sharp noted that they were at one extreme end of the storage spectrum: the only item they stored beyond a day or two was the nonda plum.[7]

To Pascoe's examples, a good number of them drawn from Gerritsen, could be added many more. Philip Clarke has provided a brief survey of evidence as to traditional storage that complements Pascoe's.[8] Clarke's examples are mainly, but not only, drawn from the arid zone. One could also add, from the wet monsoon belt, the following. In the 1970s in the case of the Wik region of CYP, where I did intensive fieldwork with people who in many cases had been born and raised beyond the reach of the British Empire, I found that:

> Limited food storage was practised. Nonda plums (*Parinari nonda F. Muell. ex. Benth.*) were dried on the rooves of shelters, or collected dry from the ground (the dry form even has a different name), and were kept for some weeks after their season of superabundance. Long yams (*Dioscorea transversa R. Br.*) were stored in the sand for weeks and even months.[9] Long-necked turtles might survive a day or two trussed up, and in the Big Lake area barramundi is said to have been cooked, wrapped in paperbark, and buried in the cool earth for eating days later. Most food, however, was eaten within twenty-four hours.[10]

Labels and definitions

In the course of discussing *Dark Emu* in this book, we engage with the problem of labels for kinds of people that are focused on their economic lives. This problem looms large in *Dark Emu*. It should not be lightly dismissed on the grounds that names for types of subsistence are merely tags. The debate here is over not just labels but the way subsistence types are classified and compared.

In a talk given in 2018, Pascoe said:

> *In 2014 I wrote a book, Dark Emu, which exploded the myth that Aboriginal people were mere hunters and gatherers and did nothing with the land. I wrote the book because I found it hard to convince Australians that Aboriginal people were farming. Using colonial journals, the sources Australians hold to be true, I was able to form a radically different view of Australian history. Aboriginal people were farming. There's no other conclusion to draw.*[11]

A little further on in this speech, he refers to '*the ancient agricultural economy' of Australia.* This central plank of Pascoe's theory is one we put to the test.

Pascoe's message is built on a simple distinction between what he calls 'mere' hunter-gatherers, on the one hand, and farmers; or between 'mere' hunting and gathering on one hand and 'agriculture' on the other. We consider that the evidence, in fact, reveals a positioning of the Aboriginal people of 1788 somewhere between these two extremes: they were complex hunter-gatherers, not simple farmers. The Old People in 1788 had developed ways of managing and benefiting from their landscape that went beyond just hunting and just gathering but did not involve gardening or farming. They were ecological agents who worked *with* the environment, rather than, usually, against it. They frequently used slow-burning fires to make their landscapes more liveable. However, they did not cut down bush to clear the land, plough and hoe the soil in preparation for planting, or then sow stored seed or tubers or rootstock in gardens or in fields.[12]

As is often pointed out, all human beings were hunter-gatherers—also known as foragers—for over 90 per cent of our history as a species, until the agricultural revolutions that began around 11,000 years ago in south-west Asia, in the Fertile Crescent. Agriculture also developed later and independently in parts of China, New Guinea, Sub-Saharan Africa, Central and South America, and the Mississippi Basin of the eastern United States of America.[13] Agriculture thus developed in what are archaeologically rather recent times on all the inhabited continents except Australia. Here, foraging, augmented by various ways of modifying the environment, was a highly successful economic adaptation, as it also remained in south-west Africa, the sub-Arctic Circle, parts of California and a number of other locations around the world, until the impact of colonisation.[14]

We do not propose here to engage in a lengthy coverage of the various debates that have been held over the semantics of the words 'foraging' (also referred to as 'hunting, fishing and gathering'), 'horticulture' or 'agriculture'. Our own working definitions used in this book are both readily understood by non-specialists and compatible with definitions given in the authoritative *Dictionary of Anthropology*.[15] For example: 'Foragers are peoples who subsist on hunting, gathering, and fishing with no domesticated plants, and no domesticated animals except the dog.'[16] As discussed elsewhere in this book, this needs to be augmented with recognition of foragers' roles as skilled ecological agents.

By contrast, 'Horticulture is a mode of subsistence agriculture that involves small scale farming or gardening practiced with simple hand

tools, such as the digging stick, and without the use of the plow or irrigation.'[17] One of the main forms of horticulture is 'swidden horticulture',
also known as 'shifting cultivation' or 'slash-and-burn'. An area of forest
is cleared and burned, and the area is gardened, and later abandoned,
after exhaustion of nutrients, for a new plot. Swidden horticulture is
practised on the larger northern and eastern islands of Torres Strait, but
was practised nowhere in pre-conquest mainland Australia.[18]

By contrast again, 'Agriculture is the deliberate growing and harvesting of plants, but the term is often extended to include the raising of
animals ... Agriculture always involves more, technically and culturally,
than just planting and harvesting crops.'[19]

The difference between horticulture and farming is usually
regarded as mainly one of scale, between small-scale cultivation and
field cultivation respectively. In German the distinction is between
Gartenbau—'horticulture', from 'garden (*Garten*) building (*Bau*)'—and
Ackerbau—'agriculture', from 'field (*Acker*) building (*Bau*)'.[20]

We regard Peter Bellwood's definition of 'cultivation' as appropriate,
and one that would have very wide support:

> *Cultivation*, an essential component of any agricultural system,
> defines a sequence of human activity whereby crops are planted
> (as a seed or vegetative part), protected, harvested, then deliberately
> sown again, usually in a prepared plot of ground, in the following
> growing season.[21]

Some peoples combine two or even three modes of subsistence. For
example, some Torres Strait Islanders, depending on which islands,
traditionally combine fishing, hunting and gathering with a little
horticulture, while others combine fishing, hunting and gathering with
intensive horticulture.

Dark Emu sets up a simple distinction between agriculturalists living
in 'permanent housing' and the 'hapless wandering' of the 'mere hunter-
gatherer',[22] choosing to conclude that the former is the truth and the
latter a widely accepted lie about Aboriginal Australia before colonisation. There seems to be an assumption here that subsistence based on
hunting and gathering is itself not complex. This is far from the truth.

Setting aside the various proactive ways in which Aboriginal people
at conquest modified their environment and its resources, the hunting,
fishing and gathering economy was far more complex than might be

imagined from the word 'mere'. As an economic process it was at least as complex as gardening or farming, if not much more so. Agriculture can get by with knowledge of a small range of flora and fauna. Hunting and gathering can't.

Hunting and gathering in pre-colonial Australia required fine-grained knowledge of hundreds of species and their habitats, annual cycles, names and generic classifications; of methods for processing them and for preparing them as food, as tools, as bodily decoration, and as ritual paraphernalia. It required what repeatedly seemed to colonial newcomers to be almost supernatural eyesight, seeing things in the far distance or among foliage that no colonial could see.

Allied to this, it required the ability to track game using often infinitesimal traces left on the ground or in foliage. It required tremendous spatial and narrative memory, of the kind many of us now have very much lost through reliance on paper maps, written records and Google Maps. It required high skills in lithics (stone tool manufacture) in order to reveal from within the rough stone the elegant tools now found in museums and in the bush. And it required deft and precise skills in using weapons and wielding digging sticks, nets, lures and traps. Spearing fish required the ability to calculate instantly how refraction through water needed to be corrected for during the throw (see below).

Even 'mere' hunter-gatherers would have been resource experts on their own ground, but Aboriginal people were hunter-gatherers-plus.

It might have been better if labels like 'hunter-gatherer' and 'horticulturist' and 'agriculturist' were not so prominent in these debates, as Harry Lourandos has proposed.[23] They can sometimes attract outdated evolutionary schemes that operate on the discredited 'primitive'

Bruce Yunkaporta spearing a stingray, Wooentoent, Kirke River, Cape York Peninsula, 1976.

versus 'advanced' scale, also known as social evolutionism. We provide evidence below that Pascoe has resurrected social evolutionism in his text, both in words and in the way records are evaluated in *Dark Emu*.

In *Dark Emu* the author uses the presence of ecological agency, such as the firing of country and the conservation of species or the storage of food, as a pathway to reclassifying pre-conquest Aboriginal people as an agricultural people. On this basis all human beings might have been classed as agricultural people for hundreds of thousands of years until the present. But this semantic shoehorning submerges a distinction that is not merely one of economic type, but one of sheer power. The differences between hunter-gatherers(-plus) and settled agricultural farming peoples have been played out in a series of unprecedented and cataclysmic shifts in human history. Bellwood, an authority on the emergence of agriculture, describes these shifts as 'episodes of massive cultural and linguistic punctuation'.[24]

The rapid emergence of settled crop-growing agricultural societies beginning about 11,000 years ago in south-west Asia, and from there reaching west to the British Isles by about 5000–4500 BP (before present), led to 'dramatic cultural change and population growth'.[25] It has been described by Israeli archaeologists Bar-Yosef and Kislev as 'a revolutionary subsistence strategy'.[26] This revolution in turn led to the conquest, displacement, assimilation and absorption of almost all of the foraging peoples of Europe within about 4000 years.

In turn, the descendants of those Neolithic farmers who moved west from the Levant region became the European nations that expanded themselves by way of colonial conquest around the globe, especially from the seventeenth century to the nineteenth. These agrarian societies were land-hungry, populous, technologically complex, armed with the modern weapons of the day, in charge of a range of domesticated animals, and imbued with the idea of their own superiority over 'natives' as part of the justification for their conquest of allegedly 'new' lands.

The shift from hunting and gathering to farming was therefore a quantum leap in human economics and geopolitical power, accompanied as it was—at least in the Eurasian case—by the unprecedented development of towns and cities, population explosion in fixed settlements, animal and wheeled transport, metals and the powerful weapons made from them, and a hierarchical social organisation that made large-scale warfare and the concerted invasion of other lands more than possible.

So, if the Old People of 1788 can be pigeonholed at all, we would prefer the label 'hunter-gatherers-plus'—not 'agricultural people', the badge of their conquerors. We go into the many varieties of 'plus' later.

Why didn't the Old People adopt agriculture?

The Australian people of the pre-conquest era did not avoid agriculture because they didn't know how plants grow. The proposition would be absurd, given they were acute observers of the plants around them and the plants' life cycles. Instead, they regarded the fertility and the reproductive spark that maintained plant populations via seeds to be spiritual, not a matter of secular human technology. Many have argued that Australia lacked plants and animals suitable for domestication and was limited by its aridity and uncertainty of rainfall, concluding that this prevented the development of agriculture. But others have pointed out that some Australian plant species are very similar to those that were being cultivated just to the north in Torres Strait or New Guinea.[27]

Plants suitable for domestication were introduced to north Australia before colonisation of that region. They were planted by visitors such as the Buginese and Macassans, and included betel nut palms, coconut palms and tamarind trees—but Aboriginal people did not adopt the practice of planting them.[28]

Coconuts also arrive irregularly on many of Australia's northern beaches, drifting in on the tides. That they have done so for a very long time is reflected in the words for coconut in several north Australian languages. While some are borrowed from English (for example, *guganat*, Burarra, *guginarr*, Yidiny), many are old Indigenous words, including *galuku* (Gupapuyngu) and *arlipwa* (Tiwi). Old words for coconut among CYP languages include *thiineth* (Wik-Ngathan), *kuunga* (Kuuku-Ya'u), *warapa* (Umpila), *olulul* (Wurriima), *gamyarr* (Morrobolam) and *wuyngkayi* (Umpithamu). There is no evidence that north Australian Aboriginal people created coconut plantations before colonisation; they did eat the coconut flesh from the nuts that drifted ashore.

Another reason why the 'lack of plants suitable for domestication' argument is flawed is that there are plenty of Australian trees with edible fruit that are readily propagated from either seed or rootstock or both, but that were not used to create orchards before colonisation. The macadamia nut, the lady apple, the nonda plum and the quandong are good examples among a very large number.

Can we be sure that an absence of Aboriginal horticulture in 1788 means that it had never been practised before then? A genetic study by Hunt, Moots and Matthews has found that the wild taro of an area near Cooktown, Queensland, breeds naturally, but the data do not exclude the possibility that it may have had a history of domestication in the past.[29] Note that another edible tuber found in the same location may have been introduced from the eastern Papuan tip, given that the Cooktown language has *wugay* for the yam species *Dioscorea sativa rotunda*. Ray Wood has sourced this term, and the equivalent term *kuthay* of north-east CYP and Torres Strait, to the eastern Papuan tip.[30] There is also the hypothesis that a species of banana (*Musa acuminata*), a wild taro (*Colocasia esculenta*) and the greater yam (*D. alata*), which are found in north and north-east Australia, may have been subject to experimental horticulture—an experiment later abandoned—during a period when Australia and New Guinea were still a single landmass, that is, more than 10,000 years ago.[31] The hypothesis remains unconfirmed.

Although domesticable species in Australia may have been limited, as a factor in the absence of adoption of agriculture it is more important that the Old People did not see any necessity to go beyond their existing environmental modifications, given their deep commitment to the maintenance of fertility through engagement with the spiritual powers left for them by the Dreaming. After all, even in regions on other continents where there were species eminently suitable for cultivation, human beings lived for countless centuries as hunter-gatherers before changing to being farmers. The economic switch was not triggered by the presence of domesticable species, but by something else, something cultural, a shift of mindset.

A reviewer of the manuscript of this book suggested that spiritual practices were no bar to the shift to agriculture in other societies. Plenty of other peoples who used religious practices to do with species propagation were also gardeners and farmers and had stopped being hunter-gatherers per se. 'Garden magic' was most famously reported from New Guinea by Bronislaw Malinowski in 1935.[32] But shifting from foraging to gardening-and-foraging does not entail the abandonment of spiritual beliefs and practices to do with the fertility of resources: it entails the augmenting of religious propagation, environmental agency and hunting, fishing and gathering with horticulture and its magic.

In Chapter 2, I provide plentiful evidence that this positive spiritual propagation was maintained in classical Australia by human reverence and direct action, but on the basis that the elemental forces of life are there forever, from the Dreaming, the spiritual ground of being. They are not created by human ingenuity. Humans can only stimulate the emergence of such latent powers in the cyclical regrowth of plants and animals, and in the supply of rain.

This commitment to the non-physical basis of reproduction in the biota was also the Old People's basis for resistance to the gardening and agriculture methods of their Melanesian neighbours at Cape York, and to those of the European colonists who tried so hard to convert them to agriculture, and who failed—not always, but mostly, at least for a time (see Chapter 6).[33]

Pascoe links gardening and cropping to the settled life—that is, to what is sometimes called sedentism. Given the extent to which *Dark Emu* owes a debt to the work of Bill Gammage, it is unfortunate that Pascoe effectively rejects him on the question of sedentism. Gammage said:

> Neither in Australia's richest nor poorest parts, by European standards, were people tempted to settle. Instead they quit their villages and eels, their crops and stores and templates, to walk their country.
>
> They were mobile. No livestock, no beast of burden anchored them. They did not stay in their houses or by their crops.[34]

Gammage also noted the way Aboriginal people rejected European gardening, and included the Torres Strait example that we discuss elsewhere:

> In the north they knew about farmers. Cape York people traded with Torres Strait gardeners, and Arnhem Landers watched Macassans and Baijini from the Indies till land and plant rice, tamarind and coconuts, build stone houses, wear cloth, make pottery and feed domestic fowls, dogs and cats. Some visited the Indies. None copied either group, instead maintaining typical Australian templates.[35]

Gammage's focus, like Pascoe's, is on defining the people's activities behaviourally and materially, not philosophically. This is economics without religion, something inconceivable to the Old People. Gammage argues, though, that they were farming but not farmers, given that they were doing most of the things farmers did but not all of them: 'So people burnt, tilled, planted, transplanted, watered, irrigated, weeded, thinned, cropped, stored and traded. On present evidence not all groups did all these, and few Tasmanians may have, but many mainlanders did. What farm process did they miss?'[36]

This sweeping passage is highly debatable, even with the caveats of 'not all groups' and 'few Tasmanians'. It bears the same crippling flaw as is found in Gerritsen's slippage from assembled fragments to continental Australian assertions, a flaw identified at the time by CSIRO research scientist Fiona Walsh:

> It will be debated if he [Gerritsen] has overstated the role of intensification and food production …
>
> Gerritsen has also, to some extent, located the practices and technologies that he reports in relation to Aboriginal socio-political and language groups. *However, his extrapolation from isolated observations across wide geographic regions is highly questionable.*[37]

Of more immediate concern here is that Gammage's assemblage of behaviours conjures up a kind of culture-free and philosophy-free zone in which these material activities—scattered, tenuously reported and never all reported together—seem to have a life of their own. It is of more immediate relevance that even though Pascoe goes much further than Gammage on certain questions, such as sedentism, both share the giving of scant (at best) attention to spiritual propagation of the whole biota and the active stimulation of certain valued species and of rain, as an embracing template on which behaviours rested.[38] Gammage's 'template' is un-sacred.

Pascoe's attempt to fit the evidence into the 'farmers' category (for example, page 26) leads him to mythologise both history and Aboriginal culture, and to ignore the spiritual propagation culture of the Old People. He is in this way as much a myth-maker as a myth-buster. He also consistently pushes the evidence of Aboriginal subsistence beyond what it can factually bear and into a European model of economic life. It is almost as if the more European the Old People can be made to seem, the better. As suggested above, this is *Dark Emu's* most fundamental flaw.

For the Old People, their means of making a living and obtaining materials for artefacts were inseparable from their commitment to a spiritual understanding of the origin of species, to conservative values in relation to change, and to a cosmology in which economics had to be in conformity to ancestral authority. Hunting, gathering and modification of the environment through fire and other means were a dimension of how the Dreaming—the ultimate spiritual foundation of life—left things forever. Practice followed cosmology. Gathering and hunting and fishing were not just economics: they were the Law.

Under that Law, people employed supernatural, sometimes esoteric ways of ensuring the regrowth of plants and the resurgence of animal populations, for successful hunting, for ensuring water flow in wells, and even, in one region, for creating pet crocodiles for use against enemies. People also engaged in ritual and musical performances to manage their meteorological environment, including making rain, fending off lightning, bringing on specific winds, preventing cyclones, and, in one case, hastening the shortening of the night at the winter solstice through song. These are all further explored in this book.

Through clan and personal totems, people also had shared substance with the species of their places of belonging, and with other phenomena. Clan totems, when they were species of plants and animals (not all were), were typically native to the ecological zone of the clan's country or estate. There were no mere plants or animals as economic objects, and there was no wilderness to conquer through cleverness.

Dark Emu as revelation

For many of those who knew nothing about the book's subject matter before reading it, *Dark Emu* seems to have come as a revelatory experience. Indeed, Pascoe is often at pains in the book to make reference to the ignorance of his fellow Australians and to the newness of what he has to say. His depiction of Australian history as telling students nothing about Aboriginal people's 'agricultural' past is correct, because no one in a true position to teach the subject has believed that was the case; but his implication that educators have failed to tell people anything about Aboriginal resource management and semi-nomadism (as against 'hapless wandering') is simply false, as we also demonstrate below. This includes students' texts covering many decades in which a 'simply nomadic' description of the Old People was rejected. We quote from them later.

Dark Emu's claims to debunking myths are unfounded. This article appeared in *The Guardian* seven years before *Dark Emu* was published:

SCIENTIST DEBUNKS NOMADIC ABORIGINE 'MYTH'
Before white settlers arrived, Australia's indigenous peoples lived in houses and villages and used surprisingly sophisticated architecture and methods to build their shelters, new research has found.

Dwellings were constructed in various styles, depending on the climate. Most common were dome-like structures made of cane reeds with roofs thatched with palm leaves.[39]

Some of the houses were interconnected, allowing native people to interact during long periods spent indoors during the wet season.

The findings, by the anthropologist and architect Dr Paul Memmott, of the University of Queensland, discredits a commonly held view in Australia that Aborigines were completely nomadic before the arrival of Europeans 200 years ago.[40]

Is it possible for the same myth to be debunked twice? Perhaps serial debunking is necessary if the public keeps forgetting previous debunkings. This is not in any way to belittle Memmott's wonderful book, but it does reflect the problem of making mass media news out of a complex subject. Sometimes, it seems, truth has to be reduced almost to ashes.

Is not that journalist's expression 'surprisingly sophisticated' a failure of respect for Indigenous people and, indeed, a metropolitan put-down? Dwellings that function to meet people's needs, whether they be elementary or more complicated, are hardly 'surprising'; and 'sophistication' here is measured against whose yardstick? Pascoe himself complains about the Bradshaw rock art of Western Australia being attributed to non-Aboriginal people long ago on the basis of its style being that of a 'more sophisticated people' (pages 193–4). Yet in *Dark Emu* he seems very focused on stressing examples of the exceptional, the ingenious, the clever, the sophisticated, the most numerous, the oldest, the permanent.

The cluster of examples of 'advancement' that appear in *Dark Emu* are themselves not new. If you read widely enough, you are aware that they have been collected and made public before.

Just as an example, there is a haunting resemblance between *Dark Emu* and archaeologist Harry Allen's 1980 contribution to a highly

Three gypsum mourning caps.

illustrated work created for the general public, *The Aborigines of New South Wales*. There, described in plain language and mostly illustrated with images, are a whole cluster of the same things that are presented by Pascoe in a revelatory framework: the gypsum mourning caps of widows (see above), claimed as some kind of precursor to pottery by Pascoe; the small 'villages' of grass-thatched huts (seasonally used); the Brewarrina fish traps (see below); the hunting and fishing nets (see overleaf); sewn skin cloaks; the ecological damage caused by introduced stock; and even explorer Major Thomas Mitchell's 1835 report of 'hayricks' and 'hay-cocks' from seed gathering. Below I make available a

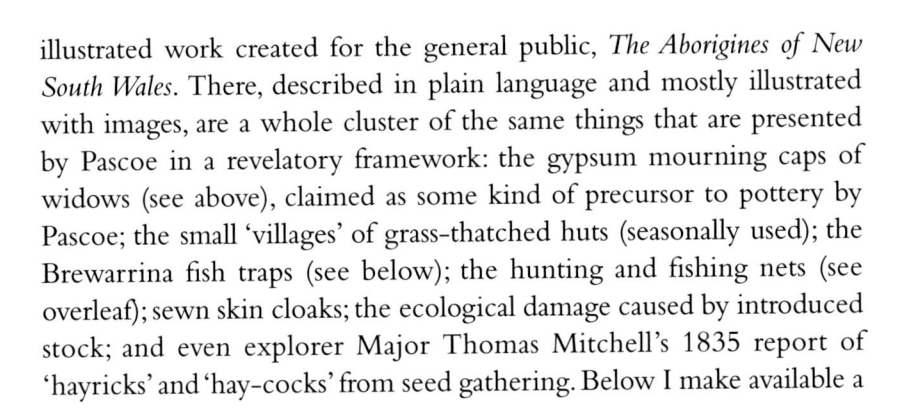

Brewarrina fish traps.

Duck net, Murrumbidgee River, 1880s.

swathe of similar introductory works of the past that make clear Pascoe is not breaking any truly new ground in relation to the economic, artefactual and technological facts presented.

In the same 1980 volume as Allen's essay, archaeologist Helen Clemens argued in a nuanced way against 'mere hunter-gatherer' descriptions:

> Aborigines took measures to assist the growth or reproduction of animals and plants that were useful to them … In other words, whilst the Aborigines have in the past been denigrated for their primitive economy, it seems that in some areas they developed techniques that *verged on agricultural practices*, and in other areas *deliberately refused to adopt such practices* when there was no advantage to be gained.[41]

Another introductory text that includes the same cluster of topics— although balanced out with regional variations and combining the ordinary with the unusual—is Philip Clarke's *Where the Ancestors Walked*.[42] There we find a familiar cast of characters. There is the refutation of the same falsehoods that *Dark Emu*, eleven years later, identified: that the Old People did nothing beyond hunting and gathering and had a passive relation to their environment (Clarke's pages 53, 62; page 65 is about fire management); that they wandered aimlessly over the landscape (page 53); that they did not store food (page 63);

that they did not sew clothing (page 88); that they did not, at least seasonally, build substantial shelters (page 82); that they were constantly on the march and did not have periods of staying in one place (page 82). Clarke also describes (as *Dark Emu* does not) the predominantly ritual ways in which people ensured the reproduction of species (page 64).[43]

Pascoe is prone to finding a localised or regional exception to a general continent-wide pattern and then suggesting the exception was the norm. Briefly, we can point out here that in contrast to what he has suggested, the eel traps of western Victoria are unique in the whole country and the Brewarrina fish traps have no equal on the inland river systems. After a wide survey of Aboriginal weirs and fish traps, Worsnop referred to the Brewarrina trap complex as 'a singular work of art'.[44] The fish traps of the Glyde River (Northern Territory), much emphasised by Pascoe, were considerably more complex than other Aboriginal fish weirs set in flowing streams, and indeed were unique to only two clans of that river (see Chapter 8). These creations were complex, but they were atypical. A more balanced story is needed. Is there something wrong with the ordinary but effective?

A common type of Aboriginal fish trap at the time of colonisation was the weir, sometimes referred to by English speakers as 'dams' even though they did not store water. Water and juvenile fish could pass through weirs, but not the bigger fish; and the bigger fish could then be readily speared without blocking the reproductive cycle of the species. In some cases, people combined weirs with nets, as in the Lake Eyre region (see below),[45] or with a conical wicker trap, as in

Remnant stakes used to divert fish to nets, Lake Eyre region.

the photo below from near Nagalarramba, north-central Arnhem Land. The latter is a slightly unusual type given it worked with tides rather than in a stream. The diversion fence was many metres long.[46]

Diversion fence with wicker fish trap, Arnhem Land, 1952.

Dark Emu's sources

Pascoe is not a trained anthropologist or archaeologist, and yet the issues at stake are complex and the relevant evidence from across the whole of Australia is voluminous. Much of it has been published in scientific journals or books written by social scientists, but much of it has also been published in introductory educational texts and even works for children. We use all of these in this book.

Pascoe has concentrated more on historical sources, especially explorers' journals, than on the evidence of Aboriginal people who have traditional knowledge.[47] In fact, there is almost no evidence in *Dark Emu* that he has asked Indigenous elders about their Old People's economic practices. He does refer to his visiting the remote community of Lockhart River, CYP (page 70). *Dark Emu* also refers to Maningrida, which is in the Northern Territory (not 'VIC' as in the index; page 174). Nothing relating to local economic traditions is mentioned in *Dark Emu* as having been learned in either of these visits to remote communities.

Nor does *Dark Emu* draw significantly on works by specialist scholars who have studied Aboriginal traditional economics and material culture under senior Indigenous expert mentoring, often through a lifetime. We seek to compensate for this omission here by giving full recognition to the elders' own knowledge of their people's pasts.

As far as we can tell, no journalist or book reviewer covering the *Dark Emu* story has interviewed senior Aboriginal people from remote communities where knowledge of the old economy is retained at least by some, and practised in an adapted way by many. Nor do members of the media appear to have spoken to any of the anthropological specialists who have learned from Aboriginal authorities and from the vast literature on their traditional ways of life. The most obvious candidate there would have been Dr Ian Keen of the Australian National University, whose 2004 book is a thoroughly researched study of multiple regional Aboriginal economies on the threshold of conquest by the British Empire.[48] He describes a rich array of cultural and economic practices, but does not find that mainland Indigenous Australians practised agriculture or gardening.

This journalistic abandonment of the academy, if that is what it is, seems to be symptomatic of a break from the past—a past in which professional knowledge and lay knowledge were more distinct, and the distinction more respected. The authority of the academy has slipped. Much worse than that, the authority of Aboriginal knowledge-holders has been ignored yet again.

Another problem in this case is that Pascoe's heavy reliance on explorers' journals is reliance on the evidence of those who encountered classical Aboriginal Australia only transiently at each location, and typically without any language in common with those they met. They were also the vanguard field agents of Aboriginal dispossession during the predatory expansion of the agrarian society of the British. They were men who were anxious to be able to map and report valuable future pastoral and agricultural environments back to Sydney and London. They were the forward scouts for the army of land-hungry farmers who would come in their wake. Waving fields of grass and stacks of seed-bearing stems, real as they were, could be easily read from a European standpoint as meadows in waiting, full of promise for the coming wave of agricultural usurpers.

We are not questioning the explorers' immediate factual observations generally, but they cannot help us much with, for example, the question of how much the Old People relied on harvesting uncultivated natural resources versus those over which they exercised a degree of management, or how often they moved camp, or whether what the Britishers saw as a 'village' was there for temporary, medium or extended use. What colonials called 'villages' were probably temporary dwellings used seasonally, with the exception of places of longer stay in the minority of areas that can be described as unusually rich in resources and hosting the highest population densities: namely, the Western District of Victoria, the middle and lower Murray River, and the east coast of CYP north of the Stewart River. We discuss the evidence in Chapter 9 of this book.

In *Dark Emu* there is little or no reliance on the evidence of those who lived on the Aboriginal side of the frontier for months on end, learning from the traditional owners of the lands they lived in and learning local languages, as in the case of trained anthropologists such as Ursula McConnel, Donald Thomson, Fred Rose and Lauriston Sharp. There is also almost no reliance in *Dark Emu* on those early castaways who lived inside Australian Indigenous societies and operated in local languages, for years on end, as in the case of William Buckley (32 years), James Morrill (or Murrells; 17 years), James Davis (Duramboi; 13 years), John Sterry Baker (Boraltchou, 14 years) and Barbara Thomson (nearly five years). Pascoe makes one fleeting reference to castaway Narcisse Pelletier, who lived among Cape York people beyond the frontier, also for seventeen years, in the nineteenth century (page 70). These unusual sources had more to say that could have been useful to Pascoe—especially Buckley, who recorded so much detail about the movements and camping places of the bands he lived with in Victoria's Western District (see Appendix 2).

Success of sorts
Pascoe's *Dark Emu* has been a print publishing and digital-media success, it has been rendered into dance performance by the famed Bangarra Dance Theatre, two children's versions have been published, and it has begun to be incorporated into school curricula.[49] It has many admirers—or perhaps one should say converts, given it is written in the style of dramatic revelation. It has been awarded two New South Wales Premier's Literary Awards (Book of the Year and the Indigenous Writers' Prize, 2016) and was shortlisted for the History Book Award

in the Queensland Literary Awards (2014) and the Victorian Premier's Award for Indigenous Writing (2014). Its offspring, *Young Dark Emu*, has won the Eve Pownall Children's Book of the Year Award for Information Books (Children's Book Council of Australia, 2020).

Noel Peemuggina and his student Peter Sutton, Ti Tree Outstation, Cape York Peninsula, 1977.

Pascoe's book purports to be factual. It offers support for propositions in footnotes that lead to an extensive list of published and archival sources, and has an index.[50] However, it is littered with unsourced material. It is poorly researched. It distorts and exaggerates many old sources. It selects evidence to suit the author's opinions, and it ignores large bodies of information that do not support the author's opinions. It contains a large number of factual errors, a range of which we analyse here. Others we could not include for want of space.

Dark Emu is actually not, properly considered, a work of scholarship. Its success as a narrative has been achieved in spite of its failure as an account of fact.

All of this success would appear to indicate, within our society and public sphere, either a profound lack of factual knowledge in relation to the peoples and history written about in *Dark Emu*, or an unconcern with facts and truth themselves, or a combination of these things. Whichever the case, the situation is troubling.

2
Spiritual propagation

In contrast to the picture conveyed by *Dark Emu*, the greater part of Aboriginal traditional methods of reproducing plant and animal species was not through physical cultivation or conservation but through spiritual propagation. This included speaking to the spirits of ancestors at resource sites, carrying out 'increase rituals' at special species-related sites, singing resource species songs in ceremonies, maintaining rich systems of totems for various species that were found in the countries of the totem-holders, and handling food resources with reverence.

It is clear from the evidence in this chapter that the practice of the spiritual propagation of species through ritual acts at particular sites ran from northernmost Queensland south, through southern Queensland and New South Wales to the lower Murray River, across most of the arid zone to the fertile south-west, and northwards through Western Australia to the Kimberley and parts of the Top End and the Gulf of Carpentaria.

The traditional rituals through which the ensuring of fertility took place are often called 'increase ceremonies' by scholars, although it is not an ideal term, as I discuss below. They are about maintenance, not the creation of more than usual.

The rituals were performed at particular locations. They have been reported from vast areas of mainland Australia, but not quite all of it. They were, however, pervasive. The most common features of the 'increase ceremonies' were the addressing of the totemic being in the site, and the 'throwing' or broadcasting of materials such as mud, sand, dust or stones so as to impregnate places elsewhere with the spiritual seeds of the resource, which would then become abundant once more. They were concerned with dissemination. Anthropologist Ken Maddock wrote:

An outsider might form the impression that Aborigines were parasites upon nature. On the Aboriginal view, however, nature and society were mutually dependent. The famous 'increase' rites performed in much of Australia were held to sustain the fertility of the species for which they were performed. In some areas rites specific to the various species were unknown, but men addressed themselves to a power or powers identified with fertility as such …[1]

Cape York Peninsula

Casual treatment of resources was much frowned upon by Wik people of western Cape York Peninsula, with whom I lived in the 1970s in bush camps and outstations. Newly killed animals were often spoken to with pity, if not regret. The carcasses of flying foxes that had been eaten had to be laid in a straight line on a piece of bark and disposed of carefully, not just hurled away. One day our party had dug yams at Uthuk Aweyn and as we were leaving the patch some teenage girls were making jokes about the long yam tubers they held. Senior man Alan Wolmby scolded them, saying in effect *'Ke'a! Inth aak aweyn, wiintha!'* 'Don't do that! That's something important, sacred/dangerous!' Sculptures of these yams played a role in ceremonies, including house openings for the deceased (see below). Reverencing food sources was therefore not confined to special 'Story Places' where species were spiritually propagated by ritual acts.

Long yam carving for house-opening ceremony, near Aurukun, 1976. Francis Yunkaporta (holding yam), Peter Peemuggina and James Kalkeeyorta.

Spiritual propagation sites are common in both eastern and western CYP. In eastern Cape York, between the Olive and Stewart rivers, anthropologist Athol Chase, assisted by colleagues, mapped thirty clan estates and hundreds of sites with traditional owners in the wet season of 1975–76. He later described clusters of initiation sites in these estates, some of which were 'manipulated through ritual' to control the movements of species. For example:

> At Kapikam muta ('blue-tailed mullet' [+ sit-down place]) for example, beating the rock with branches and 'calling', after putting underarm sweat on the site, will cause the species to congregate, but only when they are near at hand on their seasonal spawning run.[2]

A similar combination of speech and sweat as means of interaction with a sentient landscape is a major feature of anthropologist Elizabeth Povinelli's book *Labor's Lot*, about the people of Belyuen in the Northern Territory.[3] In both regions, but not universally in Australia, sweat communicates to the spirits of the Old People who you are; they are not just able to listen to you but also to smell you. In both regions sweat is often stirred into water while one is announcing or being announced as present. Your smell identifies whether or not you are a familiar of that place, and whether or not you belong to the place.

Anthropologist Lauriston Sharp, who lived in bush camps in western CYP in the early 1930s, recorded and described eighty spiritual propagation centres in the Coleman-Mitchell rivers area.[4] He referred to 'that aspect of their ritual life which theoretically supports the food economy, the annual ceremonies to increase natural species including those used as food'.[5]

Ursula McConnel, pioneering anthropologist of the Wik region to the north of the Mitchell River, published much detail on the sites where these rituals took place in the Wik countries.[6] In Wik-Mungkan these spiritual centres are called *awa* (McConnel's '*auwa*') (see opposite). This is one example:

> The Wik-nantyara have a yam *auwa*, where yams are said to have originated, consisting of a waterhole in a little creek which always remains sweet. It is said that the spirits of the dead go down into the waterhole and stop the salt water coming in to spoil the yams. Every year when rains begin, the ceremony of smoothing out the

mud in the waterhole takes place. Mud is thrown about the sides of the waterhole and the place is tidied up. This ensures a good crop of yams in the coming season.[7]

In Wik traditions, McConnel recorded that species conservation went hand in hand with spiritual species reproduction:

These *auwa* or totem-centres are sometimes the nests and breeding places of the birds, animals and plants concerned …

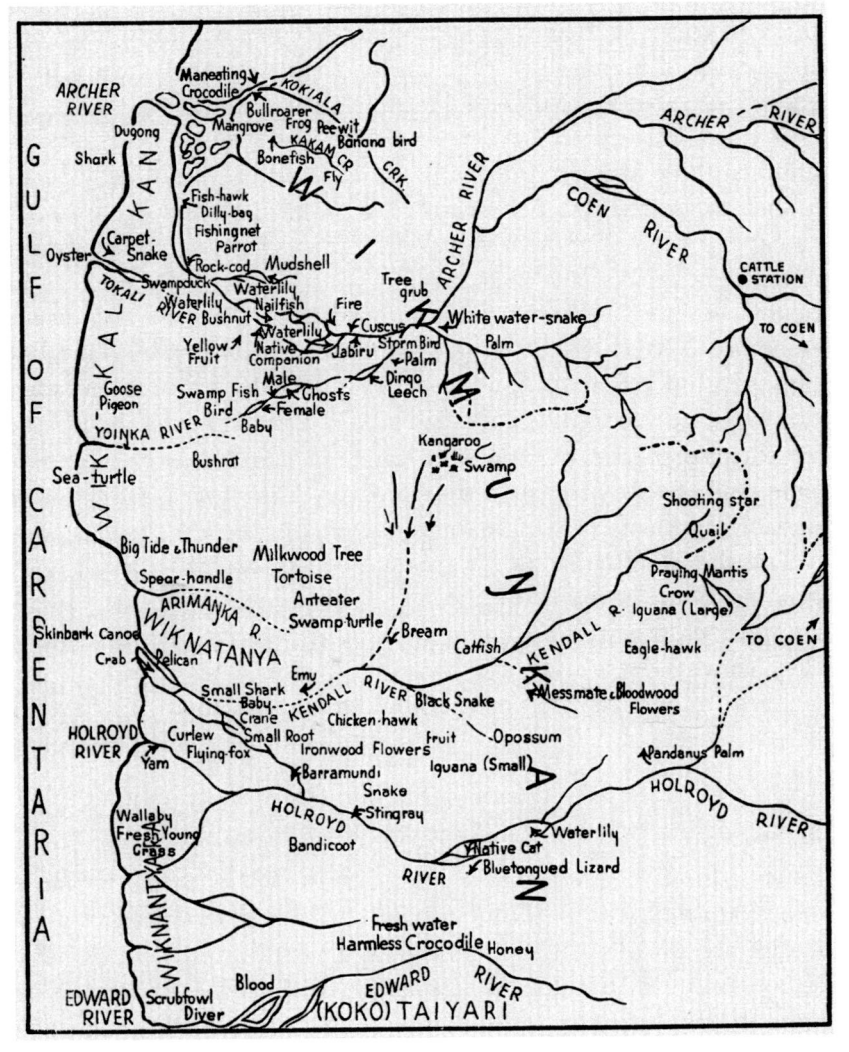

Totemic centres, Wik region.

There is always water near by in the shape of river, creek, lagoon, waterhole, swamp or well at the bottom of which the *pulwaiya* [totemic being] resides and into which the dead of the clan are believed to go. This is perhaps why plants and animals are protected near the *auwa* of their representative totem and why the killing of an animal or the injuring of a plant near its *auwa* is not only strictly forbidden but believed to be attended by grave consequences.[8]

These were ritual acts, often including songs, that caused the activation of totemic sites by 'stirring up', 'waking up' or 'spreading/throwing' the essence of the species represented at a particular site.[9] Not all such sites were to do with edible plants or animals. There are also sites for spreading diarrhoea, itchiness, blind boils, pre-seminal fluid, love affairs, greed, and so on. I have recorded many on site myself, as have colleagues. Our work mainly of the period 1969–95 yielded the mapping of fifty-three Wik totemic sites that were specifically used to reproduce and propagate a comprehensive range of animals, plants, human states, and natural phenomena.[10]

The most widespread activity that both women and men engage in at these sites of spiritual propagation in the Wik region is talking, often in a loud clear voice, and usually in the language of the location or a language its traditional owners would have understood. They are addressing the spirits of the site's Old People. To address the spirits at such places and others is in Wik-Mungkan *wik thaw*, and in English 'to talk language'. They address the spirits of their Old People both reverently and demandingly. This is demand-sharing with ancestors.[11]

A Wik barramundi maintenance site is shown in the photo opposite. This is a Story Place (*eemoeth* in Wik-Ngathan; *awa* in Wik-Mungkan) or sacred totemic site left behind by the Pungk Apelech brothers, who found barramundi (*moenchenh*) here as they created the spiritual landscape and its clan countries and languages in the northern coastal part of the Wik region. It is 2 kilometres inland from the Gulf of Carpentaria between the Kirke and Knox rivers, on the edge of a vast seasonal freshwater wetland. The focal point of the *eemoeth* is the two wells partly visible behind the tree. To ensure the reproduction of barramundi in the region, a person has to chop cuts into the trunk of the tree. This was described when we were there on 9 October 1977 by Isobel Wolmby, the senior member of the mapping party.

Barramundi maintenance site Moenchenh-nhiin, Wik region, 1977.

The slender Ray Wolmby took a tomahawk and headed for the tree. He was pulled up sharply by Isobel, who said no, the 'thrower' of the barramundi site had to be thickset so the barramundi coming up would be nice and fat. So instead she ordered her more rotund brother, Rupert Gothachalkenin, to carry out the rite.

A different example from the same region is the magpie goose egg maintenance site between Love River and Knox River (see over-leaf, top). The same kind of sympathetic logic applied to this engine of reproduction. While a senior man would cut a blaze in a nearby tree (see overleaf, bottom), the main 'throwing' of the site had to be done by women of proven fertility who had a strong link to the site. The swale (sand dune depression) holds many baler shells, which represent the eggs of the magpie goose. This large bird nests seasonally in untold thousands on the vast wetlands next to this sand ridge. On the occasion we mapped the site, on 28 October 1976, Marjorie Yunkaporta, a woman who had already borne nine children and whose paternal grandmother had been a traditional owner of the country

Magpie goose egg maintenance site, Yaad, Wik region, 1976.

Johnny Lak Lak Ampeybegan cuts a blaze in a tree at a goose
egg maintenance site, Wik region, 1976.

in which the place was located, serviced the goose egg site. She did this by throwing debris and grass away from the 'eggs' (baler shells), rearranging the shells, and calling on deceased ancestors to once again supply goose eggs.[12]

In the case of the moulting ducks species maintenance site Minhwiyumpen Nyiin on the upper Knox River, CYP, the increase rite requires women who have borne many children to chop the trunks of pandanus trees with an axe. As they do so they call out the names of swamps in the area. Mary Walmbeng and Dorothy Pootchemunka performed this rite on site in 1986, and it was recorded by David Martin (see page 2 of the picture section).[13]

Some Wik species maintenance sites could be equally 'thrown' by women and men. This included flora as well as fauna. For example, May-kuthel-aw is a species maintenance site for two varieties of swamp grass bulbs, on a sand ridge inland from Cape Keerweer. As part of the maintenance ritual, both men and women would dig out the hole with their feet while calling out to the ancestors.[14]

Cessation of species maintenance rites could cause the supply of that species to dry up. For example, bush-reared Wik woman Mary Walmbeng told Martin in 1986 that the yellow nonda fruit (*may po'al*; the sweet drink made from it is called *may ow*) had ceased being available in the Pu'iyang area since maintenance rites ceased being performed at Miilp (upper Knox River, Cape York).[15]

Among Wik people, there was also a customary but non-ritual practice carried out at swamps that was aimed at ensuring a big goose-egg-laying season. The first eggs laid at the start of the season were not collected. If they were, the other geese would be deterred from creating their nests there. As is so often the case, this example shows how spiritual maintenance and practical resource management combined to characterise the classical Aboriginal economy.

In the case of sacred sites with plant Dreamings, these rituals might be referred to metaphorically as spiritual gardening. In the Wik region, Koe', on the north side of the Kirke River, is such a Story Place. It is a maintenance centre for the reproduction of *may ka'err*, the hairy yam (*Dioscorea bulbifera*). Koe' is a tiny but dense scrub on a treeless plain. It is in such scrubs that yams of this kind were dug, leaving the stems intact to reproduce another time; I saw this done in the 1970s. These particular yams could be stored in the ground for several months, eking out the supply from *Onchen*, the season (roughly March–April) of hairy yam ripening immediately after the wet season, well into the year.[16]

Once again, the spiritual and the physical are here combined to create a unified system of resource maintenance. In many more cases, however, Wik maintenance rituals are the standalone and privileged means of keeping the country rich, with no physical accompaniment, and most resources were not stored.

In the 1970s I lived many months at outstations and bush camps in the Wik country south of Aurukun. My teachers were mainly people who had been born and raised in the bush, some to full adulthood. Apart from the practice of leaving yam stalks undisturbed while the tubers were removed (see Chapter 6 for more on this), I never heard of or saw any older practices that could be even remotely described as horticulture, agriculture or farming in the commonsense way those terms are used. Nor did McConnel in her time with people there, including living for many weeks beyond the reach of colonisation, in the 1920s and 1930s. Wik people did not grind seeds. McConnel's incredibly comprehensive collection of Wik artefacts[17] and my own careful reinvestigation of Wik material culture[18] revealed no hoes or ploughs, not even any grindstones, and indeed almost no stone tools of any kind apart from axe heads imported from far away. However, I saw many sacred sites 'thrown' (*thee'enh*) so as to propagate the species they held as totemic beings.

South-east Australia

Further south in Queensland, during her 1934 field work at Cherbourg, anthropologist Caroline Tennant Kelly recorded '[n]umerous accounts of increase ceremonies'. These related mainly to central and southern Queensland. She published three examples.[19]

The first was a rainmaking site in Kabi Kabi country. A clever man would cut pieces of the stem of a rare vine growing next to a cave on Mount Urah, and talk to Biral (the 'all-father'). He would then throw a piece of the vine stem in the direction of the territory of friendly neighbouring tribes, calling their names as he did so.

Near Maryborough, the pendulous moss hanging down from a particular tree was burned by old men in order to make rain. On the Nebine River the first native bee was created by a bat, who then chased it all around Kuwamu country until it came to the cave Ungwari. From then on, the increase rite for bees was always performed at that cave.

In the 1950s, Gaiarbau (aka Willie MacKenzie, born c1873), a Duungidjawu man from south-east Queensland, recorded fulsome details about his people's traditions with Lindsey Page Winterbotham, a GP. In his language, spiritual maintenance sites were called *mowar*, and Gaiarbau recorded details of maintenance rites for rain, kangaroos, carpet snakes, honey and eaglehawks:[20] 'All such ceremonies used to be performed a few days before they moved camp; and they expected, when in due course they returned to this old camping ground, that their requests would have been granted, and food would again be plentiful.'[21]

Anthropologist Rex Radcliffe-Brown did fieldwork in eastern Australia in the early twentieth century and found more such sites and rites in northern New South Wales in the countries of nine different linguistic groups. In Yukumbil (Yugambeh) these sites were called *djurbil*, and in Kumbaingeri (Gumbaynggirr) *mirer* or *mirera*; in Yegera (Yaygirr) they were *yerkari*.[22] The maintenance sites he recorded were for kangaroo, wattle grub, native bear, locust, big lizard, opossum, wild honey, sleep, rain-serpent, rain, yams, hot weather, cold weather, wind, babies, emu, kangaroo rat, dingo, crab, codfish, perch, oyster, an unidentified shellfish species, an edible fruit called *girguru* (Gumbaynggirr), old-man kangaroo, female kangaroo, joey, storms, diarrhoea, dysentery, tiger snake, death adder, ghosts, edible grub, duck and dew-fish.[23] In a study of the literature on Aboriginal ceremonies in New South Wales I once located a further nine literature references to what I called there 'increase ceremonies'.[24]

Further south again, AW Howitt, writing about south-eastern Australia as he knew it in the nineteenth century, called spiritual maintenance ceremonies 'charms to influence food-supply'.[25] Increase sites appear, however, not to have been a salient institution in the Victorian region. Ian Keen's 2004 survey discussed such places and rites for the Western Desert Pitjantjatjara people, the Wiil and Minong people of south-west Western Australia, the Sandbeach people (eastern Cape York) and the Ngarinyin of the Kimberley,[26] but the Kŭnai people of Gippsland apparently lacked them. Through his role as an expert witness in a native title claim in Gippsland, Keen has comprehensive knowledge of Kŭnai traditions.

Further to the west in the south-east of Australia, Ronald Berndt recorded sacred rituals of the lower Murray River that were attended by both women and men, many of which he said were 'of increase intent'.[27]

Central Australia

In a far more trying environment, the Western Desert region of Central Australia (see illustration on page 142 in Chapter 10), similar sites were described by anthropologist Robert Tonkinson as the 'ritual "technology" through which [Gibson Desert men] claim to exert a measure of control over resource production and weather conditions'.[28] Elsewhere in the desert country, anthropologist Nicolas Peterson referred to the equivalent ceremonies, including the mulga seed ceremony filmed by Roger Sandall, as rituals of 'continued reproduction'.[29] Examples of southern Western Desert 'increase centres' were published by Ronald and Catherine Berndt in their introductory text.[30]

The Lake Eyre region of Australia's south-eastern deserts was another zone where spiritual propagation sites were activated. For example, near Kanowna is a cave containing bones of the extinct diprotodon, and the cave is a 'sanctuary for the increase of the large carpet snake' or *woma*. The ritual involved men singing songs within the hearing of women, and both women and men carried out actions at the site.[31] There was also an 'increase' aspect to the emu cult ceremony called *mindiri*. Yawarawarrka people told AP Elkin in 1930 'that the due performance of the ceremony caused the emus to lay eggs and also to get fat, so that it is in some sense an increase rite'.[32] The two places he recorded as sites where this ceremony was carried out, Cutrabelbo and Kudadjiri, were themselves *mura* (Dreaming) sites.[33]

In the same region, seeds of *wirra* (*Acacia salicina*) were pounded, one at a time, by special stones at a place where this wattle species was desired to be growing, and performers danced until the supply of seeds was used up.[34] Another means of propagating *A. salicina* was to use a special white stone: 'It represented the white inside of the seed and was planted where the *wirra* tree was wanted.'[35] The symbolism was drawn from the germination of seeds, but the means of propagation was ritual use of stones, not the horticultural use of seeds.

Anthropologist Mervyn Meggitt, in his major study with the north-western desert Warlpiri people in the 1950s, wrote that in addition to the effects of specific 'increase ceremonies' at particular sites, the 'revelatory' lodge ceremonies had an effect on species reproduction no matter where they were performed. The pre-circumcision kangaroo ceremonies affected the numbers of kangaroos everywhere in Warlpiri country.[36] He added:

It is worth noting here that the term 'increase', although commonly used in the literature in relation to such rituals, is not strictly accurate. The participants are simply concerned to maintain the supplies of natural species at their usual level, to support the normal order of nature. Thus, rain ceremonies are not performed until late spring, when the first heavy cumulo-nimbus clouds appear in the north-west. The men do not believe that they can force the rain to fall at any time of the year: instead, they try to ensure that it will come in the appropriate season.[37]

Some languages contain special vocabulary for these rituals. For example, one of the Warlpiri verbs is *ngarrmi-rni* (transitive), which has been glossed as 'to increase (species) by ritual'.[38] In the Githabal language of the Warwick–Woodenbong district (southern Queensland, northern New South Wales), to cite another linguistic example, there is a specific term for 'increase corroboree', *birrbayn*.[39]

Botanist of Central Australia Peter Latz prefers the term 'maintenance ceremonies' for these forms of resource management:

> To ensure the continued existence of these plants and animals, ceremonies must be carried out at these sites. These rituals are usually referred to as 'increase ceremonies', but as this term implies a progressive unnatural increase of the particular organisms, the term 'maintenance ceremony' is probably more apt. Maintenance ceremonies are regularly carried out throughout much of Central Australia for most of the plants discussed in this book.[40]

As we have seen, maintenance ceremonies and physical resource management were not mutually exclusive. To cite another example, Norman Tindale recorded that Pitjantjatjara people of the Western Desert performed ceremonies to ensure the birth of dingo puppies around May and June, but at the same time refrained from hunting the puppies so that 'these unmolested dingo puppies become fat and soon provide a rich food for the winter months'.[41]

Among the most extensive descriptions of species maintenance rituals are those of the Arrernte area of Central Australia by Spencer and Gillen.[42] They include witchetty grub, emu, mulga manna (lerp), water, kangaroo, *irriakura* tuber, longicorn beetle grub, bandicoot, hakea, plum, euro, lizard and snake. The various Arrernte words used to name these spiritual propagation rites include the verb 'throwing'.[43] This practice of spiritual broadcasting of species and other phenomena by 'throwing' is widespread in the record of classical Aboriginal Australia. In some cases, as described by Spencer and Gillen, species were not hunted until they had become abundant following the relevant 'throwing' ceremony. Yet again, spiritual propagation was combined with physical conservation.

Anthropologist Petronella Vaarzon-Morel was with Lower Arrernte women in the Simpson Desert in 2001 when they were at a sacred sugar lerp (manna) site. They cleaned around it and then rubbed the rocks in order to ensure continued supply of the lerp. North-west of there, she saw Warlpiri women rubbing sacred rocks at a rain site in order to bring rain. In both cases the women observed the strict protocol of 'introducing themselves to the ancestral spirits of the country'.[44]

On the South Australian side of the Simpson Desert, people used to make representations of emu eggs using gypsum, the same material they used for widows' caps (see below). The Old People would 'sing'

Gypsum emu eggs sung to start emus nesting, Simpson Desert, South Australia.

these eggs at a ceremony intended to start the emus nesting.[45] They also made gypsum representations of duck eggs.[46] One side of such a coin is the maintenance of fertility of certain species for the immediate future; the other side is the conservation of the species over the long term.

The linguist and anthropologist TGH Strehlow described how the Arrernte people of Central Australia, among whom he had grown up at Hermannsburg Mission, prohibited all hunting and food gathering anywhere within the 'sacred precincts' of totemic centres. He referred to this as 'the decisive economic influence of the [sacred sites] as functioning as game reserves within each [clan estate]'.[47] He did not, however, have evidence that the sacred sites themselves 'had intentionally been created as game reserves'.[48]

There again is the principle of merging the sacred domain with a pragmatic effect—a principle repeatedly applied in classical Australia and in some regions still applied.

The south-west

Legendary ethnographer Daisy Bates (1859–1951) took a special interest in the spiritual maintenance ceremonies of the people of the south-west of Western Australia.[49] She recorded rites for the reproduction of swans and swan eggs in the Gingin district, and for salmon in the Busselton district; for honey-bearing banksia flowers and edible jamwood gum in the Swan and Pinjarra districts, and for possums;[50] and for kangaroo in the area north of Lake Nabberu.[51] A long edible bean was increased by visiting the bean's growing location in a dream, biting a bean and throwing the pieces about.[52] In the Meekatharra district there had been a site for maintaining plain turkeys, but the custodians died out, and through lack of the rituals the turkeys were dying out as well.[53]

The Kimberley and Pilbara

In the Kimberley region, Phyllis Kaberry found in the 1930s that spiritual propagation sites and rites were an important part of Aboriginal economy and religion, as also was ritual rainmaking.[54] Of the former she said:

As the totemic ancestors passed through the country they left stones or sometimes a tree, each of which is supposed to contain the *guniŋ* [totemic essence] of some animal, bird, fish, reptile, tuber, and so on.

These sites are called *bud-bud* at Forrest River, and *wulwiny* among the Lunga. By rubbing one of these or striking it with bushes and uttering a spell, the *guniŋ* will go forth and cause the species with which it is associated to go forth and multiply. The Aborigine [in this region] has no granaries, but he has, if we may use the term, these 'spiritual' storehouses, in that they insure him against starvation, and give him a sense of security and confidence in regard to his food-supply for the coming year.[55]

Kaberry also found that both women and men visited these 'increase centres' in that region.[56]

In a different part of the Kimberley, the western coastal area, species maintenance sites were known in Nyikina as *malaji*:

They are locations believed to be imbued with the spirits of specific natural species, plants, birds, animals, reptiles and insects, and also phenomena such as rain, storms, lightning, floodwaters or cyclones. The people in whose land these sites fall are responsible for the ceremonies that ensure that beneficial results lead to the seasonal renewal of game species and important plants or rain ...[57]

Radcliffe-Brown recorded a large number of these maintenance rituals and sites in the northern parts of Western Australia in the early twentieth century. In one case they were spread over a large area from the western Kimberley in the north to the Murchison River in the south.[58]

Fellow anthropologists Ralph Piddington and AP Elkin separately published quite detailed accounts of 'increase ceremonies' in the Karadjari (Karajarri) area, just south of the Kimberley in the La Grange district of Western Australia.[59] One of them was for the edible ground nut *yarrinyarri* or *nalgoo*, more widely known as yelka.[60] In the photo opposite, women who have picked up pebbles from the site, where the pebbles represent *yarrinyarri* nuts, are throwing them to form heaps on the ground.[61] The dust blows away as they do so. This is done when the westerly wind can carry the dust, so that 'the spirit *yerinyeri* may be dis-seminated over the land'.[62] It was also reportedly a general Aboriginal practice to avoid gathering these nuts at the time of year when they were germinating to create new plants.[63] Yet again the spiritual worked hand in hand with the physical.

'Increase ceremony' for *yarrinyarri* (nutgrass), north-west Australia.

South of there, in the Pilbara region, Radcliffe-Brown recorded many totemic increase centres in 1911 and referred to them by the local Kariyarra word *talu* (*thalu*), which has become used by scholars of other regions as well:

> The *talu* is a spot set apart for the performance of totemic ceremonies ... The purpose of the ceremonies is said to be to increase the supply of the animal, plant, or other object with which it is connected ... The women of the clan take part in the ceremonies as well as the men.[64]

The *talu* sites were located where the relevant animal or plant was found to occur more abundantly.[65]

The Top End and Gulf of Carpentaria

After I mapped over 200 named sites on the lower Daly River with Malak Malak people in 1979–80, it was clear to me that spiritual propagation or 'increase' sites, as against general fertility promoted by ceremonies, were rare in the area.[66] We visited only one such site.

At Wani-Woenoe, a yabby Dreaming place, Queenie Midinyan and Kitty Waliwararra collected rocks as they spoke to the place and identified themselves. They took the rocks to Wuliyana (Horseshoe Billabong) and activated the yabby totemic essence there by throwing them in. Senior Malak Malak man Jimmy Tapnguk told me the ritual was to 'make 'im plenty prawn come'.[67]

Elements of 'increase' are reported for western Arnhem Land by the Berndts[68] but again they are not prominent. South-west of there, Francesca Merlan reported a sacred blue-tongue lizard site on the upper Katherine River that was used for ensuring 'fish and other bounty' by speaking to it in the ecological agent's language.[69]

In the Maningrida region north-east of there, Jon Altman described large regional ceremonies as having 'perceived maintenance and increase functions': 'Regular performance of ceremonies is essential for the maintenance of the resource base and indirectly for the biological survival and reproduction of clan groups.'[70]

By contrast, for another part of north-central Arnhem Land, Lily Gurambara has supplied details of multiple ritual acts aimed at propagating species.[71] People go to sites associated with particular plants and animals and throw stones, mud or sand, calling out to the beings to 'Go! Go to [Place X]!' The named places are specific sites in the clan countries (estates). Sand is thrown for stingrays, mud from the place Moyadjirrpa is thrown to propagate mussels, and soil from Dhuwa moiety estates is thrown to renew the crop of long yams. This practice occurs at places as far east as Milingimbi Island in Yan-nhangu country, which is at the western extremity of north-east Arnhem Land.

In south-eastern Arnhem Land the Nunggubuyu (Wubuy) people also practised the influencing of supply at specific sites, using a unique interjection to address the site: *Jangu!*[72] This would happen at special ritual sites where diagrams were made in the ground. Although linguist Jeffrey Heath considered the abundance of food in the area rendered these rituals 'relatively unimportant in this region', he does not say unimportant compared to what, and the practice was there nonetheless.[73] For example, a young man called Yurumura told Heath in Nunggubuyu:[74]

(About) that thing. They (people) go and look around. They catch no food. They go to that dreaming place. They go along and stop there. Then they break some branches (with leaves) off (trees).

They break off some branches. They go and do that, they rub the branches on it (dreaming, for example, a particular rock) with that branch. They rub it. They call out 'Jangu! Make food abundant for us! Let there be a lot of food!' They said that. 'Jangu!'

Then they go into the water in a billabong. Then that (game, vegetable food, etc.) becomes abundant. They catch a lot of it. Long-necked tortoises, or sand goannas, or fish (whatever they want). There is plenty of food because they said 'Jangu!'[75]

Nunggubuyu people also practised rainmaking and creating the north-east, north-west and south-east winds.[76]

For the region just north of there, north-east Arnhem Land, the evidence for specific increase sites and rites is at best sketchy, although there is a general fertility theme prevalent in major ceremonies, the key one having a name that is sensitive and that I do not use here. Lloyd Warner wrote of that region, where the clans have wide arrays of animal and plant totems:[77]

The Murngin [Yolngu] in their logic of controlling nature assume that there is a direct connection between social units and different aspects of nature, and that *the control of nature* lies in the proper control and treatment of social organization. Properly to control the social organization, the rituals must also be held which rid society of its uncleanliness. The society is disciplined by threat of what will happen to nature, the provider, if the members of the group misbehave. This brings on an identification of the social organization with nature, and they are treated as one and expressed as such in the rituals.[78]

He did not, however, report specific 'increase sites' at which species were propagated ritually.[79]

Ian Keen, who worked in the same region over forty years later, noted that 'at least one "increase" site has been recorded in the country of Djinang-speakers' at the western end of the region, but that the Yolngu philosophy was that the Dreaming (*Wangarr*), as one man put it, 'provided game and vegetable foods as "a gift"'.[80]

Ronald Berndt, who carried out extensive fieldwork with people of north-east Arnhem Land and elsewhere, contrasted the localised and 'compartmentalised' increase ceremonies of Central Australia with 'the northern pattern of general fertility'.[81] Of those northern regions he also said:

> The great fertility cults of the north and north-western-central part of the continent are designed to activate—through a combination of male and female elements—the natural forces surrounding man. Life is a continuing process of birth and re-birth, decay and revival, in nature, and in man. To ensure that this process is not jeopardized, spiritual intervention is necessary.[82]

South-east of that region, on the south-west of the Gulf of Carpentaria, John Bradley has long been learning from Yanyuwa and Garrwa people. They have taught him about the local spiritual propagation centres and how they were controlled by people of prestige who had the knowledge and local authority to activate them. The example he gives is the increase site for cycad nuts. He translated the following from Ida Ninganga, who told him this in 1988:

> They would be asking him my brother, his name was Jayungkurri, they would ask him, 'Make the cycad nuts come out in abundance, so next year there will be more, make it so there will be much food so we will not starve.' He would say, 'Mmm. Alright but you will get a sea turtle for me.' They would say yes to that. Then he would go and get a stick, a small one, he would put his sweat from under his armpit on it, he would strike a cycad kernel and then he would throw it into the palm fronds, one here, another over there, yet another further away, all the way like that. When he threw the cycad kernel he would call out in the following manner, 'Cycad kernel! Cycad kernel! May you become many! May there be an abundance!' That was it, he would come back and they would give him a turtle, maybe a kangaroo, alright they would wait and next year there would be too many cycad nuts, nobody would go hungry ...[83]

Given that the cycad nuts here are said to have been thrown onto the tops of plants already established, this ritual should not be confused with broadcast seeding.

Elsewhere Bradley said, 'In many respects the Yanyuwa and Garrwa peoples do not see themselves as managers of the environment, but rather as peoples who are in constant apprehension and negotiation with it, following the Law established during the formative activities of the Dreaming.'[84]

Centres of what some would call 'natural abundance' are often given a special term in Australian languages, although the category 'natural' is foreign to Aboriginal tradition, given that everything is designed by the Dreaming. These places are called *wirriwangkuma* in Yanyuwa, which means 'country where people can come together on a seasonal basis and expect to share in the resources that are abundant there'.[85] Places of species abundance are referred to in Burarra as *gumbomboli*.[86] In Wik-Ngathan a location with plentiful vegetable food is *aak may mu'em*.[87] In the eastern Western Desert dialects, the prevalence of a species of plant in a particular area is indicated by doubling the name of the plant.[88]

While one might metaphorically call these places 'gardens', they are not sown plots, and they are not human creations.[89] Their fertility is inherent.

East of Yanyuwa country is Mornington Island, where rituals are carried out by Lardil people 'to ensure a supply or the increase of a resource':

Kelly Bunbujee describes part of the increase ritual at the Wild Grape story place in his country: '… if you want black grapes to ripe, you brush them with bush, any bush'. Other ritual methods include hitting or poking a particular story place with a stick and shaking bushes at places. These actions are performed at the Barracuda, Mudcrab and Goanna story places, as well as many others.[90]

Paul Memmott has recorded eighty-six Lardil sacred sites 'that were increase ritual centres for biological, meteorological and planetary phenomena'.[91]

The dominant mode of resource management

Aboriginal traditional maintenance of the fertility of the biota in many different regions by spiritual means is ignored in *Dark Emu*. There is a brief mention of Keen's 2004 study that showed how 'economies were embedded in the prevailing kinship and cosmological systems of particular groups' (page 136). Instead, *Dark Emu*'s focus is completely on material methods of species cultivation. Yet Aboriginal spiritual management of species fertility was clearly the dominant mode by comparison with physical species management practices. It was dominant, but the two were often complementary.

The earthly environment was not the only target of Aboriginal spiritual management. Nicolas Peterson witnessed a Warlpiri winter solstice ceremony in July 1972. The people sang songs before and after sunset: 'The explicit purpose was to get the Milky Way to move across the sky more quickly and so reduce the length of the night.'[92] I was once in a bush camp south of Cape Keerweer, CYP, where we were sleeping in the open, and an unseasonal thunderstorm began to break out during the night. The senior Wik man in the camp, Billy Landis Gothachalkenin, harangued the lightning and storm in no uncertain terms, to get it to stop. His sister Isobel Wolmby, on fearing approaching lightning during the wet season we spent based at Watha-nhiin Outstation in the same region, would take a sharp knife and slash the air in its direction, 'cutting' the dangerous flashes to make them stop.

And Wik people had a firm rule about digging wells: if people with no right to the country dug a well, it would cause cyclones supernaturally; and if anyone failed to refill a well after digging it, that also would bring down storms and cyclones. This influencing of the meteorological went hand in hand with a practice that prevented both trespass and the fouling of wells—another blending of the spiritual with the pragmatic.

Has Pascoe in *Dark Emu* simply reflected a modern Eurocentric attitude in which physical resource management is central, separable from the spiritual domain, and clearly the preferred medium for showing 'advancement' and 'sophistication' beyond 'mere' hunting, gathering, trapping and fishing?

If you're looking for 'sophisticated' complexity in classical Aboriginal society, you will find it above all in the intricate webs of kinship and social structure; in the richness of the grammars of the languages; in the innumerable mythic narratives that bind place to place and engage the full range of the emotions; in the thousands of song series and the prodigious feats of memory by which they have been locally maintained; and in the elaborate intertwining of totemic religion, linguistic group organisation and land tenure systems.

In the deeper European past, species fertility was also heavily reliant on religious acts, such as sacrifices to the gods of various crops and domestic and wild animals, or monotheistic prayer. These mostly survive now only as folkloric memory gestures in the case of crop gods, or, more sincerely, in the case of, for example, Lutheran wheat farmers praying for rain. A secularised notion of Aboriginal cultivation, devoid of spiritual dimensions, did not exist in Australia before conquest.

3
The language question

Culture is to a very significant degree reflected in language. In *Dark Emu*, Pascoe does not consider how Aboriginal people have classified their economic world or their economic artefacts in their own languages. If, as he says, they traditionally *hoed* and *tilled* and *ploughed* the earth, made *gardens*, selected and *sowed* seed or *planted* tubers, *irrigated* their crops, *reaped* the results and stored them, and thus were *farmers* on *farms* doing *farming*, should he not have tried to demonstrate that these categories and terms were present in at least some of the approximately 260 distinct languages of Australia in 1788?

Almost the only venture into language in *Dark Emu* is this: 'It seems even the name of Lake Killapaninna [*sic:* Killalpaninna] has within it the word for the harvest grass variously spelt pannana or parrara. The evidence, while now difficult to find on the surface of the land, is still embedded in the language' (page 47). Killalpaninna (more accurately Kirlawirlpanhinha) actually translates from the original Diyari not as 'harvest grass' but as 'In the Vagina', a name arising from the site's sacred mythology according to the highly trained linguist Peter Austin, who wrote a study of the language of the Diyari people whose country includes Lake Killalpaninna.[1] Pascoe describes his own etymology here as 'evidence'. The actual and contrary facts, however, appeared in a published paper by Austin twenty-eight years before Pascoe's appeared.

The basic pattern with regard to the possession of specifically 'horticultural' vocabulary in traditional Australia is that it is found only in the Torres Strait, where horticulture (gardening) was in fact traditionally practised to a degree, on the western islands, and to a greater degree in the east and north.[2]

In their popular *Macquarie Aboriginal Words*, Nick Thieberger and Bill McGregor sampled seventeen representative Australian languages. If you look up common words like 'to dig' or 'to die', all seventeen languages have a term.[3] If you look up things that have a limited environmental distribution, there are fewer entries: 'oyster' has six, and 'paperbark' has four (out of seventeen languages). If you look up 'garden' and 'to sow, to plant', there is only a single entry in each case: Meryam Mir, the language of the eastern Torres Strait.[4] This is not an Aboriginal language. It is a Papuan language within Australia's borders.[5] The very different western Torres Strait language, Kala Lagaw Ya, has been described as a Papuan language with a significant Australian substratum.[6]

Both the western and eastern Torres Strait languages have considerable gardening vocabulary,[7] as in the terms in tables 1 and 2, recorded long ago by linguist Sidney Ray.[8]

Table 1: Gardening vocabulary in the Mabuiag language, western Torres Strait, recorded by Sidney Ray in 1907.

Mabuiag	English	Reference
naguli, M. n.	gardens. Probably yam gardens.	Ray:113
gowa, n.	a trench, ditch. Cf. K. pari-goua, ditch.	Ray:99
pagi, v.	stick in, go in, pierce.	Ray:116
gowa-pagi, v.	dig up garden.	Ray:99
pa, n.	a fence for garden; a stockade. Plural: pal.	Ray:116
sai-palat, v.	to plough.	Ray:117
baradar saipalaiza, n.	a plough.	Ray:120
pa-pagai, v.	enclose, as a garden, fence in.	Ray:116
pa-pagi, v.	make a fence.	Ray:116
sowagai, n.	weeds, 'small bush in garden', grass.	Ray:122

Table 2: Gardening vocabulary in the Meryam Mir language, eastern Torres Strait, recorded by Sidney Ray in 1907.

Meryam Mir	English	Reference
gedub,[9] n.	a garden, plantation.	Ray:143
irukill,[10] v.	make fence, enclose.	Ray:145
itara,[11] n.	clearing of bush for garden, carrying away of scrub, etc.	Ray:145
kebe-le, n.	a man who borrows a garden.	Ray:147
kebe-le tonar, n.	ceremony for closing gardens.	Ray:147

Meryam Mir	English	Reference
nauwareb zogo, n.	the zogo [sacred object] of a certain garden.[12]	Ray:155
sule, n.	a man who lends a garden, that is, who goes away.	Ray:160
wek,[13] n.	an ornament placed in a garden, 'to make him flash'.	Ray:164
no-sumez, n.	weeds.	Ray:156

Long-term cultural influence on Australian mainlanders of Cape York Peninsula by Torres Strait peoples was manifest in ritual, including masked dancers, grass skirts for male performers, and the skin drum.[14] That mainlanders were not closed to also absorbing some economic technologies from their northern and Papuan neighbours is clear from their adoption of outrigger canoes and the detachable-head harpoon. Horticulture, however, and the bow and arrow did not travel south along with these influences.

The story of how northern and eastern Cape York peoples came to have outrigger canoes—watercraft not found anywhere else in Aboriginal Australia in 1788—is complex. It is also a good case for showing how language reflects technical innovation or borrowing. In the area from north of Cooktown to Princess Charlotte Bay, the languages reflect the adoption of double outrigger canoes not from Torres Strait but from eastern New Guinea, as Ray Wood's 2018 paper lays out in detail.[15] Given that culture and technology are usually reflected in language, it is natural that specialised outrigger canoe terminology in that area is not found in other regions of Australia. In the 1970s I recorded the words in Table 3 from Johnny Flinders, who was born in the area, at Cape Melville, in about 1900. Where the Old People did not have such a maritime technology, they had no such vocabulary.

Table 3: Canoe-related vocabulary in the Flinders Island language, recorded by Peter Sutton in the 1970s.

Flinders Island language	English
akála	boat, vehicle (generic)
akála aapa (kala:pa)	outrigger canoe
aapa	pontoon
athindhin	pontoon struts (vertical)

Flinders Island language	English
arparr	pontoon struts (horizontal)
alpayi	prow of canoe
thurriini	stern
opungul	rope for straining up pontoon
wirabo	paddle
ondul	anchor
thorro	sail
ngulma thorro (ngulma = nose)	jib sail

The only mainland Australian Aboriginal language I have found with a word listed under 'garden' that is not a loan from English has this rather opaquely curious entry in Wathawurrung (Victoria): *'English*: "garden (of Eden)"'. *Phonetic*: "wo(r)det". *Sources*: "wordet tus, woddet tus".[16] An etymology is not available.

I have consulted dictionaries of around forty Aboriginal languages looking for words glossed as 'farm', 'farmer', 'to farm', 'garden', 'to sow', 'hoe', 'crop', 'to plant', 'weed' and 'to plough'.[17] Almost invariably there are no such terms. What appear to be the exceptions are usually adaptations of existing terms to new activities, such as the extension of 'bury' or 'insert' being used for 'to plant something'; or to 'sprinkle' or 'broadcast a story' being used for 'to sow'—but in fact even these are rare. The *Noongar Dictionary* is rather exceptional in having a verb *niran* 'to plant in the ground', but there is no more detail.[18] Given that house posts and spears were planted or stood up in the ground, it may have been an old word adapted to new uses.

The Burarra dictionary (Northern Territory) has an entry that also seemed to me exceptional: *'lamaja* ... [to] plant so will grow, as of bananas, coconuts etc., and figuratively of establishing a story, teaching a belief'.[19] Burarra cultural expert Lily Gurambara of Yilan in Arnhem Land informs me, via Geoffrey Bagshaw as translator, that this verb means 'to put vertically', 'to stand (something) up', 'to leave behind standing', 'to establish'; and, with regard to plants, it is used *only* for introduced garden plants such as bananas, coconuts and watermelon, plants introduced by missionaries ('*Balanda* [European] food' as Lily says) and tamarind trees, introduced by the Macassans, who may have done so by discarding the seeds after eating.[20]

One dictionary, of the desert language Anmatyerr, although lacking the other terms I have mentioned, has a verb *alpent-wem* with the meaning of 'to broadcast a story', with a second meaning 'spread seeds, sow seeds, scatter seeds'. A sentence example for the latter is translated as: *Spreading the mulga seeds around so that they grow.*[21] This is an interesting rarity and reflects a seed-broadcasting practice, but its antiquity or recency is not established.

There are words for 'to grow' but they are mostly based on a verb meaning 'to rear (a person)', 'to bring up' or 'to make someone/something get up'. A typical example is Jingulu (Northern Territory): 'binjam: V[erb]. rear (children), adopt, cultivate, plant, sow. *Wawa binjamangaju.* I'm raising a child. *Ngayirni binjamangaju babirdimi.* I grow potatoes.'[22]

Note that the only example of a plant being grown here is an introduced one: potatoes. Actually, *babirdimi* is an old term for yam, here extended to cover potatoes.[23]

In one case (Kaytetye) an intransitive verb meaning 'to grow, to sprout, to rise' (*aytenke*) has a transitive counterpart using the same stem (*aytelh-aylenke*) that means 'to make a plant grow; to plant something'.[24] Although there is no indication in my source as to how far back this second usage goes, it is of note that Kaytetye and Anmatyerr have adjoining language countries in Central Australia.

Sometimes the relevant word is clearly a loan from English, such as Tiwi *katini* for 'garden', or Wiradjuri *bilaw-ir* for 'hoe', derived from English 'plough' (*bilaw*).[25] Wiradjuri also has a verb 'to plough', *birrga-n-bi-rra*, which is derived from a verb stem meaning 'to scratch'.[26] Such adaptations are common in post-contact vocabularies. The first thing settlers and missionaries usually did on taking up residence was to start a garden. They brought a vocabulary with them for the things that were familiar as well as foreign. Terms absent from Aboriginal lexicons could be borrowed from English or an old term could be adapted to a new use. A frequent example is of verbs for 'to write', something that arrived newly with the colonials. In Wiradjuri it is the verb that meant, originally, 'to spear, stick or prod with a spear'.[27] Usually it is the old verb 'to scratch/scrape', in my experience.

Wiradjuri also has a verb *gunga-m-bi-rra* 'to harrow or plough', which appears to be derived from the verb 'to comb', *gunga-rra*.[28] I would be confident that this meaning developed after the arrival of ploughs with the Europeans. Curiously, no word for 'to sow' is listed in my Wiradjuri source, even though there are seven words for seeds listed.[29] There are, however, three words for 'spade' and a verb 'to scrape with the spade', 'to dig [with a spade]', which probably reflects a specialisation in the gathering of roots, ground nuts and so on using wooden spades.[30]

Spades were not widely used in Aboriginal Australia—wooden bowls, baler shells and digging sticks were the main digging tools—but there is another example from the Adelaide region. In the Adelaide language (Kaurna) *tuku* means 'spade', and *karku* is a she-oak species that also gave its name to a small spade or scoop used for digging for grubs and other things. No word has been recorded in Kaurna for 'garden', 'to sow' or 'to plant'.[31]

4
Ecological agents and 'firestick farming'

In *Dark Emu*, Pascoe suggests that 'Indigenous Australians wandering from plant to plant, kangaroo to kangaroo in hapless opportunism' is 'the accepted view' (page 12). It has to be asked: accepted by whom? This has for generations been the ignorant and lazy view among those unwilling or unable to look into the subject for more than five minutes. People who take the question at all seriously, or who have read any reliable introductory published material of the kind I point to below, or who have found similar guidance in person or on television or the internet, know better.

Without survey evidence it would be hard to know for certain whether the educational efforts of the past fifty years or so, which I examine later, have made so faint an impression on the Australian public in the way Pascoe has suggested. In Chapter 10 of this book I cite numerous examples of introductory texts written for students and others over the past few decades that do not espouse this 'accepted view' that Pascoe positions in stark contrast with his own message.

Firing the country

Pascoe traces the discovery that Aboriginal people were ecological change agents who used fire to manage their lands to archaeologist Rhys Jones's paper of 1969 (page 49). But Jones himself acknowledged a predecessor in Norman Tindale.[1] In 1959 Tindale had published a paper, which Jones cited, containing these passages:

> Man, setting fire to large area of his territory at all times of the year convenient for his hunting, often causes destruction far beyond that done by nature [that is, lightning].

Thus man probably has had a significant hand in the moulding of the present configuration of parts of Australia. Indeed much of the grassland of Australia could have been brought into being as a result of his exploitation ...

Perhaps it is correct to assume that man has had such a profound effect on the distributions of forest and grassland that true primaeval forest may be far less common in Australia than is generally realised ...

Next to the firestick the womans [sic] digging stick was probably the most effective instrument in altering the patterns of plant growth, removing a considerable portion of the more edible forms of vegetable life.[2]

Anthropologist Fred McCarthy referred to this passage at a conference in 1961; his conference paper was published in 1963.[3] Ronald and Catherine Berndt cited the same passage in the section of their introductory text where they discussed traditional resource use by Aboriginal people.[4] The same passage survived unaltered over the next few decades as the Berndts' textbook went into multiple revised editions at least until 1988.[5] For many years this was the standard introductory text on Aboriginal traditional life, past and present. Hundreds if not thousands read it.

It follows that Tindale's proposition on the huge role of human-made fires was already on the public record in the 1950s and 1960s, when Pascoe was a young man and before Jones came up with a fetching label for Aboriginal fire use. Gammage, often relied upon by Pascoe, cites the Berndts' book[6] but not their reference to Tindale, nor Tindale's own early flagging of the environment-changing and economic roles of fire itself. However, Gammage does acknowledge many of those who came after Tindale, from the 1960s onwards, and who found 'sense and purpose in Aboriginal burning'.[7]

Tindale had his own problems with newness and resistance, on this very subject, back in the 1950s. In the same paper he said, 'The picture of man's effect on the Australian environment, lightly sketched in the above paragraphs, is not seen by all ... It was thus possible even as late as 30 years ago [1929] *to dismiss the Australian aboriginal as an ecological agent.*'[8]

In Jones's and Betty Meehan's fifteen months in the bush in Arnhem Land in the early 1970s, they saw fires lit almost every day between

March and January. The main purposes people gave them for firing the country in modest and mosaic patterns were to clear (and 'clean') it for ease of walking and tracking, and as an instrument of hunting. Game was harvested from freshly burned patches. Subsequent providing of green pick for marsupials and maintenance of grasslands free from trees do not seem to have been local objectives, or they were not mentioned, at least, in Jones.[9]

In his 1969 paper on 'firestick farming', Jones listed reasons why people burned 'the bush': for 'fun' or 'custom' (reasons I would not take at face value only); signalling one's presence to others; to clear the way for travel and get rid of vermin; hunting; regeneration of plant food; and 'extending man's habitat'.[10] He did not commit to a view that the last of these was deliberate.[11]

In the paper, Jones put quotes around the term he had invented: 'fire-stick farming'. I do not believe he meant this literally, but it works very well metaphorically. He later said, 'It was not entirely with tongue in cheek that I once called this "fire-stick farming".'[12] Even later, he said, 'So, when I use the word "farming", it isn't just a tongue-in-cheek term. I meant to indicate that through the use of fire people were affecting the land in such a way as to increase the food available to them.'[13] The fact that he did not literally identify this ecological agency as agriculture is made clear in the same paper, where he mentions the first successful claim to native title in Australia: the test-case claim on Murray Island (Mer) by Eddie Mabo, David Passi and James Rice on behalf of their families:

> As a side issue I think it's very interesting that Eddie Mabo came from that one tiny part of the present Commonwealth of Australia which was actually occupied by gardeners [that is, Torres Strait]. You know, these people are Papuan gardeners and, perhaps it's too difficult to discuss these days because there's so much politics attached to any discussion of these issues [that is, *terra nullius*], or any dissenting view. But it is interesting that the Mabo case was in that part of Australia that was occupied by gardeners, and I still wonder—had the [native title] test case been a place occupied by hunters and gatherers, would you have had the same result?[14]

The main purposes older Wik people gave me for firing patches of country in the 1970s were to harvest macropods and small grass-dwelling animals (especially mice and reptiles), and to make the country open and safe from snakes, safe for travelling on foot, and open enough to see long distances beyond camps, in case of threat. People indeed kept firing the country (see below[15]), especially in the season known as *kathuk* ('burn-grass time' in local English). If people want to metaphorically call that 'firestick farming', as Jones did in his 1969 paper, they well may, but producing young grass was never their main motivation in engaging in grass firing in the extensive Wik grasslands and thickets. I never heard of people intending fire to maintain grasslands free from trees, although this may well have been an effect of their actions.

The smoke also dissipated dangerous spirits, and kept the country tamed rather than feral. The adjective they use in Wik-Ngathan to turn 'domestic dog' (*ku'*) into 'dingo' (*ku' thayengun*) means 'wild' or 'untamed'. Country not regularly burned would become *aak thayengun* 'feral country', and could be said to be *aak wuut-ul* 'country that has become reprobate' (literally 'an old man-already'). People also knew that firing incidentally led to green pick that drew marsupials to recently burned areas, but this was not its main purpose. The same observation that green pick was not a primary purpose of bush firing was made for the southern Tanami Desert people by Vaarzon-Morel and Gabrys.[16] Latz and Griffin found the same for Central Australia more generally:

Wik people firing the country, middle Kirke River, Cape York Peninsula, 1977.

Fire was used mainly for short-term advantage in daily hunting and food gathering. People were conscious of the abundance of food plants after fire but saw this largely as a result of ceremonies performed to increase rain and food … Once burnt and the appropriate increase ceremonies performed, only then would the food plants produce in abundance.[17]

In his introductory essay to Marcia Langton's 1998 book *Burning Questions*, Arnhem Lander Dean Yibarbuk has given us one of the best descriptions of the cultural, spiritual and economic roles of fire in a specific monsoon-belt Australian cultural location, in this instance the upper Cadell River of the Northern Territory.[18] Similarly, Vaarzon-Morel and Gabrys have given us a rich account of contemporary firing in the Tanami Desert.[19] An excellent continental survey of traditional fire use is provided by Philip Clarke in the chapter called 'Fire-stick ecology' in his 2007 book *Aboriginal People and Their Plants*.[20]

Resource managers

By the early 1980s it was well recognised among anthropologists of Aboriginal Australia that the pre-colonial economy was one in which people managed resources in a variety of ways, including firing the bush. Nancy Williams and Eugene Hunn put out a volume of papers by various authors on this theme in 1982 called *Resource Managers: North American and Australian Hunter-Gatherers*. In the introduction they said:

Yet a common finding unifies this collection: hunter-gatherers *actively manage* their resources, whether through strategic ecological or economic courses of action via social controls and political maneuver, or by virtue of the power of symbol and ritual. We can firmly reject the stereotype of hunter-gatherers as passive 'food collectors' in opposition to active, food-producing agriculturists.[21] [emphasis in original]

In *Burning Questions*, which is not mentioned in *Dark Emu*, Professor Marcia Langton had already announced the death of the idea that pre-colonial Australians were simply hunter-gatherers and not also ecological agents. This was sixteen years before *Dark Emu*. She wrote:

Furthermore, as botanists, zoologists, anthropologists and geologists continue to investigate the complex relationships between Aboriginal culture, the plant communities, animal species and the physical environment in general, it emerges that *complete dependence on natural bounty is a poor characterisation of the Aboriginal economy*. It now appears that this economy has had a substantial impact on the environment which we characterise today as characteristically Australian.[22]

Eight years before *Dark Emu,* Langton reiterated the fact that the 'mere hunter-gatherer' model of Aboriginal people before European contact was something that lay in the past:

> Economic approaches to pre-European contact history *have evolved from an initial view of prehistoric Australians as simple foragers* to a greater understanding of the complex connections between the social and physical dimensions of resource exploitation in hunting and gathering societies.[23]

Langton was nevertheless happy to describe the pre-conquest subsistence system of the peoples of Cape York Peninsula, perhaps by way of a convenient shorthand, as 'their hunting, gathering and fishing economy'.[24] No evidence of pre-conquest horticulture or agriculture can be found in Langton's writings on the people of south-east CYP, with whom she carried out fieldwork for her PhD on their relationships with country.[25]

Tindale, long before Langton's 1998 statement, was an explicit opponent of a simple 'hunter-gatherer' pigeonholing of Aboriginal economies:

> In the past it has generally been assumed that the aborigines have always been a nonagricultural [*sic*] people and this may be true, yet some practices suggest that the very first steps may have been taken in areas along a path or paths leading to gardening, irrigation, and the partial domestication of animals …
>
> Were the Mara and Alawa on the verge of becoming rice growers? They went each year to the same areas. Only one step, deliberate planting, was missing. The Alawa had even learned to store surplus food such as water lily seed in paperbark-lined pits in rock shelters; *however there is no suggestion that this was ever used for planting.*[26]

These people were, in short, gatherers and storers but not cultivators, at least not in the material sense.

The regionally differing degrees to which people intervened in the reproductive cycle materially, as opposed to ritually, are well illustrated here. Perhaps at the opposite end of the spectrum is Phyllis Kaberry's description of the bush harvesting practices of the Aboriginal women among whom she lived in the Kimberley in 1934–36:

> It is not the steady strenuous labour of the German peasant woman bending from dawn to dusk over her fields, hoeing, weeding, sowing, and reaping. The Aboriginal woman has greater freedom of movement and more variety …
>
> Women then do not appear to be embryonic agriculturists in this part of Australia, in spite of the fact that many have worked on the stations and know something of gardening.[27]

Narcisse Pelletier's seventeen years living with bush people in eastern CYP beyond the limits of colonisation apparently did not reveal any signs of agriculture of a kind familiar to a European. He was recorded as stating: 'No-one plants and no-one sows';[28] 'They seldom stay long in one place';[29] and 'It would seem that these tribes spend their lives in hunting, fishing, and fighting, and never attempt any kind of cultivation.'[30] However, he did make an early observation of plant management using fire: 'I cannot see among these tribes any other branch of industry which seems to be even in the embryonic state, unless, from the agricultural viewpoint, we wish to consider the care the savages take in firing the woods where the yams grow so that the tubers of these plants develop more extensively and their crop is more plentiful.'[31]

No one-way street

Tindale provided several additional concrete examples of practices from different parts of Australia (also discussed in *Dark Emu*, though presented as if being revealed for the first time), including the turning-over of soil that is not a prelude to planting but a by-product of extraction, and the replacing of yam stems after the tuber had been removed, seed grinding, storage, and use of hunting nets.[32] He even used the term 'proto-agriculture':

> One of the important elements of *proto-agriculture* present among the Iliaura [Alyawarr] and other konakandi [hairy armgrass] users

seems to have been the idea of storage. Food sufficient only for current needs was milled ... Gathered surpluses were stored in caves for months so that women did not have to go food-gathering every day. That storage is not quite unknown elsewhere is indicated for both the Ualarai [Yuwalaraay] and Wadjari as indicated in later paragraphs; *however the storage was always for use and never for returning to the soil.*[33]

'Proto-agriculture' is not agriculture. It may well have been, instead, a long-term stable skill beyond which it was unnecessary to venture, and therefore was not proto-anything. We should not assume that it was 'on the way' to something other than its own continued effectiveness. The same applies to 'incipient animal husbandry'.[34] All these 'incipient' and 'proto' words, and expressions such as 'on the pathway to agriculture', suggest unfulfilled potential and assume an inevitable progression that has not been completed.

That a shift from hunter-gathering to horticulture and/or animal husbandry is not in every case a one-way journey is proven by those peoples who have shifted back from horticulture and pastoralism (stock herding) to foraging. For example, there was a reversion to hunting and gathering in the South Island of New Zealand between the initial settlement of Aotearoa by the horticultural Māori in about 1300 CE and circa 1700 CE.[35] Around 5000 years ago in parts of Europe there was 'a reversion to foraging in areas where agriculture had been practised'.[36] In Africa, it is documented that Maasai and Kikuyu herders have at times reverted from pastoralism to hunting and gathering, and 'some San communities have oscillated between foraging and cattle herding over several centuries—perhaps for millennia'.[37] As Layton, Foley and Williams say, 'These examples underline the danger of perceiving the transition between hunting and gathering and specialized husbandry as a one-way process that in some absolute sense constitutes progress.'[38]

The 'incipient' model of Aboriginal ecological agency suggests a deficit theory of Aboriginal culture. We need to grow out of that one-directional evolutionary mindset and respect classical Aboriginal culture and practice for what it was and is, not for what it might have become.

Although *Dark Emu* refers to Ian Keen's 2004 book on pre-conquest Aboriginal economies (pages 130, 136), it does not consider his discussion of where these economies lie on the spectrum between foraging and agriculture. It is not possible here to do justice to Keen's 436-page study, but after summarising regionally varying traditional Aboriginal ways in which bush resources were managed, he says:

> These practices change our picture of Aboriginal hunting, gathering and fishing as a mode of subsistence. It involved a more radical intervention in the ecology than was recognised earlier, and, as Beth Gott remarks, the boundary between foraging and farming is blurred. The writings of David Harris are particularly relevant here; he constructs a continuum from dependency on wild plants and animals to dependency on domesticated ones. Even where production of wild plant-foods and animals dominates, it may be combined with cultivation involving small-scale clearing of vegetation and minimal tillage, and/or the taming, protective herding, or free-range management of animals. Larger-scale clearing and systematic tillage comes further along the continuum. 'Agriculture' involves more or less exclusive cultivation of domesticated plants, livestock raising by settled farmers, or transhumant[39] or nomadic pastoralism …
>
> In light of these discussions, although I have used the expression 'hunters and gatherers' to characterise Aboriginal subsistence practices, it might be more appropriate to classify Aboriginal subsistence production as that of hunter-gatherer-cultivators.[40]

Keen has since revised his opinion and removed '-cultivators' from his description.[41]

If you read Keen's 2004 book from cover to cover you will find plenty of references to vegetable food foraging, seed harvesting, fishing, hunting, and the use of fire to modify the environment, but there appears to be no evidence of soil preparation followed by sowing of seeds or tubers, which are the usual components of cultivation. This is in spite of one of Keen's chosen areas of focus being the Barwon/Darling rivers region and the Western Desert, where there was extensive harvesting and grinding of seed foods.[42] His extensive index has no entries for garden(ing), sowing, planting or, indeed, cultivation. Pascoe's presentation of his findings as new, and his frequent assertion of the ignorance of the Australian public, appear at least partly based on an unwillingness to acknowledge this kind of highly relevant published discussion and the direct teachings of Aboriginal people.

The limits of theory

Pascoe does not appear to have ever probed the agriculture or gardening issue with senior and knowledgeable Aboriginal people who grew up living off the land, or whose older family members did. None of his topics appear to have been explored with elders who have retained traditional knowledge. He quotes white explorers freely, but not the words of traditional owners of Aboriginal land, and only occasionally the reports of those who have carried out in-depth research on Aboriginal traditions with living Aboriginal people. Pascoe is an armchair theorist.

In the early twentieth century, when cultural anthropology was still a developing social science, there were the great 'armchair' anthropologists of metropolitan Europe and America, who published books using the observations of others, and then there were the fieldworkers. Bill Stanner wrote that 'the damage to our appreciation of Aboriginal life really came from the men of the armchair, who write from afar under a kind of enchantment'.[43]

By the 1920s, professional field anthropologists were practising 'participant-observation' studies with Indigenous peoples (for example, Ursula McConnel; see below). This meant living among the people for extended periods of months or years, being immersed in local

Fieldworker Ursula McConnel writing for the *Sydney Morning Herald.*

culture and language, and becoming socially competent in their hosts' way of life. In the language of the times, their task was to understand things 'from the native point of view' and then educate their readers by translating that view into systematic knowledge and writing in a metropolitan language. One of the topics they usually covered in some detail was how people made a living—that is, how they obtained food and raw materials.

To do all of this well required a strong dose of empathy, and it is well known that anthropologists historically have frequently translated that empathy and acquired knowledge into support for their hosts, politically as well as in defence against racial slurs and what in the early twentieth century was called 'maltreatment of natives'. Anthropologists like AP Elkin, Donald Thomson, McConnel and Olive Pink were in the vanguard of the fight against the assimilation policy decades before it was rescinded. I have elsewhere gone into the evidence for this activism by anthropologists in the Australian case in the years 1925–60.[44] Since that time, Australian anthropologists' activism in support of Indigenous causes has only increased. It has not been an absence of goodwill that has prevented them from saying that the Old People were practising agriculture.

On the basis of what I have learned from senior Aboriginal mentors over a period of fifty years, it is clear to me that the non-adoption of horticulture and agriculture by the Old People was not a failure of the imagination but an active championing and protection of their own way of life and, when in contact with outsiders, resistance to an alien economic pattern. These were and are people easily confident in the bush, and proud of their ability to run an economy that had minimal negative impact on their countries.

Resistance to horticulture and agriculture

Anthropologist Athol Chase worked long and intensively with people of north-east CYP, who are now mostly based at Lockhart River settlement. He made a special study of people's relationships with the flora and fauna of their world, including their botanical knowledge and their hunting, gathering and care for their countries. He reported on their resistance to gardening and agriculture:

> For the Umpila, Kuuku Ya'u, and other Aboriginal peoples of this immediate area, agricultural practices are a wasteful and illegitimate

activity in the landscape—'It is not our way; it is alright for other people. We get our food from the bush' ... Despite enormous pressures by a government of European derivation to assimilate them into a European perspective of society, economy, and religion, there is a stubborn resistance to such shifts in beliefs ...[45]

Such pressures were exerted by mission and government authorities alike as in the case of Lake Condah (Victoria): 'The Aborigines will not cultivate their own gardens unless some pressure is brought to bear upon them to compel them to do so.'[46]

Early Northern Territory missionary Father Francis Xavier Gsell recalled local reactions to the first establishment of a mission garden on Bathurst Island (see below):

Watching us sowing, they grumbled: 'What a pity to lose all this food, these potatoes, yams, and ground-nuts. In the earth they will go bad and be of no use to anybody. If,' they said finally, 'you really want something to eat, sing a song to the spirits, dance a dance, and you'll get all the food you want.'[47]

From a similar source and era, Yirrkala missionary Wilbur Chaseling recalled that 'When it came time for planting it seemed ridiculous to

Catholic missionaries: Sisters of the Order of Our Lady of the Sacred Heart of Darwin.

the nomad to bury good sweet-potatoes instead of eating them …'[48] During the same phase at Milingimbi, Ella Shepherdson recalled:

> Garden work has always been an uphill struggle because our Aborigines were not very interested in it. However there are now a number who have gardens of their own and work hard in them.
>
> When we first went to Milingimbi, the men had to be taught to use the old Fordson tractor for ploughing the ground and preparing it for crops of cotton, maize and millet in the first instance then sweet potatoes, cassava and peanuts at a later stage. When they saw good food being put into the ground, this to their way of thinking was a waste, and often it would be dug up and eaten.[49]

Ronald and Catherine Berndt reported a snapshot of this kind of resistance from their own experience in a nearby region:

> An Arnhem Land woman once said, in effect, rather patronizingly, as she watched a Fijian missionary working in his mission garden, anxiously concerned because a few of the plants had died: 'You people go to all that trouble, working and planting seeds, but we don't have to do that. All these things are there for us, the Ancestral Beings left them for us. In the end, you depend on the sun and the rain just the same as we do, but the difference is that we just have to go and collect the food when it is ripe. We don't have all this other trouble.'[50]

They followed that passage with examples of traditional resource conservation such as not collecting all the yams from any one location, 'sprinkling seeds around' (details not given), preserving valuable trees, and not spearing stingrays when they were breeding.[51] They added: 'Holding this view, that nature is their garden, and one which they need not cultivate or "improve", means of course that the Aborigines were not able to vary the range of foods available.'[52]

In 1974, I participated in a field trip to map Johnny Flinders' country and its neighbours in eastern Cape York. Flinders spoke with a briefly visiting geographer, David Harris of University College London, who asked him why his people did not sow plants to make food. Flinders' brief reply was: 'No, he grow himself!'

In the early 1980s senior Kuku Yalanji man Johnny Walker of Bloomfield, south-east Cape York, told anthropologist Chris Anderson that the Old People were mystified by the missionary obsession with agriculture. He said something like: '*Bama* [Aboriginal people] know where to get *mayi* [vegetable food] already, why should we stay in one place and have to hoe and bother with a farm!?'[53]

And yet there are also many accounts of people adopting the planting of sweet potatoes, watermelons, pumpkins, cassava and similar exotics, with missionary support. This kind of horticulture occurred at Garttji Lagoon in Arnhem Land after missionary Edgar Wells introduced it to local people,[54] and Lazarus Lamilami recalled his age group being taught how to grow things, including potatoes, corn, cassava and pumpkins.[55]

In classical Aboriginal philosophy, the Dreaming basis of the biota ensures an eternal cycling of birth, life, death and renewal. Warlpiri elder Engineer Jack Japaljarri explained this to me once by using native honey bees as an example. Twirling his forefingers in a rotating movement, he said, 'That Dreaming, he rollin', he rollin', like honey bee, live one, dead one, live one.' This was not Asian reincarnation belief, it was the depiction of an unchanging cycle of life and a subsistence system underpinned by the Dreaming ground of being. It was not valorising the achievements of clever, ingenious, creative human beings. And it was embedded in a philosophy free from the ambiguous enchantments of notions of progress.

5
Social evolutionism rebirthed

Reviewing Pascoe's essay collection *Salt*, in *Inside Story*, Professor Tom Griffiths said of *Dark Emu*:

> Pascoe often over-reads the sources—and for what purpose? To prove that Aboriginal peoples were like Europeans? *Dark Emu* is too much in thrall to a discredited evolutionary view of economic stages …
>
> There is concern that archaic evolutionary hierarchies should be revived just when we thought that such a northern-hemisphere mode of thinking had been transcended in Australia.[1]

It could be added: *Dark Emu* is in effect an argument against cultural relativism. It is in favour of the resurrection of the view that agricultural peoples who live in permanent housing in populous villages are more 'advanced' than semi-nomads whose traditional year cycled through seasonal phases of high and low mobility, and smaller and larger camps. Under this Eurocentric and now thoroughly discredited model, Aboriginal people would look like primitives unless they could be retrospectively remade into farmers. There are moments in *Dark Emu* where a medieval European peasant economy seems to be held up as the progressive target for Australians before conquest, or even claimed as its 'achievement'.

This might leave the less discriminating among Pascoe's readers with the very attitude he is anxious to get rid of: denigration of a people whose mobility (regionally variable) was central to their use of country; whose housing was in most cases temporarily occupied, seasonally variable, and regionally differing depending on how much people were sedentary; and whose frequent (and again regionally varying) light clothing, nakedness or near-nakedness was not a matter for embarrassment, as it seems it is for Pascoe. Nudity was not a matter for shame in the classical Aboriginal world.[2]

The anthropologist Lloyd Warner lived among Yolngu people in Arnhem Land in the 1920s. His admiration for the people is evident in the name of the book he published about them: *A Black Civilization*. He wrote:

> The days in Arnhem Land are always warm. No clothes are needed for comfort. The occasional cold nights are made comfortable by windbreaks and small fires built to provide ample warmth ... [The Aboriginal person's] naked condition before the coming of the white man was far more appropriate to the country he lived in.[3]

The nakedness was not absolute. Among the various bodily adornments Warner listed were belts, bands, necklaces, and 'men's and women's pubic covering'.[4] This is generally the picture for most of the monsoon belt, although there were other instances where people wore more coverings than these, and less (see Chapter 7).

Yet under Pascoe's model, the Gunditjmara of Victoria must have been 'advanced' people, and the Yolngu of Arnhem Land or the Pitjantjatjara of the Western Desert must have been 'less advanced' people, given the contrast in their degrees of nomadism, their use or non-use of clothing, and their interventions (or relative absence of them) in the world of natural resources.

Evolutionism in *Dark Emu*

Pascoe frequently uses the language of nineteenth-century social evolutionism, even though his concentration is not on social organisation but on subsistence and technology. He is not so close to his major source, Gerritsen, on this subject. Gerritsen made an explicit attack on social evolutionism.[5] Pascoe offers an apparent rejection of social evolutionism (pages 12, 126, 154) but then proceeds to employ it. These are his own words on the subject:

> These [explorers'] journals revealed a much more complicated Aboriginal economy than the *primitive hunter-gatherer* lifestyle we had been told was the *simple lot* of Australia's First People.

Hunter-gatherer societies forage and hunt for food and do not employ agricultural methods or build permanent dwellings; they are *nomadic*. (pages 11–12)

Colonial Australia sought to forget the *advanced* nature of the Aboriginal society and economy ... (page 17)

The idea of agriculture was so well *advanced* that seed was traded as a cultural item. (page 30)

The scholar Rupert Gerritsen assembled a large body of material about the *progression* of people worldwide *towards* sedentism and agriculture. One of the tests for this *progress* is the domestication of plants. (page 35)

It may be that not all Aboriginal peoples were involved in these practices but if the testament of explorers and first witnesses is to be believed most Aboriginal Australians were, at the very least, *in the early stages of an agricultural society* and, it could be argued, *ahead of* many other parts of the world. (page 47)

Permanent housing was a feature of the pre-contact Aboriginal economy and *marked the movement towards agricultural reliance.* (page 73)

Pottery is one of the tests applied by Western archaeologists to the *developmental level* reached by civilisations. Australian Aboriginals would, at first glance, appear to have failed this test ... If *the test of sophistication* were whether or not all were fed regardless of rank or whether all contributed to the spiritual and cultural health of the civilisation, Aboriginal Australia might have *a much higher rank than some of the nations considered the hallmark of human evolution.* (page 105)

It would seem that Aboriginal and Torres Strait Islander civilisation was *on a trajectory towards greater and more sophisticated* use of pottery ... (page 111)

China was probably the most *advanced* nation on earth until the eighteenth century ... (page 111)

Near the end of *Dark Emu*, Pascoe poses a question to which he provides no clear answer: 'Anyone reading this book and the books which form part of its research will wonder why *the trajectory of development* in Aboriginal Australia did not lead to a full blown scientific and agricultural *advance*' (page 155).

He raises, as a possibility, the role played by population size as a causal factor in 'innovation'. The implication is that a larger society may have been more 'advanced'. But, he adds, 'perhaps there is a philosophical, as well as evidentiary, reason for Aboriginal civilisation'(page 155). I strongly support this 'philosophical' emphasis, as is clear from Chapter 2, but it cannot be used to explain a putative low achievement on an imagined 'trajectory of development'.

Talk of degrees of advancement and 'early stages' of agricultural development are the words of economic and technological evolutionism. Pascoe regards the possession of pottery, sewn clothing, agriculture, permanent settlements, and houses that employ stone rather than tree limbs, grass and bark as hallmarks of a more 'advanced' or more sophisticated society. He appears to regard nudity, residential mobility, economic reliance on hunting and gathering, and the use of minimalist shelters as signs of lack of 'advancement'.

If Australian societies were, as Pascoe argues, on a 'movement towards agricultural reliance', was this same movement going on for over 50,000 years? If people devised these adaptations 50,000 years ago, have they been stuck in a time warp of 'lack of advancement' ever since? Why should we believe things would have necessarily gone any further along this 'trajectory' but for the fact that they were cataclysmically interrupted by European conquest in 1788 and later? If these shifts were 'advancement', as Pascoe says, does a failure to get any further over thousands of years mean that Aboriginal people were 'less advanced' than the rest of the world by 1788, perpetually treading water?

False assumptions and Eurocentric thinking underlie these questions. Unfortunately, they are directly encouraged by Pascoe's evolutionary scheme. There are better questions: What is wrong with a stable economic system that maintains the integrity of the environment and people's relationships with it, using minimal interference with natural cycles?[6] Had people in fact achieved states of 'equilibrium' or settled relationships with the environment that enabled their stable continuation for extensive periods?[7] Why should this be characterised as an unfinished project, as Pascoe suggests? Or was it in fact accomplished, bedded down for long eras, and adjusted to climatic and sea-level changes over centuries? Was not a minimal footprint in fact the key accomplishment?

Archaeologist Heather Builth prefers the latter understanding of the Lake Condah fish traps of Victoria's Western District: 'Indigenous people occupying the landscape of the Mount Eccles lava flow at the time of European contact had already achieved *sustainable development* by adapting appropriate extractive technology to an enhanced local ecological systems [*sic*].'[8]

Tom Griffiths again:

I think it's a mistake to treat the concept of agriculture as a timeless, stable, universal and preordained template, to apply a European hierarchical metaphor, an imperial measure of civilisation, to societies that defy imported classifications. One of the great insights delivered by that half-century of scholarship is that Aboriginal societies produced a civilisation quite unlike any other, one uniquely adapted to Australian elements and ecosystems.[9]

Pascoe's approach appears to resemble the old Eurocentric view held by the British conquerors of Aboriginal society. Those were the people who organised mass theft of Aboriginal country and many of whom justified the killing of people who resisted them, really out of greed and indifference, but often under an ideological flag of social evolutionism. They assumed they had a right to profit from the 'survival of the fittest' and were the 'superior race'. The 'less advanced' had to make way for the 'more advanced'. Pascoe risks taking us back to that fatal shore by resurrecting the interpretation of differing levels of complexity and differing extents of intervention in the environment as degrees of advancement and evolution and cleverness and sophistication.

Innovation, conservation and Aboriginal religion

Pascoe's book is an essay in admiration of creativity and invention. Readers are encouraged to feel rushes of wonder for ingenious devices, for 'achievements'. This is dangerously close to a Western notion of culture focused on constant innovation, competition, progress and, in its lighter moments, gadgetry, gimmickry, smartness, novelty.

Classical Aboriginal societies were not so enamoured of the idea of human creativity and invention and were completely averse to the shallow glamour of novelty. In fact, they were hyper-conservative: change was generally frowned on very seriously, and new ways usually had to be sanctioned by developments in Dreaming mythology, or by introduced sacred ceremonies, or by having been 'found' (not created) in dreams and then sanctioned by elders. The fish traps of Brewarrina and eastern Cape York were not claimed as the ingenious works of human beings, but were regarded as having been put there in the Dreaming, by Dreamings. The Brewarrina traps are the creation of culture hero Baiame.[10] There are many similar examples of ancient creations being attributed to non-human Dreamings, from the great shell mounds of Cape York Peninsula,[11] to the ancient pecked engravings at Helen Springs, Northern Territory (my own fieldwork).

Yir-Yoront people of CYP, many still living in the bush in the 1930s, made no watercraft. Given that their location was in the wetlands of the Mitchell River system and on the coast, this example stands out as evidence for the role of spiritual traditions in the adoption of technology:

Among the bush Yir Yoront the only means of water transport is a light wood log to which they cling in their constant swimming of rivers, salt creeks, and tidal inlets. These natives know that tribes forty-five miles [72 km] further north have a bark canoe. They know that these northern tribes can thus fish from mid-stream or out at sea, instead of clinging to the river banks and beaches, that they can cross coastal waters infested with crocodiles ...

For them, the adoption of the canoe would not be simply a matter of learning a number of new behavioral skills for its manufacture and use. The adoption would require a much more difficult procedure; the acceptance by the entire society of a myth, either locally developed or borrowed, to explain the presence of the canoe, to associate it with some one or more of the several hundred mythical ancestors ... and thus establish it as an accepted totem of one of the clans ready to be used by the whole community. The Yir Yoront have not made this adjustment, and in this case we can only say that for the time being at least, ideas have won out over very real pressures for technological change.[12]

Archaeologist Harry Allen was sceptical about the proposition that 'the Aboriginal totemic philosophy maintained the economic [foraging] status quo by providing ritual substitutes for practical action and by morally discouraging technological innovation'.[13] His basis for doubt was the archaeological history of innovations in lithics, religion and social organisation in the Darling Basin. But these all seem to me minor variations on a theme, not revolutions in economic or social structure, such as from foraging to shifting horticulture, from foraging to settled agriculture, or from nomadic pastoralism to hunting and gathering. Donald Thomson made this broad generalisation:

> The Australian aborigines are extremely conservative, and before absorbing any important element of culture, social or material, they generally give it a place in their myth pattern and bring it within the totemic scheme. This provides a background in tradition and so gives a charter for its use.[14]

Technological changes that occurred elsewhere may well also have been legitimised through spiritual pathways, but surviving evidence of this is usually lacking. One of Pascoe's focal subjects, the milling of seeds into flour for the making of seedcakes, is a relevant case. Use of millstones for grinding seeds was adopted through much of arid-zone Australia and nearby beginning somewhere around 4000 years ago.[15] This was a significant shift in technology and subsistence practices that occurred after about 46,000 years of occupation of the continent. Grindstone mythology is rich in certain regions, such as the Flinders Ranges–Simpson Desert area. There, in the Simpson Desert version given by Mick McLean Irinyili, the Grinding Stone Men travel from Pirlaka (Beelaka Well) to Marrinha (Marree) and on to Mount Termination west of the Flinders Ranges, for ceremonies.[16] The economic practice of seed grinding certainly had mythic and ritual accreditation by the nineteenth century in that region.

   Dark Emu bypasses the widely based evidence for the introduction of seed grinding around 4000 years ago and instead uses the isolated Cuddie Springs site case as evidence that Australians had begun grinding seeds, and were the world's 'first bakers', around 30,000 years ago (in the Pleistocene period), 15,000 years before the Egyptians (page 30). *Dark Emu* recycles that material from an unpublished manuscript by a non-archaeologist, Eric Rolls.[17] Professor Mike Smith, senior archaeologist at the National Museum of Australia (NMA), after a detailed discussion of the evidence, concluded instead: 'In this context, claims for late Pleistocene seed-grinding implements at Cuddie Springs … are *tenuous*.'[18]

   Pascoe's *Young Dark Emu* does not mention the common seed-grinding evidence of the last 4000 years but picks out the tenuous

Cuddie Springs case as the first port of call and almost the only one.[19] It is exceptional in more than one way, and quite unrepresentative of the picture. And instead of being 30,000 years old, in *Young Dark Emu* it suddenly becomes more than twice as ancient—65,000 years old:

> She swept her hand through the grass heads at Cuddie Springs ...
> She glanced around, selected two stones, and ground the seeds into
> a powder ...
>   That was 65,000 years ago. The next people to try to bake bread
> were the Egyptians 13,000 years later. That woman came up with
> an idea far more important to humanity than the moon landing.
> That's genius isn't it?[20]

If the *Dark Emu* figure of Egyptian baking starting around 17,000 BP is correct (page 30), which it is not (it's about 8000 BP),[21] then Cuddie Springs grindstones would be allegedly not 13,000 years earlier but 46,000 years earlier. There is some confusion here.

In any case, there is no scientific consensus on an Aboriginal arrival date in what is now Australia any earlier than about 55,000 years ago (see Appendix 1). More recently Pascoe has been quoted as saying that Aboriginal people 'cultivated land' over a period of 120,000 years.[22] There is no evidence whatsoever for this assertion.

This is just one example of Pascoe's repeated focus on large numbers—oldest dates, largest dwellings, highest population densities, and biggest villages. But is bigger better? The idea is an expression of Western progressivism. It is a Texan view of quality.

6
The agriculture debate

Over the decades that followed scholarly rejection of a simple 'hunter-gatherer' label for the Old People of Australia and such people around the world, there have been various attempts to create a new category with a new label. Ian Keen's 'hunter-gatherer-cultivator' was one, but it has now been abandoned.[1] Another is 'complex hunter-gatherers'.[2] An earlier one was 'band societies',[3] a handy term that referred to residential type rather than economic mode per se. Lesley Head discussed the label problem under the title of 'Australian challenges to the categories'.[4]

The problem is that the 1788 economy actually fell somewhere between simple hunter-gathering and agriculture, but was neither. Referring to certain regionally specific Aboriginal economic practices as 'incipient agriculture', as 'proto-agriculture' or as being at 'an early stage in the development of agriculture' is to suggest an unfulfilled developmental journey. We seek here to avoid this deficit model of the Old People, which is why we prefer the term 'hunter-gatherers-plus'. It describes people accurately without attempting to place them in some supposed one-directional evolutionary scheme.

Rhys Jones suggested that it only required 'intensification' of the Australian hunting and gathering economies to produce horticultural or arboricultural (tree-growing) economies like those of the Malayo-Melanesian region.[5] In my view it would have required more than just intensification of practice along an established trajectory: it would also have required a shift of worldview. That would have been a vast cultural and philosophical leap, not a case of merely adding an incremental stage of material change.

Dark Emu makes this extraordinary claim about the early colonial period: 'Large numbers of people engaged in various agricultural pursuits were observed throughout Australia' (page 44). If this refers to the extraction of fruit, seeds and other plant products it is easily supported, but the claim that this vegetable food gathering constitutes 'agriculture' 'throughout Australia' is simply untenable. Let us begin with seed collection and grinding.

Seed collection and grinding

Pascoe refers to Norman Tindale's map of the distribution of seed-grinding peoples (see below),[6] but instead of reproducing it, draws his own version (see overleaf, top), which shows a greatly expanded depiction of the spread of this activity, even down to where the suburbs of Melbourne now spread.

The distribution of large millstones actually indicates a rather larger area of seed grinding, minus the Melbourne extension, as was published in 1957 by Davidson and McCarthy (see overleaf, bottom).[7] Archaeologist Mike Smith has overlain the Davidson and McCarthy map on Tindale's and produced a composite map (see page 77).

Tindale's 'Grassland areas exploited by aborigines [sic] as important sources of grain food with some of the names of tribes'.

2
5
6
7
3
4
1
aboriginal grain belt
(after Tindale 1974)
contemporary grain belt

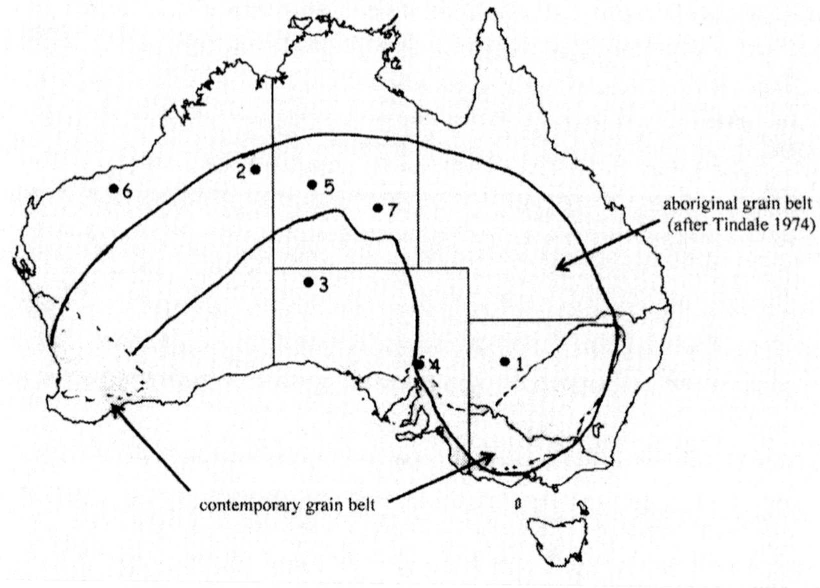

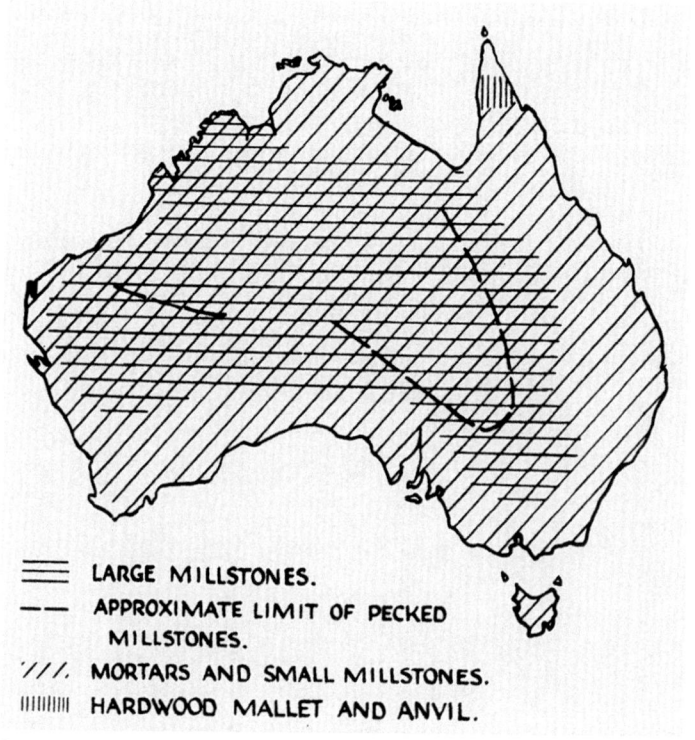

Pascoe's 'Aboriginal grain belt' (page 29).

LARGE MILLSTONES.
APPROXIMATE LIMIT OF PECKED MILLSTONES.
MORTARS AND SMALL MILLSTONES.
HARDWOOD MALLET AND ANVIL.

Davidson and McCarthy's seed-grinding area.

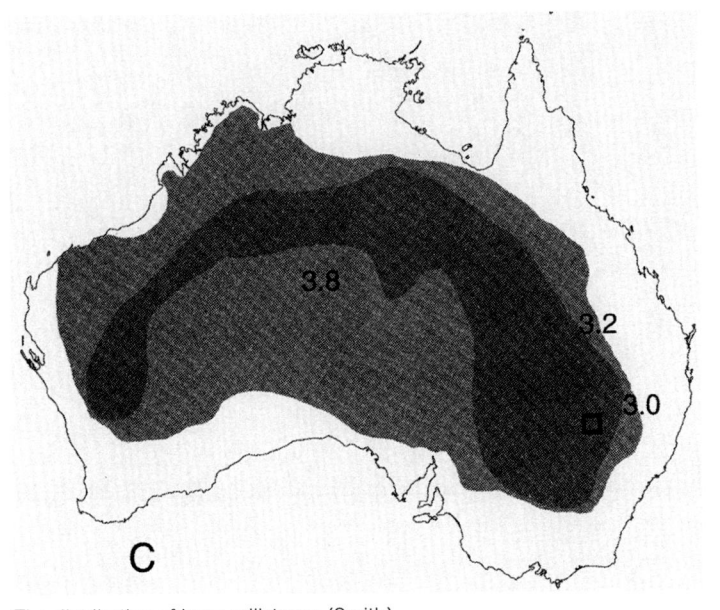

The distribution of large millstones (Smith).

Smith's map showing the archaeological distribution of large grinding millstones is also, very approximately, a map of most of the low-population regions of Australia at 1788 (see Radcliffe-Brown's map overleaf). Most Aboriginal people in 1788 lived in the south-west, in the south-east, along the eastern coast, along the Murray River, and in the monsoon belt across the north. This is compatible with Pascoe's statement: 'Areas beyond the high rainfall zones of the coastal regions favoured grain as the staple crop whereas in wetter areas yam production took over' (page 28).

In short, some Aboriginal people in the pre-conquest era ground seeds, and most did not.

Among those most famously reported as seed-grinding people were those of the Darling River Basin. *Dark Emu* contains numerous references to this area and its people. A major study of old sources on the traditional economy of the Darling Basin peoples by Harry Allen repeatedly refers to seeds and roots being 'collected' and 'gathered'.[8] But Allen mentions no evidence of 'sowing' or 'planting' or 'irrigating' of seeds or roots. In fact, he explicitly concludes that plant 'cultivation', 'horticulture' and 'agriculture' were unknown in the Darling Basin before conquest.[9] Pascoe, who cites this important study as a

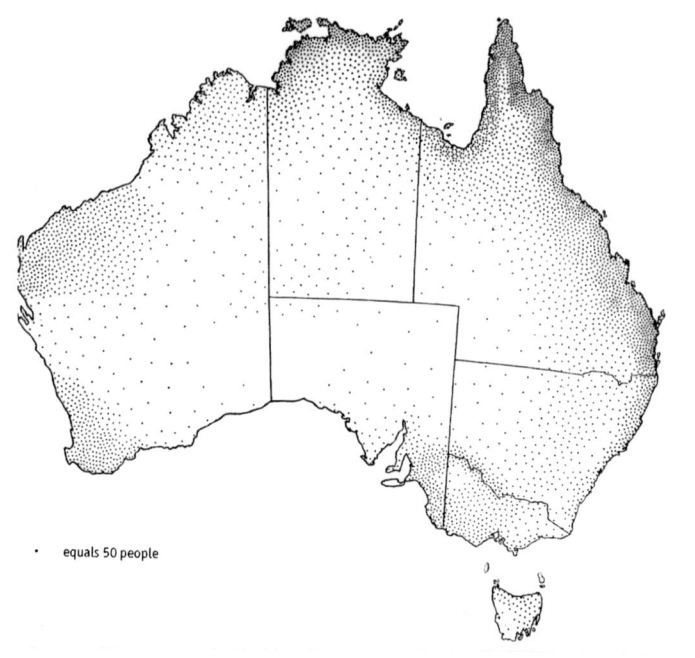

equals 50 people

Radcliffe-Brown's 'Estimated number and distribution of Aboriginals in 1788'.

reference in *Dark Emu* (page 160), does not engage with this rich body of evidence that contradicts his theory.

Keen's *Aboriginal Economy and Society* (2004), also not engaged with by Pascoe, studies traditional economies in seven widely dispersed parts of mainland Australia (see opposite). Keen's regional survey approach had had a predecessor long before: Roger Lawrence's *Aboriginal Habitat and Economy* (1968).[10] Lawrence focused on five regions: Central Australia, riverine south-east Australia, coastal south-east Australia, eastern Cape York and western Cape York. The approach of Lawrence and Keen is a great technique for appreciating the rich variety of traditional Aboriginal economies and escaping the temptation to make grand continental generalisations about 'Aboriginal people'. For a start, Keen's study found considerable diversity in traditional Aboriginal economies, not the uniformity suggested so often by Pascoe's generalisations. Secondly, he found no evidence of horticulture or agriculture as those terms are normally understood. And he avoided deficit–model expressions like 'incipient-' or 'proto-'.

The seven case studies of Ian Keen.

Tuber conservation

By contrast, back in the early 1960s in their text for young people, Tindale and Lindsay saw one of the old plant management practices as incipient horticulture: 'On Cape York Peninsula, when a woman dug up the wild yam, she would scold a shoot of the plant, command it to grow a bigger tuber next time, then replace it and cover it with soil. This is the very beginning of gardening.'[11] But it is not gardening, which involves the planting of seeds or tubers from a previous crop. It is conservation of an existing plant. Why is it a 'beginning' rather than a successful and stable customary method?

In the bush south of Aurukun, Cape York Peninsula, in the 1970s I observed a different practice. Certain yam species were extracted by digging a hole on one side of the plant, removing the tuber and, leaving the stem and vine undisturbed so it could grow another tuber in time, then backfilling the hole. Rhys Jones and Betty Meehan observed exactly the same procedure, minus the backfilling, during their fifteen months at Blyth River in Arnhem Land with the Anbara group.[12]

This was not 'planting' or even 'replanting' but rather conservation of plants in situ. It was not gardening or agriculture. Nor was it simply garnering without care for the future.

Ursula McConnel, who also observed yam conservation when she lived in the Wik bushlands in the 1920s, said, 'Sometimes the top of the yam is left adhering to the stem of the vine and replanted, only the lower part of the root being taken for food, which is interesting *where agriculture is unknown*.'[13] McConnel's finding about yam stem replanting is often referred to, but the last part of what she said is seldom included in quotations.

McConnel was born and bred on a farm, the mixed stock and cropping property Cressbrook, on the upper Brisbane River in southeast Queensland. In Cape York in the 1920s and 1930s she spent many months in the bush and camped out with people who were born and bred beyond the reach of colonisation. For a few months in 1928 she lived among people who were still pursuing the old life in their own countries far from the reach of the missions and the police, on the Kendall and Holroyd rivers. Taking a specific interest in people's plant use, she collected botanical specimens and had them identified scientifically by Cyril White, government botanist at the Queensland Herbarium.[14] She was also a trained and highly intelligent social scientist. When she said agriculture was unknown to the Wik people, she knew what she was talking about.[15]

Having carried out two seasons of ethnobotanical research with Wik people myself in collaboration with ecologist and botanist Dr Dermot Smyth in the 1970s, and having published a dictionary in which first-order botanical results were included for just one of the languages investigated, I have long taken a special interest in Wik people's knowledge and use of vegetable foods.[16] I have lived with Wik families on remote outstations and in temporary camps where we had no imported protein and were hunting and fishing almost daily, and people still occasionally dug yams and picked wild fruit, although this was all combined with plenty of damper and rice, tea and sugar. On that basis I can say that, out of the many dozens of fruits, root vegetables and swamp plants we investigated, this 'replanting' practice was confined to only one class: the yams. Of these, five species were identified, but probably only two species of yam were replanted or conserved in situ: the long yam and the hairy yam.[17] This alleged link to 'farming' does not make classical Wik society an agricultural one or even a horticultural one.

It was hunter-gatherer-plus. To claim it was 'agricultural' is to stretch the facts on a gigantic scale.

An early ethnobotanist in Australia was Edward Palmer, leaseholder of Canobie Station in Far North Queensland, whose 1883 paper detailed 106 local plants and mentioned about fifty others, the scientific names of which had not yet been ascertained. He was struck by the fact that, in addition to names for useful plants, people had 'names for a great number of plants which they do not use'.[18] Nowhere in that early and rich source is there any mention of plants cultivated in gardens or fields as crops. Palmer was not alone among earlier generations of non-Indigenous Australians who took Aboriginal plant knowledge seriously and learned a great deal from the Old People. Salient examples are JH Maiden (1889)[19] and Len Webb (1948).[20]

One of the most intensively researched Aboriginal botanical worlds is that of the people of remote Groote Eylandt, the Anindhilyakwa of the Northern Territory. In their detailed ethnobotanical works Dulcie Levitt and Julie Waddy make no mention of horticultural or agricultural practices.[21] The nearest is perhaps this:

> Sometimes, part of the [long] yam was removed and the soil was replaced in the hole so that new yams would be available later, about August. These yams never grow to the size of the original yam but allowing the plant to produce new yams was a way to ensure food later in the dry season.[22]

Transplanting species

There are isolated and scattered but informative records of the Old People expanding the distribution of some wild plants and animals.[23] This is one facet of the '-plus' in 'hunter-gatherers-plus'. Mary Gilmore, who spent her childhood in the Riverina in colonial times, recollected that possums were caught where they were plentiful and released elsewhere 'in order that they might breed in the renewing locality'.[24]

Lazarus Lamilami (1908–1977), a Maung man of western Arnhem Land, narrated that his father's father transplanted waterlilies from 'some other place and planted them in his country'. He also transplanted the root *guralal*, brought freshwater tortoises and put them in the billabongs and creeks, and planted the banyan and other trees and cabbage palms.[25] This account is unique in the number of natural resources that are said to have been given expanded distributions, assuming it has historical foundations. It does have some of the key features of a creation myth: the key character is a patrilineal ancestor and a transformative figure.[26]

Vegetation planting myths are on the record. One Murinbata (Murrinh Patha) myth described by Stanner involves the Rainbow Serpent telling his daughters to plant a baobab tree on Nganangur Island in the north-west of the Northern Territory. The Murinbata people interpreted the sporadic distribution of this species as a sign of 'human intent'. He also commented: 'Many Murinbata resent being told that horticulture and agriculture are unknown to them. They cite [the Rainbow Serpent's] instructions to his daughters that "making a garden" is an old Aboriginal custom.'[27]

The problem with interpreting this literally, instead of as evidence about mythological propagation, is that a recent fine-grained and authoritative study of plant use traditions of the same people and their neighbours, by Jeff Hardwick,[28] has produced a great deal of detail but nothing that even suggests that they practised horticulture or agriculture prior to conquest. The baobab myth is thus a case of spiritual propagation. Indeed, just a year before the quotation above, Stanner himself wrote this passage on Aboriginal traditional life:

> They had no idea that plants could be cultivated or animals domesticated but in any case there were no suitable plants, or animals except the wild dog, which they gentled [tamed] into human service. Nor did they know anything of the manufacture of metals: their tools, utensils and weapons were made of stone, bone, shell and wood. Nevertheless, they lived everywhere confidently, even where food and water were exiguous [that is, scarce] and, in most regions and at most times, they not only lived well but sweetened existence by spirited pursuits of life in no way concerned with mere survival.[29]

In the 1970s David Harris was told at Lockhart River in Cape York that yams were sometimes planted on offshore islands to extend their distribution and to ensure a 'reserve' supply,[30] but at the same time there was 'no evidence that they were formerly cultivated, but neither were they indiscriminantly [sic] gathered', because access was regulated.[31]

Bob Ellis has analysed the distribution of the native orange[32] in the Flinders Ranges (South Australia) in relation to traditional camp sites (see opposite). They cluster at those sites and these clusters together form an outpost of the species, which is mainly found widely distributed north-east of the region some distance away. He suggests the fruit was brought to the ranges by people travelling from elsewhere, and possibly established by people defecating near camp sites.[33] In the *mura* (sacred history) corollary of that likely historical spread, the *iga* trees arrived as Dreaming people coming from Queensland via the Cooper Creek area. Where the Iga people stopped, trees of that species grew. In the end, the Iga people returned to their own country, leaving behind the trees, which are a favoured food and shade source.

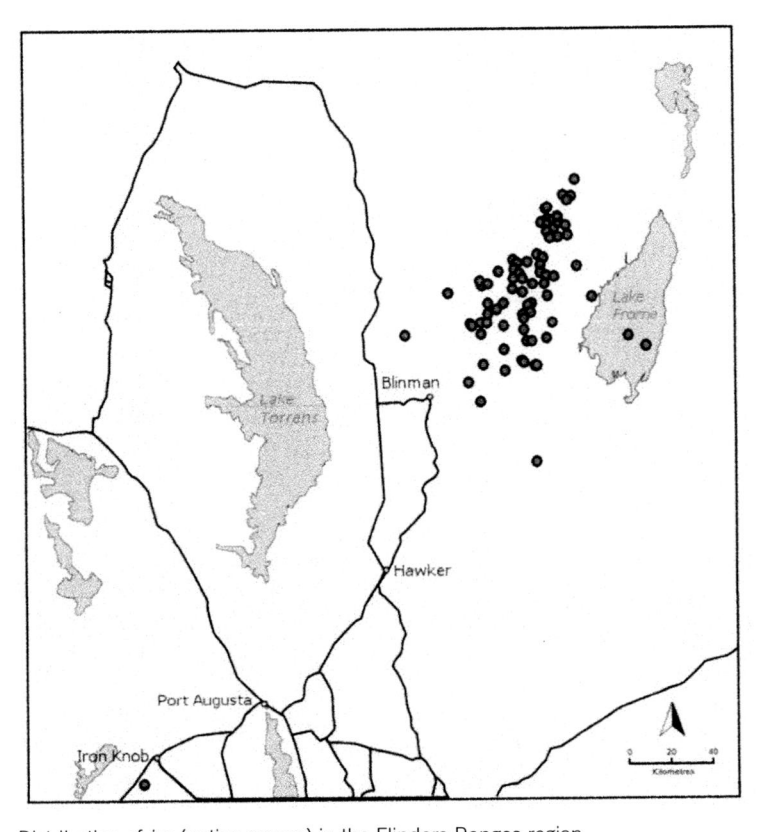

Distribution of *iga* (native orange) in the Flinders Ranges region.

The secular explanation here refers to what has been dubbed 'domiculture' by Hynes and Chase.[34] Essentially, this is the process by which discarded fruit residue, including seeds, accumulates close to camp sites and leads to the growth of those species at those sites. The Hynes and Chase evidence was especially from CYP. Jones observed the process in north-central Arnhem Land when he and Meehan spent over a year camped with outstation people:

> [Apart from firing] [t]here are other ways in which they 'look after' the country—they clean and curate the wells, and in an insouciant [that is, casual] way distribute their fruit trees, by carrying and then eating the fruits and dropping them in their middens … Discarding some Syzigium[35] seeds on the edge of a shell midden one day at the end of the dry season in 1972, Frank Gurrmanamana, noticing my glance, said of them 'By and by they will grow—all the same gardeni.'[36]

Jones and Meehan did not, however, report any tradition of gardening or agriculture in the region.

In 1985 archaeologist Roger Cribb and I were being shown the Love River country of Cape York Peninsula by Wik people led by Rex and Cecil Walmbeng, and we were recording, among other things, the extensive shell middens of that area. The mounds were all held to be of mythological origin (see below and opposite).[37] Archaeologically they

Rex Walmbeng with shell midden at Punth-Kuunteng, near Love River, Cape York Peninsula, 1985.

Cecil Walmbeng at
Waathem, Wik country,
Cape York Peninsula,
1985.

were formed where people in past centuries discarded shells after
cooking and eating shellfish. Growing on the top of most of these
middens are plant species originating in the vine scrub communities some distance away. This was another case of domiculture. The
fieldwork led to an article pertinently named 'Landscape as cultural
artefact'. There is no evidence that these patches of vine scrub were
created intentionally.

If 'horticulture' and 'agriculture' are to be apt terms for Aboriginal
interventions in the reproductive cycles of plants, then there has to
be, at a minimum, *intentional* sowing of seeds or planting of tubers
or rootstock.

The fact that, as do grain farmers and flour millers in agricultural
societies, some Aboriginal people harvested seeds, ground them and
often baked the resulting loaves does not make the Old People agriculturalists. The most important difference culturally is the one to do with
the creation of plant life itself. That is where things start. It is at this

critical, central point of fertility and fertilisation that Aboriginal culture in 1788 assigned the creative role to the Dreaming, to speaking with the spirits of the Old People, and to the activation of totemic centres through ritual. You don't have to grow seeds in gardens—in a case of domiculture[38] you discard the seed and 'he grows himself'. Of all the defining elements of agriculture, planting is the most crucial—without planting, the garnering of wild plant foods remains part of a foraging strategy, not a gardening or farming one.

Is there evidence of cultivation?
It is notable that detailed studies of Aboriginal seed use in the seed-grinding region characteristically make no suggestion of the physical cultivation of crops through sowing of seeds stored from previous seasons. Had this practice been widespread it would have been observed and recorded ubiquitously.

Absence of evidence is not evidence of absence, but when a whole-volume study of traditional plant use by Yankunytjatjara people (Central Australia), for example, gives details of seed foods and accounts of their garnering and processing in the Yankunytjatjara language by highly knowledgeable women elders, and there is not the slightest suggestion of preparatory tilling, sowing, fertilisation, or irrigation, it is clear that neither 'horticulture' nor 'agriculture' were Yankunytjatjara traditions.[39]

The lifelong ethnobotanical work of Peter Latz, carried out very widely in Central Australia, has resulted in a truly rich account of Aboriginal use of plants in that region. He has not found evidence of cereal cultivation anywhere there. Central Australia is in the middle of the traditional seed-grinding belt (see the map on page 76). He does say of the narcotic plant commonly called pituri: 'Nowadays [pituri] seeds are sometimes spread around to ensure a future crop but it is possible that this is a recent innovation not practised in the past.'[40] Pituri is a drug, not a food staple.

The term 'cultivation' is fairly variable in meaning. For most people it requires something like gardening, where soil is prepared, seeds are sown, weeds may or may not be removed, there may be fencing against animal intrusions, and perhaps irrigation is carried out. This is the way I use the term here. For some other people, almost any interven-tion in the life conditions of a species—such as burning off, or the replacement of tuber stems after removing the tubers, or leaving some yams while taking the rest—counts as cultivation. One source used by Sylvia Hallam and a few others is FR Irvine, who even used the term 'semi-cultivation'[41] but managed to cite only one very ambiguous case for Aboriginal Australia, that of the bunya nut. 'Semi-' has the problems we have identified with 'proto-', 'incipient' and so on as qualifiers: they are negatively based.

One can legitimately interpret these stretched definitions and uses of qualifiers such as semi-(cultivation) and proto-(agriculture) as Eurocentric wishful thinking. They start from a fully-fledged economic production type known in England or China (etc.) and work backwards to Aboriginal practices that didn't quite make it to the fully-fledged stage. One should be cautious about the directional flow of ideas here. They can, as we have seen, take us back to social evolutionism and the idea of the primitive society. What, one may ask, was supposedly partial or not fully-fledged about traditional Aboriginal environmental agency? Why not just accept it as the concluded cultural development that met peoples' needs and used their finely honed subsistence skills?

Pascoe in *Dark Emu* does not quite ever define agriculture, but he gives a definition borrowed from Gerritsen:[42]

When Europeans began their classification of eras and the peoples of the world they decided that five things signified the development of agriculture: selection of seed, preparation of the soil, harvest of the crop, storage of the surpluses, and large populations and permanent housing. (page 19)

But this is not what Gerritsen said. On those pages he was citing authors, mainly of the 1980s and 1990s, on the question not of what constituted the 'development of agriculture' but of what factors were preconditions for 'incipient agriculture'. It is astonishing that Pascoe's definition says nothing about planting seeds or tubers, and mentions only 'selection of seed', the latter not being described by Gerritsen (who does mention 'availability of domesticable plant species'[43]). No evidence about selection of some seed over other seed in Australia for cropping purposes in 1788 is advanced by Pascoe, in any case. I know of no such evidence anywhere.

Evidence for seed planting is assumed by Pascoe (page 96), but in fact it is remarkably thin and narrowly sourced and often ambiguous, as we shall see below.

Alastair Campbell's 1965 paper on 'elementary food production' by Aboriginal people had a section called 'Planting of seeds',[44] but the only seemingly reliable report of this he had found was the isolated source of Mary Gilmore. She reported that in her Riverina childhood Aboriginal women gathered seeds from plants that had survived fires and planted them where the burned ones had stood. She also reported seeds of ground-berry and quandong being planted after the flesh had been eaten. Campbell commented on the rarity of this kind of statement, and that it was required 'to be treated with some reserve'.[45] It did not hinder Gilmore from writing: 'The aboriginals, on the other hand, were a nomadic people in a whole continent.'[46]

An example of a tenuous, at best, account of seed sowing is that of Arabana man Walter Smith, as quoted by Dick Kimber. It refers to six language groups in Central Australia throwing tiny amounts of seed onto the ground at favourable localities: 'Wouldn't be a handful. [They] chuck a little bit, spread it [in a broadcasting fashion] you see—one seed there, one seed there ...'[47] No indication is given as to how often this might happen. There is an explicit denial that the seeds were watered in by people,[48] and no mention of preparing the soil for planting. Given the better survival of traditional knowledge in Central Australia than in most other parts of Australia following European colonisation, it is striking that no one else has been recorded giving a matching description. Kimber refers to this description as one of 'planting'[49]—too strongly 'agricultural' a term in my view, when tiny amounts are said to have been thrown. In any case, it is not explained how less than a handful of seed could produce any significant amount of food even at a favourable location. It sounds much more like an 'increase ceremony' or species maintenance ritual (see Chapter 2).

In turn, Gerritsen picks up this fragment of evidence from a single informant, Walter Smith, and refers to it as 'broadcast seeding' and reproduces Kimber's map of groups over that title.[50] He adds, without basis, 'it could be over in minutes or hours'.[51] Or seconds?

Further on arid-zone seed use, Pascoe cites Dix and Lofgren[52] for the information in this passage:

In the north-west [sic: north-eastern] goldfields of Western Australia people sowed the seeds of kurumi (Tetracornia [sic: Tecticornia] arborea) in cracks in the clay pans to ensure propagation in the wet season. They created a stone arrangement on the bank to record the story of the collection, preparation and consumption of the harvested kurumi. (page 41)

Dix and Lofgren actually said the identification of the species was only tentative, and that this was the only clay pan in the vicinity that had the plant on it,[53] so 'clay pans', plural, is Pascoe's generalisation.

Of more seriousness is Pascoe's omission of the caveats expressed by Dix and Lofgren, caveats that were reflected in the title they chose for their paper: 'Kurumi: *Possible* Aboriginal *incipient* agriculture associated with a stone arrangement'. They also said that many sites in the area were 'not well understood by their custodians in traditional terms', and that because of postcolonial migration people had assumed custodianship of sites 'which they imperfectly understood'. 'Because of these factors, the meaning associated with this particular site may well be at variance with older traditions.' On top of this, they said that the

reference to a type of incipient agricultural activity is fascinating in this Australian context, but must be considered in the light of the relative sophistication of the informants. They have a small garden next to their camp well, including both native and domesticated plants, and have been taught some aspects of successful irrigated gardening. However, they insist that the sowing of *Kurumi* seed in the clay pan was traditional, taught to them by their ancestors.[54]

Given this site has mythology and a stone arrangement/dancing site, and given the inconclusiveness of Dix and Lofgren's account, it may more likely have been a species maintenance site than an exercise in 'incipient agricultural activity'.

Incipient development or stable solution?
Tindale was fond of the 'incipient' expression, but he combined it with a scientist's caution:

[In the grassland areas of Australia] [t]here is evidence for the *incipient* development of grain storage, and in two situations[55] *a suggestion* that the effectiveness of seasonal flooding of grassed plains had been modified by damming stream beds prior to the advent of summer rains, *implying incipient* interest in irrigation.

Examination of activities associated with other foods such as wild rice, water chestnuts (*Eleocharis*), and *Dioscorea* yams *encourage a suggestion* that many of the activities of northern Australian people were already akin to those associated with the earliest gardening cultures, *lacking principally the idea of the deliberate preservation and sowing of new seed.*[56] Thus a *suggestive* subtitle for this paper could well have been 'Pre-dawn of Agriculture in Australia'.[57]

To be sure that something is 'incipient', you need evidence from the present case or other parallel and adjacent cases that the incipient has later turned into the fully-fledged. The fact that other parts of the world developed a fully-fledged agriculture proves nothing about the temporary or long duration of Aboriginal practices, or their age in any respect. Why were these practices not read as evidence of a long-term stable relationship with the biota, as an achievement of relative equilibrium, rather than unfulfilled steps up some supposed ladder of progress?

The 'incipient', 'pre-dawn', 'proto-' and 'early' labels associated with a one-directional model of economic and technological development, and with social evolutionism, are also the language of impoverishment. They provoke questions such as: 'What held people up, for around 55,000 years, from making progress?' The question is false. It glamorises agriculture, and fails to respect the spiritual propagation philosophy of the Old People. Their grounding of species regeneration in the Dreaming and in ritual was not a defect, and not a gap of knowledge. It was a tapping of creative energy that lived in their commitment to the presence of the life principle in the world as they knew it, not in a world that human beings created, because they did not. As they understood it, it was there from the start.

As touched on earlier, there is much terrible irony in *Dark Emu*'s struggle to shoehorn classical Aboriginal Australia into the supposedly advanced world of agriculture. The agricultural complex was that very world that, along with the pastoral industry, was the main driver of Aboriginal conquest, dispossession and murder, after the convict colony at Port Jackson initiated conquest with the blessing of the British Government under the Crown. If 'agriculture' was the way of life of the Old People, why did they not segue smoothly into the domestic gardening—and the broad-field ploughing, sowing and cropping—of the British settlers? The latter tediously and repeatedly claimed that many of the people they encountered were averse to horticulture and agriculture both. They were great horseback musterers and game trackers, but averse to hoeing, weeding and planting. Knowing—as the Old People did full well—that plants grew from seeds and tubers, ignorance played no role in this rejection of farming. It was cultural resistance, and loyalty to their own ways.

Pascoe's reliance on the Dix and Lofgren source, the Walter Smith source, and the Alice Duncan-Kemp example discussed immediately below—sources that are equivocal and ambiguous at best, highly local-ised, rare, and combined with the absence of clear-cut examples of seed sowing on farms—suggests an almost desperate search to find some-thing to back up the belief that the Old People sowed seeds for crops and were thus agricultural people. This overstretching of inadequate evidence actually reinforces the general picture of an absence of crop cultivation in mainland Australia before conquest.

Pascoe quotes Alice Duncan-Kemp on one of her memories from the early twentieth century on the Diamantina River: 'From their woven dilly bags the gins sprinkled seed food over the ground ...',[58] and so on. Pascoe calls this the 'Katoora ceremony'. Actually it was a 'Wompoo' or rain increase ceremony, and the *katoora* (barley grass) seeds were not planted out for cropping but laid out in 'little hillocks' onto which water was poured during the ceremony.[59] This is an increase ceremony. Not cited by Pascoe were Duncan-Kemp's references to 'the hard, nomadic life that they have had to lead since the beginning of time' and 'a terrible struggle for existence'[60]—conventional views that we, as much as Pascoe, would say were possibly misjudged in their severity.

These scattered, isolated and often tenuous sources on what Pascoe calls 'sowing' or 'planting', even if they were valid exceptions, would be exceptions that proved the rule. After a careful search of the literature, Douglas Yen came to the conclusion that 'The closest parallel to planting practice in Aboriginal gathering pertains to the *Dioscorea* yam in subtropical and tropical Australia. Observations of replanting ... entail a rather casual replacement of the stem-attached top of the tuber at harvest ...'[61] He also concluded: 'In summary, it is worth re-stating that the element of plant domestication is absent from the Australian hunting-gathering systems, but that domestication of the environment in which those plants grow is not.'[62]

Isolated and indeed one-off records of Aboriginal ecological agency ('domestication of the environment') do not form a wider pattern that can be interpreted as 'Aboriginal people practised agriculture'.

For example, Campbell mentions women moving flower branches 'five miles' (8 kilometres) to a ghost gum where the bees established a hive.[63] He also cites the case of people cutting swamp oak saplings and piling them up on the intertidal zone on rivers in south-east Queensland so as to encourage an edible grub called 'cobra'.[64] He cites another case where the tops of living grass trees were broken off to allow decay and thus encourage bardis (witchetty grubs). The grubs were harvested by breaking the grass tree to pieces.[65] In the Mitchell River area of Cape York, the trunk of a young tree (either *Thespesia populneoides* or *Hibiscus tileaceus*) was bent over and its top secured to the ground. A year later it would have sprouted a number of straight vertical stems that were perfect for making spear shafts.[66]

None of these practices were general. Each of the scattered records of them is unique to one locality.

The very thinness and scattered nature of the evidence for soil preparation and seed sowing or tuber planting, not to mention that evidence's ambiguities, itself then becomes evidence, instead, for the view we express in this book—that is, that at conquest Aboriginal people were practical and spiritual managers and modifiers of their environment, skilled hunters, adept fishers and trappers, and very botanically knowledgeable foragers who had long come to grips with the problems of making a living in a wide range of ecologies. A minority harvested grass seeds and ground them into a paste that could be cooked or eaten raw. They had not, however, become farmers who created and tended fields, sowed crops and lived in permanent villages. Nor had they become horticulturists (gardeners). They had their own way. This way should be cherished.

7
Patterns of apparel

'[M]any Australians were surprised when Aboriginal women were featured at the 2006 Melbourne Commonwealth Games opening ceremony wearing magnificent possum skin cloaks. The pervasive idea', writes Pascoe, 'is that Aboriginal people wore nothing or animal skins' (page 89).

That may be so. But the sentence that follows this looks like a very sweeping generalisation: 'And they did wear skins but they were sewn, had sleeves for the accommodation of infant children, and could be used as rugs and bedding' (page 89). The reader fresh to the subject would have to be forgiven for taking this to mean that most Aboriginal people wore clothes in the form of sewn animal skins. The fact is that many did but the majority did not. The regional differences were graphic. The authoritative map from 2005 (see page 3 of the picture section), designed for the general non-academic reader and widely available nine years before *Dark Emu* appeared, shows the distributions.[1]

But this is a seasonal map. Wearing a possum or kangaroo skin cloak in high summer would have been unbearable, at least during daytime. It follows that even in the regions where cloaks were worn, people were largely unclothed in hot weather. The northernmost record of a 'possum skin rug' is from the Townsville area in the 1850s or 1860s.[2] In south-west Western Australia, people wore kangaroo skins rather than possum skins (see overleaf). In the Darling River region, Major Mitchell noted that prominent men wore skin cloaks during a ceremony while other men did not.[3] The practice of clothing was not always just pragmatic.

Men of south-west Western Australia, 1870s–1880s period.

Gender differences are widely reported in the use of body cover-ings. For example, writing of the Western District of Victoria in the nineteenth century, a region with a bracing winter climate and where people certainly did sew possum skins to make cloaks and rugs, James Dawson said:

> During all seasons of the year both sexes walk about very scantily clothed. In warm weather the men wear no covering during the day time except a short apron, not unlike the sporran of the Scotch Highlanders, formed of strips of opossum skin with the fur on, hanging from a skin belt in two bunches, one in front and the other behind. In winter they add a large kangaroo skin, fur side inwards, which hangs over the shoulder and down the back like a mantle or short cloak ...

Women use the opossum rug at all times, by day as a covering for the back and shoulders, and in cold nights as a blanket ... A girdle or short kilt of the neck feathers of the emu, tied in little bunches to a skin cord, is fastened around the loins.[4]

William Buckley recorded that when women of the Colac/Indented Head region of Victoria engaged in fighting, or in ceremonies where they used their 'rugs' as musical instruments (for pounding the beat), they went naked.[5] There is no record of which I am aware that the skin cloaks of the colder regions were worn over any kind of undergarment.[6] There is an early record of a skin cloak being worn under circular rush mats by a woman Mitchell and his party met in the area of the Glenelg River, south-western Victoria, in 1836 (see below). The first people Narcisse Pelletier encountered after surviving shipwreck in the Cape York Peninsula in 1858 were 'three women,

Mitchell's 'Female and child of Australia Felix'.

who were entirely naked',[7] but he also described women wearing 'a
fringe of cords extending from the waist to half way down the thigh'.[8]

Sandals were used to walk on superheated or extremely prickly
ground rather than worn all year round, but are reported only from
some regions.[9] One should not underestimate the toughness and ability
to weather discomfort that traditional people enjoyed.

The regionally differing spectrum of items worn on the body in
1788 was in fact very large. In their introductory text referred to elsewhere here, the Berndts gave a brief but wide-reaching summary of this
variation.[10] A generation or two of students and interested lay readers
would have been exposed to this survey, given the book remained in
print for over thirty years.

Skin cloaks and the paperbark aprons unique to Tiwi women[11]
(see below) are at the maximal covering end of the spectrum. In other
regions people usually were more lightly clad, including those regions
where people were largely unclothed, even in very cold weather.

Tiwi women and girls wearing traditional paperbark aprons, Bathurst Island, 1913.

By 'largely unclothed' I refer to the very common pattern whereby different people wore a pubic tassel, or a hair belt, a headband, a pearl-shell pendant, bracelets and necklaces and other adornments, but no general skin covering.[12]

A Kimberley example comes from Rev. JRB Love, who was a missionary there from 1927 to 1940:[13] 'Except for the pubic tassel worn by the younger women and growing children the Wo'rora roam the bush completely naked.'[14] He failed here to mention the substantial hair belts worn in the same region, but described them elsewhere.[15] There are hundreds of published photographs from colonial and later days, on the edge of the advancing imperial frontier, showing people in many different degrees of covering and adornment, from being fully swathed in sewn possum skin cloaks to being fully naked (see below).[16]

People were not prudish about nudity but valued modesty, expressed in sitting positions and in averting the gaze, for example. An early record of this etiquette is from First Fleet member David Collins at

Man with two wives and children, Tomkinson Ranges, 1903.

Port Jackson: '… and although entire strangers to the comforts and conveniences of clothing, yet they sought with a native modesty to conceal by attitude what the want of covering would otherwise have revealed'.[17] Elsewhere Collins recorded for the Port Jackson area the possum-fur string apron worn by girls until married.[18] A more nuanced account based on deep anthropological field work from 1927 to 1934 among the Wik people of Cape York Peninsula comes from Ursula McConnel (see below and opposite, top):

> Clothes in the European sense are non-existent. Men and women go naked. Aprons are worn by women only on certain occasions with a special significance. A young girl … first wears an apron when she returns to camp after separation at the onset of puberty [menarche], and after each ensuing separation for a similar reason [menses], either as a mature girl … or as a married woman … When a mother returns to her husband's camp at the end of her isolation during childbirth, she wears a brand new apron … Aprons are also worn by women on ceremonial occasions, as when they take part in dances, and especially for the mourning dance.[19]

Wik girl on plains south of Aurukun, western Cape York Peninsula, 1927.

Wik women performing mourning dance, western Cape York Peninsula, 1927.

Omitted there by McConnel were the grass skirts worn by men during certain ceremonies (see below). She also omitted the 'women's utility pad' made of paperbark which was used when a woman had her period, or to prevent penetration by leeches while extracting tubers or corms in swamps.[20]

Wik men in ceremony, western Cape York Peninsula, 1927.

What is most impressive about classical Wik adornments of the body is that, perhaps with the utility pad as a sole exception, all of them are symbolic statements rather than primarily a means of comfort or covering. Women's aprons mark certain distinctive states—developmental stage, post-partum condition, ritual performance. Similarly, people wore, at different times, these: healing and protective strings tied around the affected body part; strings while hunting (worn by men); strings while diving for waterlilies (worn by pregnant women); shell nosepegs; pearl-shell pendants; necklaces and headbands; pandanus armlets (men); large wooden ear-cylinders in the lobe (men); a collar of wood studded with red beads (men); cowrie shell girdles and crossovers (women); mourning strings (women); mourning necklets (women); a woven betrothal ring; lover's strings; and umbilical-cord pendants.[21] Embellishment outranked 'clothing'.

8
'Aquaculture' or fishing and trapping?

Dark Emu refers to several kinds of traditional fish trap (pages 53–71). Those given the most prominence, generally, are the ones that constitute exceptional creations. The Lake Condah eel trapping system, the Brewarrina River fish traps and the Glyde River fish trap are prominent in the 'Aquaculture' chapter but there is little to compare them with anywhere else, perhaps except for the Brewarrina traps. There were hugely numerous but different and more basic coastal fish traps that used tides to capture wild fish. Weirs, not highlighted by Pascoe and not included in *Young Dark Emu*, were widespread. The curriculum guide *Dark Emu in the Classroom* illustrates only one kind of fish trap: the exceptional case of Brewarrina.[1]

Is it accurate to refer to these successful devices as 'aquaculture', as Pascoe does (page 53), rather than as 'trapping wild fish'?

Most people's understanding of 'aquaculture' would define it as the protective breeding, rearing and harvesting of aquatic animals. Raising fingerlings in captivity, where they are protected from predators, is usually integral to aquaculture enterprises. That is, there is domestication of the reproductive beginnings of the relevant fish population. While the Old People did this through ritual and through communicating with aquatic spirits, there is no evidence they did so using physical technology. In the case of the eels of Western Victoria (see Chapter 13), they spawn far from human beings, swimming 'anything up to three or four thousand kilometres to a spawning ground in deep water somewhere in the Coral Sea off New Caledonia'.[2]

That is, there is abundant evidence that Aboriginal people in different regions of Australia harvested wild fish by spearing, angling, netting, grabbing them by the gills, and creating weirs and stone traps, but no evidence that they physically bred, fed, protected and reared them as captive fingerlings and then introduced them into the environment.

This is from the Australian Government's Department of Agriculture, Water and the Environment website:

> Aquaculture is defined by the Food and Agriculture Organization of the United Nations as the farming of aquatic organisms including fish, molluscs, crustaceans and aquatic plants with some sort of intervention in the rearing process to enhance production, such as regular stocking, feeding and protection from predators.[3]

Complicating the issue is the fact that the World Heritage listing of the Budj Bim Landscape in western Victoria describes the fish trapping system as 'aquaculture': 'The three serial components of the property contain one of the world's most extensive and oldest aquaculture systems.'[4] Perhaps two distinct meanings of 'aquaculture' are now established in Australian English usage: a technical sense covering breeding of spawn in captivity, and a broader sense covering trapping of wild fish by modification of water flows.

Pascoe raises the Glyde River (Northern Territory) fish trap in the context of the phrase 'for example', and indeed it is an example of invention using bush materials. However, it is completely unrepresentative of Aboriginal fish trap technology. It is unique in the Australian record, and even unique in Arnhem Land, and in fact unique to only two local clans of Yolngu people on a single river in Arnhem Land. It was named *gorl* by Donald Thomson's teachers:

> The *gorl* technique is not in general use throughout Arnhem Land but is confined to a small area on the north coast lying between the Glyde River in the west, and Buckingham Bay in the east ... the right to use the *gorl* is regarded as the exclusive property of two of these groups—Ngalladar Tjumbar'poingo and Kalbanuk group of Liagallauwumirr—and its use is restricted to these.[5]

Pascoe reproduces a photo of this particular fish trap, and says, 'When I show this to students of Aboriginal Studies they turn to me in astonishment, as if I'm pulling their leg' (page 65). This may be true, but photographs of this same trap have been published multiple times over decades. It is ironic then that Thomson's 1938 paper was originally called 'A *new* type of fish trap ...'[6] It was new, then, to anthropological publication in 1938. Photos of this Glyde River fish trap have since been repeatedly published, in two publications by Thomson[7] and in works by Wiseman,[8] Keen[9] and Memmott.[10] The trap has also been described in print in Thomson,[11] Blainey[12] and Memmott and Fantin.[13] This unique creation is the only fish trap illustrated in *Young Dark Emu*.[14] No ordinary traps are represented. The normal is excluded.

Pascoe's use of the striking Thomson photo is marred by multiple errors of fact, which can be detected if you compare his description with Thomson's 1938 original. Thomson's 1937 photograph was of two men sitting, not standing as Pascoe says. Pascoe also says the tubs were made of paperbark; Thomson says they were made of Darwin stringybark. Pascoe's caption for the photo describes the image as 'Queensland fishing system' (page 65). The Glyde River is in Arnhem Land: the nearest part of Queensland is over 500 kilometres away to the south-east.

Moving offshore, Pascoe here asserts that 'large, organised fishing expeditions by watercraft were observed all around the coast' (page 66). If 'the coast' here is the Australian coast, then the statement is false. Large parts of the coast had people with no seagoing craft at all, only inland still-water bark canoes. Some had no boats but used floating logs, for example to cross rivers.

Watercraft were absent from the greater part of the south-western coasts. There were also no watercraft in most of the interior. These distributional contrasts have been on the published record for many decades,[15] and the National Maritime Museum has published an authoritative map of watercraft distributions (see below). Pascoe

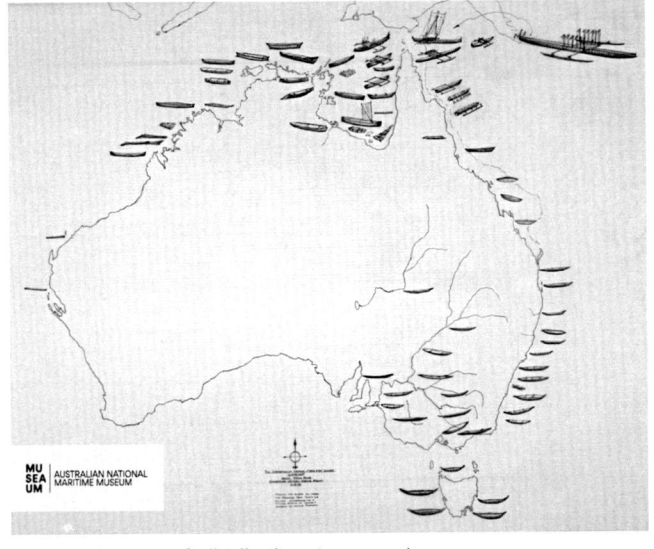

Aboriginal watercraft distribution at conquest.

seems to have ignored this evidence in a now familiar pattern: towards uniformity, largeness, and a social evolutionist expectation of 'advancement'.

The *Macquarie Atlas of Indigenous Australia* contains a mainly compatible map (see page 3 of the picture section). This atlas was aimed at the educational market of young people and people new to the subject of Aboriginal studies. It has sold well and gone through two editions, and there is a downloadable teacher's guide.

9
Dwellings

Sleeping under the stars with nothing more than a windbreak being needed for shelter from wind at night was certainly a regular practice in the largely dry months in north Australia and the arid zone. Having had the pleasure of sleeping under the heavens countless times there, I can recommend it. Wet seasons in the north and wintry seasons in the centre were different, and people made substantial huts for sleeping in. In the daytime, when not on the move, people used natural tree shade, or constructed bough-sheds, or combined the two. But is it truly the case that, as Pascoe suggests in *Dark Emu*, 'Permanent housing was a feature of the pre-contact Aboriginal economy and marked the move-ment towards agricultural reliance' (page 73)?

Pascoe provides only fragmentary evidence from a single part of Victoria, namely the Western District, that dwellings were 'permanent' (page 91). There is also no convincing evidence that they were con-tinuously occupied over decades. No cases of stone-based permanently occupied year-round housing are advanced in *Dark Emu* for anywhere else but this one district.

James Dawson's account of Western District dwellings, written in the nineteenth century and discussed, but only briefly, by Pascoe, presents a picture that cannot possibly be interpreted as that of a people who lived only in permanent and substantial houses. Instead, it states that families had their 'permanent' dwellings but did not dwell in them all of the time:

> While travelling or occupying temporary habitations, each of these parties must erect separate wuurns [habitations] …

These comfortable and healthy habitations are occupied by the owners of the land in the neighbourhood ...

When it is necessary to abandon them for a season in search of variety of food, or for visiting neighbouring families and tribes, the doorway is closed with sheets of bark or bushes ...

Temporary habitations are also dome-shaped, and are made of limbs, bark of gum trees, scarcely rain-proof, and are smaller, opener, and more carelessly erected than the permanent residences. They are only used in summer or for shelter while travelling, and have a large open side, with the fire in front. In fine warm weather, a few green bushes, placed in a half circle to windward of the fire, suffice for a temporary dwelling.[1]

Close by, the early protector William Thomas, a man who lived in Aboriginal camps soon after the invasion of the Melbourne area in the 1830s and on whom Pascoe relies at times, observed of the people of 'Australia Felix' (the Western District):

About once in three months the whole tribe unite,[2] generally at new or full moon, when they have a few dances, and again separate into three or more bodies, as they cannot get food if they move *en masse*; the chief, with the aged, makes arrangements for the route each party is to take. *In their movements they seldom encamp more than three nights in one place, and oftener but one.* Thus they move from one place to another, regardless of sickness, deaths, births, &c. ...

... They seldom travel more than six miles [10 km] a day.[3]

This early eyewitness account from Victoria is not cited in *Dark Emu*. It could have been challenged by comparison with Dawson's more nuanced account of seasonal variation, but is not. As I show elsewhere, William Buckley's records of the eastern part of the same Western District region pre-colonisation gave factual details of a wide range of stopover length, from days to months to many months. None of the residential periods were described by him as permanent (see Appendix 2 for details). The recurring pattern, all over Australia, was one of seasonal and other variation in lengths of stays in one place. No group is ever described, at the moment of colonisation, as living year in, year out, in one single place. Degree of mobility varied from region to region, and from ecological zone to ecological zone, but it was always there.

Nor are Thomas's remarks on dwellings among the same people mentioned or challenged in *Dark Emu*: 'In warm weather, while on the tramp, they seldom make a miam [hut]—they use merely a few boughs to keep off the wind; in wet weather a few sheets of bark make a comfortable house. In one half-hour I have seen a neat village begun and finished.'[4] Colonial use of the word 'village', as employed here, does not necessarily imply permanency. A cluster of temporary huts was an 'encampment' or a 'village' just as much as the more substantial sets of stone footings supporting bough walls and thatch.[5]

One of Pascoe's central sources, Peter Beveridge, an early colonist in the Swan Hill area of Victoria, was a rather dismissive dissenter on the use of the term 'village' by his contemporaries of the nineteenth century:

> It is just possible, by the stretch of a very fertile imagination to assign the name of village to an assemblage of aboriginal huts, but such a liberty with the English language could only be permitted to one possessing a highly poetical organisation, as a number of these habitations gathered together in one spot is merely an encampment, and one of the very rudest too.[6]

Use of stone in dwellings

Dark Emu cites Paul Memmott citing others who found 'hundreds of stone buildings on High Cliffy Island off the Western Australian coast' (page 94). 'Stone buildings' is going too far, and indeed Memmott himself never used the word 'buildings' in this context.[7] If we go back to Memmott's source for High Cliffy Island, we find that the archaeologist Sue O'Connor refers to them as 'stone structures' and 'hut bases', and cites an earlier archaeologist, Valda Blundell, who in 1972 was told by Aboriginal informants that 'the structures were house bases whose walls had been formed by wooden uprights with bark coverings'.[8] These stone structures were no more than a metre high.[9] They were footings or supports for walls, not walls.

It is consistent with this that the stone structures at High Cliffy Island were constructed on sandstone surfaces, an environment where more typical wooden structures involving posts driven into the soil would not be possible; and wood and bark were not available on this rocky outcrop.[10] As in the Victorian cases recorded by Buckley and Alfred Kenyon (see below), the use of stone footings for boughs seems to have been partly prompted by scarcity of organic materials rather than simply chosen. O'Connor suggested that the local islands were used on a 'sedentary or semi-sedentary basis' and High Cliffy Island 'on a sedentary basis throughout the wet season'.[11] That is not permanent occupation.

In a later publication, O'Connor surveyed the ethnographic evidence and came to an inconclusive position on how seasonally or permanently the High Cliffy Island shelters were occupied.[12] Particularly problematic is her less than critical use of Tindale's view that the relevant language group territory was a population isolate.[13] This would be contrary to the normal patterns of intermarriage between linguistic group members and intergroup visits, and would recycle Tindale's confusion of a descent-based country-owning group with an on-the-ground population of residents.[14]

Pascoe does not define 'permanent housing'. Does it mean housing in which people resided permanently, or does it mean durable and lasting housing that was used for defined periods such as seasons of local food abundance? Substantial dwellings, such as those made with log supports, grass or bark covering, and sealed on top by upended turf or clay roofing, could last until revisited in the following cold and/or wet season, when some refurbishment may have been needed. That may be permanent housing without permanent dwelling. We even have a monsoon-belt record of wet-season huts made of purely organic materials sometimes lasting long enough to be refurbished the following year during seasonal visits.[15] Heavy wooden wall supports for small huts have lasted in the Simpson Desert at some sites since at least 1899 into recent decades.[16] In Tasmania, mobile bands moving along the west coast travelled from one group of huts to the next, 'occupying old huts or building new ones as occasion demanded'.[17] Once again, the relative permanency of the dwellings did not mean they were permanently inhabited.

Stone, naturally, is the most permanent dwelling material—but it is also the rarest in the Aboriginal record. We have an eyewitness account of the use of stone combined with reeds in housing in the Western District of Victoria from before effective colonisation, in the form of a recorded memory of William Buckley. This account is in a source listed by both Gerritsen and Gammage,[18] but not by Pascoe. None of these authors discuss Buckley's information as set out below:

We ... proceeded to the borders of another large lake, which they call Yawangcontes, in the centre of an extensive plain. There we made our huts *with reeds and stones, there being no wood*; so bare was it indeed, that we had to go nearly three miles [5 km] for fuel to cook our food with.[19]

This suggests that use of stone was the exception rather than the rule in the region of Buckley's extensive travels in the Western District. It also suggests stone being used as a substitute for wood, and resorted to in the absence of the latter. This is supported by all of Buckley's other descriptions of housing:[20]

During my first day's lonely march, I saw, at a distance, about a hundred natives, in and about some *huts built of bark, and boughs of trees*, and others of the Tribe making towards me. (Morgan, page 8)

We proceeded in this way until we came to their huts, *two small turf cabins*—in each of which there was just room enough for two persons to lay at length under their shelter. (page 16)

My friendly natives, or rather new acquaintances whom I had accompanied, took me to their homes, which were merely *branches of trees thrown across each other, with slips of tea-tree and pieces of bark placed over* as an additional shelter. (page 22)

After the skirmish just mentioned was over, the tribe to whom the boys belonged retired farther into the bush, when we made our huts, as I have described, *with boughs and bark*. (page 27)

Having arrived at a place good for this purpose, as they thought, we pitched, or rather erected *our bark tents*. (page 31)

… after a while we all moved on to a place they call Godocut [Point Addis], near the sea side, where we pitched *our bark huts* on a high projecting piece of land … (page 42)

The next place we went to was called Ballackillock [Ballark], where we found a tribe already settled, if a few days' residence under *sheets of bark and branches of trees*, may be so called. (page 48)

Having erected their *bark huts* near ours, they remained peaceable enough for several days … (page 69)

Here are eight descriptions of huts made from branches, bark and turf, and only one made from a combination of rocks and reeds, the latter being a case of necessity due to distance from sources of wood. By highlighting rare stone structures and ignoring other sources, including Buckley, Pascoe is citing the exceptional as exemplification of the usual. This is not a scientific approach.

Still in Victoria: stone was used as a substitute for wood on treeless plains in western Victoria in another case provided by Kenyon:

> The structures [on the Mount Elephant run, near Derrinallum] were shelter-circles, erected in situations *where neither … brushwood nor bark could be obtained* for building mia-mias [huts] … These circles are common on the plain or eastern part of this property (Purrumbete), *where branches of trees could not be procured for giving shelter … The circles are generally formed of large stones set on their edges and bedded in the ground close together, without any other stones on the top,* thus forming good protection from the wind as they lay around the fire.[21]

Dawson made the same observation based on his experience in colonial Victoria, suggesting that stone was not the preferred dwelling material: 'In some parts of the country *where it is easier to get stones than wood and bark for dwellings*, the walls are built of flat stones and roofed with limbs and thatch.'[22]

It seems clear that in *Dark Emu*, stone is proposed as the preferred, the more advanced, building material. It is crucial to Pascoe's task of proving the sophistication of the Old People. Those people evidently had the opposite view: organic materials, light and easily adjustable, were the preferred building mediums. Stones were used as a last resort.

Kenyon discussed the stone circles in the Lake Condah–Mount Eccles area of the Western District, and quoted Alexander Ingram as having been told in 1898 by elderly people at the Condah Mission that they had been roofed over with boughs and bark.[23] Keryn Walshe discusses this particular area in Chapter 13. Kenyon also referred briefly to explorers Flinders and King having found 'huts with stone walls, in both instances in the north'.[24] I will deal first with Matthew Flinders. The King example is dealt with further below.

The reference here to Flinders very likely comes from Thomas Worsnop.[25] However, the arranged stones Flinders saw, according to Worsnop, were not of Aboriginal origin: 'It was evident that these people were Asiatics …'[26] This was not mere speculation by Worsnop.

Here is Flinders' original published record from the Sir Edward Pellew group of islands in the Gulf of Carpentaria:

> Besides pieces of earthen jars and trees cut with axes, we found remnants of bamboo lattice work, palm leaves sewed with cotton thread into the form of such hats as are worn by the Chinese ... but what puzzled me most was a collection of stones piled together in a line, resembling a low wall, with short lines running perpendicularly at the back, dividing the space behind into compartments ... Mr Brown saw on another island a similar construction, with not less than thirty-six partitions, over which was laid a rude piece of framework ...[27]

In his masterly survey of Aboriginal traditional dwellings, Paul Memmott presented only a few examples of stone used in buildings. His chapter 'The stone architecture of Aboriginal Australia'[28] opens with a two-page spread showing a photograph of a circular stone structure. Not until late in the chapter is it revealed that this is not a house but a hunting device, a bird hide. The Australian Alps also feature briefly, in a drawing of 'stone houses of Aboriginal Druids'.[29] It is possible that these 'stone houses' were representations of caves rather than houses, given that stone-house remains have not been discovered in the Australian Alps, and 'druids', in English folklore, are frequently typecast as cave-dwellers.

In support of this possibility is the report from William Thomas in Brough Smyth that an old man from the Australian Alps, Kul-ler-kul-lup, had spoken of:

> a race living in the Alps who inhabited only the rocky parts, and had their homes in caves; that this people rarely left their haunts but when severely pressed by hunger, and mostly clung closely to their cave-dwellings; that corroborees were conveyed by dreams to Kul-ler-kul-lup's people and other Australians; and that men of the caves and rocks were altogether superior to the ordinary Aboriginal.[30]

These details have all the hallmarks of religious mythology.

Be that as it may, Pascoe makes this very large claim: 'Early travellers in the Alps remark on the small villages of stone houses and the large populations' (page 91). The source he gives is 'Peisley Papers, 2012'. The bibliography shows four sets of papers by 'A. Peisley', possibly Annette Peisley, dated 2010a, 2010b and 2011 and one undated. None of these sources are publicly available, so there is no way a reader can test Pascoe's sweeping assertion here. It has not been justified with evidence.

It is then highly problematic for Pascoe to go on to say: 'These structures [stone arrangements] have been found *all around the country*, as have stone houses similar to the Lake Condah buildings' (page 96). The evidence does not bear out the term 'stone houses' for Lake Condah (see details in Chapter 13).[31] These had wooden wall structures and thatch on the walls and roofing, based on about two layers of stones used as footing for the upright posts. No mortar was used, and the naturally formed rocks were not trimmed. That is not a stone house. Without mortar, it is not possible to create house walls of up to 2 metres, from floor to roof, without using a massive pile of flat rocks, as in a corbelled vault, or arches or domes of close-fitting stones. In these senses, no stone houses have ever been reliably reported for Aboriginal Australia before conquest. The modern reconstruction in the photo is faithful to the sources for western Victoria (see page 4 of the picture section).[32]

A footnote at the end of Pascoe's sentence on 'stone houses' being found 'all around the country' leads us to believe the statement is based on, or supported by, Memmott. But when we go to that page in Memmott's book to check, there is no such statement, and instead Memmott comments: 'There is extensive ethnographic and archaeological literature on stone structures, *but unfortunately little published on stone buildings per se*.'[33]

Pascoe asserts that 'Foundations and walls are still visible despite the pilfering of their stone for European dwellings and dry walling, two hundred years of damage by cattle and sheep, and the sudden advent of uncontrolled fires' (page 91). But a paucity of record may well mean, simply, that there is a paucity in fact.

Memmott, evidently having difficulty locating evidence of any more than a dozen possibly pre-colonial stone-dwelling structures across Australia's 7.7 million square kilometres, cites Worsnop as a source on what he refers to as 'stone buildings'.[34] But if we go to Worsnop, we find there a quoted source from the explorer Phillip Parker King, who visited Careening Bay in the Kimberley in 1820.[35] Here is the original passage in King to which Worsnop, and then Memmott, and then ultimately Pascoe, refer:

> Besides the huts on the beach, which were merely strips of bark bent over to form a shelter from the sun, there were others on the top of the hill over the tents, of a larger and more substantial construction. One of them was thus erected:— Two walls of stones, piled one upon the other to the height of three feet [0.9 m], formed the two ends; and saplings were laid across to support a covering of bark or dried grass: the front, which faced the east, was not closed; but the back, which slanted from the roof to the ground, appeared to have been covered with bark like the roof.
>
> The other huts were made somewhat of a similar construction, as they are represented in the woodcut [see below], but all differed in shape ...[36]

These structures do not fit the usual meaning of the term 'stone buildings'. They are consistent with stones being used to support posts where the ground is too hard to sink the posts. Memmott, as an architectural anthropologist, refers to this as 'buttressing'.[37]

Woodcut of shelters at Careening Bay, Kimberley, in 1820.

Given his career-long specialisation in the anthropology of Aboriginal architecture, Memmott is likely to be aware of more examples of dwellings employing stone than anyone else. Nonetheless, the only ones he can identify are, in summary of the above:[38]

1. King's huts in the Kimberley using stones to buttress posts (Memmott, page 185).
2. George Augustus Robinson's roofed stone-based houses in western Victoria (page 189).
3. Kenyon's low stone circles in western Victoria roofed over with boughs and bark, as discussed earlier (page 189).
4. An 1843 sketch of 'stone houses' in the Australian Alps, inhabited by druids, possibly caves instead, quite possibly mythological (page 185).
5. Basedow's observation in Central Australia of roofing using flat stones as a regional exception to organic-only shelters, as discussed below (page 185).
6. A family tradition of unproven antiquity relating to the Warringah area in Sydney, Memmott's source dating only from 2000, presented without any archaeological substantiation.[39]
7. The Lake Condah case of Victoria, which has been controversial. Memmott has recently stated regarding the Lake Condah stone circles: 'I would hypothesise that the stones (if positioned by humans) were low stone walls. They were windbreaks.'[40]
8. Dawson's references to houses with stone walls in western Victoria (page 198).
9. High Cliffy Island in north-west Western Australia (pages 199–201).
10. The Georgina River (Queensland) circular and square stone structures that may have been in use before European contact or in response to it (page 201).
11. Worsnop on 'near Arnhem Land' (page 204); these are 'low stone walls'.[41]
12. Worsnop on 'Prince Regent River Basin' in Western Australia (page 204). Described as a stone structure, and as possibly an oven or an altar, by Worsnop's source (Bradshaw), but not as a dwelling.[42]

In a country of 7.7 million square kilometres, the extreme leanness of this record, even if we include the controversial and questioned cases, is obvious. It is less than minimal. On the factual evidence, use of stone in making dwellings in pre-conquest Australia was extremely rare and atypical, even if we include stone windbreaks. There is no scientific evidence that Aboriginal Australians, before conquest, made stone houses with stone walls rising all the way from ground level to roof level at, say, a height of 2 metres—that is, giving enough room for most adults to stand in. This paucity of the record for stone being used in constructing shelters in pre-colonial Australia seems to have led Pascoe to grasp at straws, and to suggest that what has been found only here and there was more common or even universal.

Dwellings and the seasons
The general pattern, which Pascoe does not acknowledge, was that in each region people used the least elaborate structures under the most warm and dry conditions, and the most elaborate structures under the coldest and/or wettest conditions. This meant a seasonal oscillation between open-air form—such as windbreaks or camps under shade trees, covered sleeping platforms and bark huts—and more substantial huts sometimes sealed with mud or clay and, in one sole recorded instance, flat stones.

This impulse by Pascoe to overstress sedentism ignores a corrective made long ago in which the anthropological literature recognised that people of different regions engaged in different degrees of mobility, and that the mobility varied ecologically and seasonally. Western Desert people's mobility patterns are well known from multiple records.[43] In their case, frequent movements and wider dispersal in the cooler months, where there were scattered ephemeral waters, alternated with contraction to longer-held camps on more permanent waters in the worst of the hot weather.

The people of the northern monsoon belt were mostly immobilised for the roughly three months of the wet season but varied in their mobility through the rest of the year. Western Cape York Peninsula coastal people made wide use of multiple base camps and temporary camps through the seasons preceding the wet, ranging widely on the beaches and in the peri-coastal country, and with forays further inland. By contrast, on the east coast of CYP north of Stewart River, the 'people of the sandbeach' were more sedentary in all the seasons, often moving only short distances along the beach as camp sites became fouled and firewood short.[44] No camp site was itself permanently inhabited.

Dry-season shelter, western Cape York Peninsula.

The striking thing about the western Victorian stone structures (see Chapter 13) is not that they present Aboriginal Australia generally in a new light—they were detailed in print many years ago—but that they are so exceptional to the continental pattern. Australian dwellings before conquest were designed to be appropriate to the different seasons of the year. Given that the continent spans the temperate zone in the south through to the monsoon belt in the north, those seasons themselves vary a great deal, although Aboriginal seasonal calendars typically recognised four to six seasons depending on latitude. Aboriginal people of the monsoon belt have calendars most commonly of five (sometimes six) seasons.[45]

Pascoe is incorrect in claiming that the peoples of Cape York and Arnhem Land, 'where the seasons were divided into wet and dry, usually had two seasonal camps and two different styles of housing' (page 86). His assessment here is one of many elementary errors that a proper peer review process would have corrected. A two-season northern year is a non-Aboriginal idea. Table 4 shows the Yawuru season names pertaining within the country in which *Dark Emu*'s publisher, Magabala Books in Broome, is based, alongside approximate English equivalents.[46]

Table 4: Yawuru season names.

Season name	Time of year
Man-gala	Wet season, December–March
Marrul	Late summer, April
Wirralburu	Autumn, May
Barrgana	Winter, June–August
Wiriburu	Spring, September
Laja	Early summer

That monsoon-belt people used a range of forms of housing and shelter—not two, as announced by Pascoe—has been on the public record for many years.

Paul Memmott and Shaneen Fantin published a well-illustrated chapter on 'Northern monsoonal architecture' in Memmott's 2007 book.[47] There (on page 161) they illustrated the seven different shelter types recorded among the Wik people by anthropologist Donald Thomson and published by him in his 1939 paper. They also illustrated twenty-two types of shelter recorded by Thomson in Arnhem Land in the 1930s (page 165). Earlier, Lloyd Warner had published descriptions of seven different styles of shelter used in the same region.[48] Having accused others of making Aboriginal technology out to be far simpler than it really was, it could be argued that by claiming monsoon-belt people had only two camps per year, and only two styles of housing, Pascoe was himself guilty of this oversimplifying.

It is worth noting in this context that in pre-colonial Australia, and still in some places, people's sole source of heat for cooking, keeping warm, and providing a hearth area daunting to both snakes and spirits at night was firewood. Collecting it was often a task especially, but not only, given to elderly women and to children (see overleaf). The only means of transporting it to a camp before the age of the vehicle or the beast of burden was to carry it on foot. As the radius of collected suitable wood expanded over time, wood became harder to find and had to be sought further out. The fuel-based incentive to move to another location thus increased with length of stay.

Pascoe cites work by Memmott on the subject of the 'domed' wet-season dwellings of traditional Arnhem Land.[49] Here he refers to Thomson as a photographer and includes an image showing a very large and tall domed thatch structure, bearing the caption 'Pointed dome house'. But this was not one of the domed structures photographed by

Firewood collector, Wik region, Cape York Peninsula, 1927.

Thomson and was actually not even from Aboriginal Australia but from the Melanesian region of the eastern Torres Strait, where the people speak Meryam Mir. This is a language belonging to the Trans-Fly family of languages of Papua New Guinea, speakers of which are tradition-ally swidden horticulturists and fishers.[50] This domed-structure photo taken by Pascoe from an unacknowledged source is the same as the one in Memmott's book, where it is correctly described as being from eastern Torres Strait and sourced to the Queensland Museum.[51] In the second edition of *Dark Emu*, the image was replaced by a photograph of the framework of the same hut minus the grass thatching.[52] In *Young Dark Emu* both the hut and the framework are shown as 'dome house', with no note that it is Melanesian and not Aboriginal.[53]

Several design features of this 'Pointed dome house', repeatedly used by Pascoe, mark it out as being not at all typical of Aboriginal Australia: the pointed peak with a high protruding centre-pole, the sheer height of the room space, and the degree of symmetry and exactitude—and hence the labour investment—of the framework and lashings. This is a hut one can stand and walk around in. Most Aboriginal people's huts were low-ceilinged, designed for sitting and lying down, and assembled with an economy of effort appropriate to their needs and their minimal-impact economic philosophy—the latter being what Stanner called their use of 'least-cost' solutions.[54] I know of only one image of an Australian hut that resembles this one to a significant extent: the one photographed at Tully, a rainforest location in Far North Queensland, by Walter Roth.[55] Roth's photo is of a hut tall enough to stand in, but that may have been unusual, as his records of this hut type state: 'the height is usually well under four feet [1.2 m]'.[56]

Economy of effort in the material domain went along with the conservation of energy and of resources, all part of a minimal-impact lifestyle. Spending time in the bush with people in remote Australia and walking through the various environments shows how light were the footprints of the Old People, as you notice how people part branches rather than snap them off, and how a camp can be quickly established without very much clearing or removal of what was there—just enough for comfort. By contrast, ceremonial and martial events could be performances of high energy and competitive display, often of great length, requiring tremendous stamina and commitment of effort. Rituals lasting weeks and involving singing all night till dawn were not unusual. For the Old People, cultural elaboration was more highly valued than technological elaboration.

Camp and band sizes

We have many records of the numbers of people seen camping and travelling together on or beyond the frontier. Large groups numbering in the hundreds are part of this record but not typical of cases generally. Escaped convict James Davis (Duramboi), who spent thirteen years (1829–42) living among Aboriginal people in south-east Queensland beyond the reach of the colonists, was recorded as having seen 'a muster of about a thousand' people at an initiation ceremony.[57] In the 1920s, RM Williams of later bootmaking fame, then working as a young camel-boy for missionary William Wade, encountered people in the desert far to the west of Oodnadatta. He reckoned about a thousand were gathered at one location, being there to trade with a dingo scalper.[58] These examples are at the high end of the estimates of temporary bush gatherings beyond the frontier.

There is only space here to cite a selection of more precise examples from different regions.

In the mid dry seasons of 1939 and 1955, patrol officer Gordon Sweeney contacted bush groups in the Liverpool River region of

Arnhem Land. Some had assembled for joint ceremonies, others were 'hunting groups' or undescribed. His reports gave the residential group sizes shown in Table 5.[59]

Table 5: Residential group sizes recorded by Gordon Sweeney in the Liverpool River region, Arnhem Land.

Place	Number
Juda	77
Jarala	81
Gunbatgari	60
Budugaduru	34
Nanja	19
Imairut	63
Nabalagorrorji	36–46
West of Liverpool	14
?	15
Juda	c79
?	at least 46
Gunbatgari	28
Madei-Japa	36
Imimbar	c70

Nicolas Peterson and Jeremy Long published not only these censuses but a much more substantial number drawn from the northern monsoon belt and the interior desert, in a chapter called 'Residential group censuses'.[60] All were very detailed observations of camps met by recorders travelling beyond the effective frontier. Table 6 is drawn from their analysis of those details.[61]

Table 6: Residential group sizes in the northern monsoon belt and interior desert, according to Peterson and Long.

Region	Mean no. of people per camp	Camp size range
Western Desert	13.6	4–28
Cape York Peninsula	14.6	8–22
Bathurst Island	15.6	6–32
Groote Eylandt	21.4	11–27
Mainland Arnhem Land	32.7	18–63

We would expect camp sizes in the extremely rich Western District of Victoria to have been on average larger than these, and the people sedentary for longer periods. Buckley's observations of the eastern half of that district prior to colonisation are in Table 7.[62]

Table 7: Camp sizes in Victoria's Western District, according to William Buckley.

Buckley's description	Camp size
'... we came to their huts, two small turf cabins—in each of which was just room enough for two persons to lay at length under their shelter ...' (page 16)	accommodating 4 people
'About a hundred men came to meet us, but the women remained digging for roots, which they use as food: their huts being situated near an extensive lagoon.' (page 22)	possibly numbering in the low to mid hundreds
'... we left this place and joined a friendly tribe, about fifty in number ...' (page 27)	about 50
'Before we left this place, we were unexpectedly intruded upon by a very numerous tribe, about three hundred ... On the hostile tribe coming near, I saw they were all men, no women being amongst them.' (pages 32–3)	about 300 men assembled for battle (probably recruited from multiple bands)
'... reaching the appointed place of rendezvous, we found about eighty men, women and children gathered together ...' (page 38)	about 80
'Another tribe soon after joined us, amounting to about one hundred men, women, and children.' (page 58)	about 100
'One day we saw a large party of natives coming towards us ... There were about sixty of them ...' (page 59)	about 60; war party (so perhaps all men)
'With my adopted children, and two families only, I now went to a place they called Bearrock ...' (page 72)	probably less than 20
While at the above, they were joined by a man, his wife and family, then: 'Our small community remained in perfect harmony for many months ...' (pages 74–5)	perhaps 25 or so
'By one accession and the other our numbers had now increased to more than two hundred men, women, and children ...' (page 76)	200+
'... we were visited by two of the tribes I have already mentioned ... They mustered about two hundred strong, men, women, and children.' (page 95)	about 200

Throughout Buckley's reminiscences, groups of people are joining each other, often summonsed by a messenger, and then splitting up and returning to their own base camps. In short, the numbers in Table 7 are snapshots of events, rather than descriptions of groups each with a constant composition. Residential groups (bands) in the old Australia are usually regarded as having had fluctuating memberships.[63]

Harry Lourandos collated membership numbers of what he called 'bands' in the Western District of Victoria,[64] but I have not used those figures here because they appear to be membership numbers for named descent-based land-owning groups, not land-occupying groups or camps (bands). As we know from elsewhere in Australia, bands or land-occupying groups were commonly composed of members of more than one land-owning group or clan, averaging six clans represented per camp in the Arnhem Land and Cape York cases listed in my 2003 book about native title.[65] They also lacked formal names. Lourandos does however offer an estimate of Western District camp sizes:

> The information on the size of groups of huts indicates that most references [in early sources, e.g. GA Robinson] are to groups of 2–5 huts, with a significant percentage referring to groups of 6–13 huts or more. This information therefore falls within the range of between 20 and 100 or more individuals, if we assume an approximate occupancy of about 8 persons per hut.[66]

Rhys Jones summarised early Tasmanian observations of camp sizes between 1792 and 1831 (see Table 8).[67]

Table 8: Observations of Tasmanian camp sizes between 1792 and 1831.

Location	Camp size
SE Tasmania	48
SE Tasmania	42
Oyster Bay	25–30
Huon River	20 'families'
Robbins Island	50
Hobart	64
Hobart	50
Bruny Island	about 50
Port Davey	40
West Point	40
not stated	50–80
not stated	60–80
not stated	19

In these figures there is probably a sliding scale whereby the Western Desert people had about the smallest average camp size, and the numbers increase as one moves to the monsoon belt, then to Tasmania and, at the very high end, the Western District of Victoria. Degrees of mobility versus sedentism are roughly in line with this scale. It follows that blanket descriptions of 'Aboriginal people' inevitably hide a wide range of sizes of residential groups and patterns of mobility. Camps numbering in the hundreds were not the norm.

Dark Emu for children

In the children's version, *Young Dark Emu*, there are four images of dwellings. One is a hypothetical reconstruction of a 'Gunditjmara village' of stone-walled houses in Victoria,[68] one is George Augustus Robinson's drawing of a 'village' of substantial huts in south-western Victoria,[69] and the other two are the same images of the framework and then the thatched version of the domed hut from the island of Mer in the eastern Torres Strait.[70] There are no images of the most frequently recorded range of dwellings in the old Australia: modestly sized, low huts that one entered by crawling, shelters made by folding bark over a support, leaf shelters set up for shade, and semicircular windbreaks.

The teaching resource book, *Dark Emu in the Classroom*, shows only one dwelling: the same Mer-style domed and pointed construction discussed here. There is no image in the book showing anything representative of Aboriginal Australian dwellings. The text indicates that the authors mistakenly believe Aboriginal and Torres Strait Islander people to have had the same traditional economic system: 'Research suggests that Aboriginal and Torres Strait Islander peoples had an agricultural economy in which seeds were propagated, irrigated, harvested, stored and traded across regions.'[71] This is plainly erroneous. The authors also suggest that the Old People 'had systems of *agriculture, aquaculture,* housing, food storage and land management, inconsistent with hunter-gatherer societies' (emphasis in original).[72] Put in this distorted and simplistic form, the message serves only to seriously mislead secondary students exposed to this material.

This teaching resource book should be withdrawn by any educational authority currently using it, and rewritten. When students exposed to its false narrative later encounter evidence of the high mobility of desert peoples or the seasonal oscillation between stationary wet-season camps and frequently moving camps of the various dry seasons in Australia's north, for example, or catch sight of one of the

Punga-style dwelling, Lake Eyre region.

plentiful published images of Aboriginal old–style dwellings, such as are shown here (see page 116 and above), will they make uncomplimentary comparisons? Or just be confused?

Thomson long ago illustrated a range of dwellings from the Cape York region (see below). His illustration, published in 1956, reflected not just the requirements of different seasons, but also the way people travelled during the year as they enjoyed the wide range of resources that were unevenly distributed across their domains.

Cape York Peninsula dwelling types, illustrated by Donald Thomson.

10
Mobility

In *Dark Emu*, Pascoe contends that Aboriginal peoples at the time of white invasion were not complete nomads and that they had a high degree of sedentism, commonly residing in a single place, and that these truths have been hidden or suppressed.

Given that the Old People of the Western District of Victoria were at the very high end of Australian sedentism in the pre-conquest era, they are a good test case for the proposition that at least some people stayed permanently in one place for year after year after year. Buckley's information on band mobility and sedentism in the eastern part of the Western District—an area roughly enclosing Barwon Heads, Bannockburn, Lake Colac and Cape Otway—contains the following information (drawn from Appendix 2). (Note that we have no information on what proportion of Buckley's thirty-two years in Victorian camps beyond the colonial frontier is covered by the account published by John Morgan.[1] Buckley's numerical estimates of miles have been converted to kilometres here; other less specific estimates like 'a few miles' have been left as they were.)

Distances travelled between camps: some miles, a few miles, two or three days walking, about 64 km, 14 days' march, at least 60 km, about 13 km, one day's walk, two days' walk, about 8 km, about 10 km, about 18 km, about 40 km.

Length of stays in one place: a few days, a few weeks, a very long time, probably a few days, some months, many months—perhaps a year or two, many months, a short time, some months, awhile, a few days, many months, many months, one night, several months, many months, a month or less, some time, a very long time, several months, many months.

Named locations (total 23): Maamart, Yawangcontes, Kongiadgillock (Lake Corangamite), Kironamaat (Lake Gerangamete), Moodewarri (Lake Modewarre), Bermongo (on Barwon River), Beangala (Indented Head), Liblib near Bangeballa (north-east of Colac), Godocut (Point Addis), Palac Palac (Paraparap), Boordek (possibly west of Colac), Morriock (Mount Moriac), Ballackillock (Ballark), Monwak (Aireys Inlet), Moodewari (Lake Modewarre), Koodgingmurrah, Booneawillock (near Buckley Falls, Geelong), Nellemengobeet (lagoon at Barwon River mouth), Karaaf (Bream Creek, now Breamlea), Nullemungobeed (Murgheboluc Flat), Bearrock (near Gerangamete), Banor (near Cinema Point), Jerringot (Waurn Ponds).

It follows that the people among whom Buckley lived were not settled in permanent villages year in, year out. They stayed at different locations for a few days, for some weeks, for some months, and often for many months. This degree of sedentism is only matched in a small number of other regions, notably on the Murray River and eastern Cape York Peninsula (see details later in this chapter).

Norman Tindale has also provided evidence of relatively sedentary peoples:[2]

To the east [of Adelaide] were a series of tribes of people occupying small territories, dependent on the waters of the Murray River and Lake Alexandrina for their livelihood. They were *relatively sedentary* except for free movements up and down the river within the limits of their hordal[3] territories and somewhat less free movements to the hordal territories of their kinfolk in whose areas they had some rights, derived either from mother or from wife. (page 60)

Tribes living along the New South Wales coasts appear to have been *relatively sedentary*, having little communication with people over the inland ranges ... An early account by Clement Hodgkinson ... of conditions in 1842 shows that the natives of Bellinger River, presumably the Kumbainggiri, had *very stationary habits*. There was a local abundance of food and the broken intervening country was such as to discourage travel. (page 127)

Compressed into the toe of Fleurieu peninsula [*sic*] with the center of their territory at Ramong (Encounter Bay), [the Ramindjeri] appear to have been not only *sedentary* but also hemmed in by later comers in the Tanganekald and Jarildekald ... (page 133)

The general term Kakarakala, which seems to have originated with the Mandi tribespeople who live on the deltaic land at the mouth of the Gascoyne River, is applied to the tribes between North West Cape and Shark Bay ... It is not clear whether it also covers *the sedentary Mandi population* of the mouth of the Gascoyne River. (page 145; see also page 247)

These statements by Tindale are in one of the basic texts on Aboriginal people and their relationships to their countries. This work is not cited by Pascoe, other than as a source for a map of the Aboriginal grain belt (see the map in Chapter 6 on page 76).

The monsoon-belt peoples more generally alternated wet-season sedentism with considerable mobility in the other five (or four) non-wet seasons of the year. The most mobile people were those in the arid zone, perhaps the most highly mobile being people of the Simpson Desert and the vast Western Desert (see the map on page 142).

However, there are odd records from well-watered areas describing frequent camp moves—for example, that of James Morrill (or Murrells) who lived seventeen years with Aboriginal people beyond the frontier in what is now the Townsville region of Queensland:

They never stay long in a locality; as one place becomes a little exhausted of food, they travel to another. In the wet and cold season they put up small gunyahs to live in, but in no particular order ... They get their living by fishing, hunting, digging in the earth for roots, gathering fruits, &c.[4]

There is at least one other monsoon-belt account of mobility through-out the year. Paul Memmott and Robyn Horsman, in their 1991 'Student Text', reported that the Lardil people of Mornington Island were quite mobile even in the wet season. Wet-season camps were occupied only for 'up to six weeks' before people shifted.[5] They also gave accounts in the people's own words:

> For whatever reason, the Aborigines were constantly moving around Mornington Island, as the comments of these elderly people show: 'My mother and father no more [= did not] sit down one place … walk about everywhere. They move around all over the place' …[6]

That was followed by a long quotation from Elsie Roughsey describing the pleasures and difficulties of a long journey she made as a girl.

As noted earlier, elders' accounts of the old foraging life, both in their own languages and in English translation, have been long in the public domain, but are not considered in *Dark Emu*. One such source is the book *Warlpiri Women's Voices*, in which desert women gave accounts of where they lived and travelled in their youth.[7] None refer to permanent camps or to gardening or to the sowing or planting of seed crops. Another example, from the Cairns rainforest region, is Tilly Fuller's account in Yidiny of a day's foraging activity in the bush in her youth.[8] She refers to gathering ten plant species, to toxic nut processing, to gathering thatching materials, and to constructing fish traps—but at no point is there any mention of behaviours characteristic of horticulture or agriculture.

We should listen to these voices freely speaking in the peoples' own terms and tongues, and others like them. These voices do not appear in *Dark Emu*.

Restricted by a simple distinction between foragers and farmers, Pascoe has no place for the halfway house, as it were, of alternation between periods of being settled interspersed with periods of being on the move. The usual term for this is the 'semi-sedentary' pattern of land use. This was the term chosen by Sylvia Hallam for the *warran* yam–using people of central west Western Australia.[9]

'Semi-sedentary' is not mentioned in *Dark Emu*, but it is a way of life that is extremely widely reported in the anthropological literature on Aboriginal Australia as well as in evidence from the 'white blackfellows' who spent years living in Aboriginal society beyond the frontier. I will provide a sample of that evidence, much of it eyewitness evidence, below.

A hidden history?

Pascoe is certainly right that there were ill-informed views in materials used in education contexts in the past. Here are some examples:

Baldwin Spencer (1927): 'They are *pure nomads*, the members of a tribe hunting over the land that has belonged to their ancestors, and not encroaching on that of others.'[10]

Charles Barrett (c1936): 'The aboriginal, within the restricted limits of his totem country, is *a true nomad.*'[11]

JW Bleakley (1961): 'Because of their nomadic habits, there is *no idea of settled home* or village life, although suitable camping places may be occupied for short periods while certain food supplies are plentiful, and even returned to at the proper season.'[12]

Charles P Mountford (1969): 'The tribal aborigines are an *entirely nomadic* people, changing camps to collect food, at the times and places which Nature provides.'[13]

Although Spencer was an early professional anthropologist and zoologist, neither Bleakley, Barrett nor Mountford was a trained anthropologist. Bleakley was a bureaucrat, Barrett was a journalist, and Mountford, although he published widely on Aboriginal art and mythology and earned a D.Litt degree for it, was a Post Office mechanic and self-taught ethnographer who did not begin fieldwork with Aboriginal people until he was middle-aged.[14] Mountford actually, though weakly, qualified his nomadic description in the same source, called *The Aborigines and Their Country*: 'Except in the higher rainfall areas, the life of the aborigines is one of continuous movement in search of food.'[15] That was a very large exception, given that the great majority of Aboriginal people lived in the higher rainfall areas (see the map on page 78 in Chapter 6).

It doesn't get much lower than the ignorant and hostile views of Charles Chewings, a geologist and amateur ethnographer, who wrote in 1936: 'Like animals, they make no provision for tomorrow's food. All have the "wanderlust". Make no permanent shelter or camp, and *camp any and everywhere.*'[16]

By 1936 those views were already long dead and buried among informed people. Chewings was a dinosaur. However, in 1969, the same year that Mountford published the simplistic work just discussed, AW Reed published *An Illustrated Encyclopedia of Aboriginal Life*, written 'at the elementary level'.[17] It was not an academic work, but it had been checked for accuracy by professional scholars AP Elkin and FD McCarthy.[18]

Reed 'was neither a scholar nor a gifted writer, but wrote commercially successful books based on simplifying and popularising secondary sources'.[19] His *Encyclopedia* contained in part the following summarised entries, which made clear that Aboriginal people were ecological agents and not simply hunters and gatherers constantly on the move. People in well-watered areas stayed in one place for much longer than people in the desert (page 34). In the Darling River–Cape [*sic*: Lake] Eyre region, widows wore caps of clay (page 36). Aborigines used fire to hunt game and also 'as a means of increasing the fertility of his tribal territory' (page 65). 'Fish traps were used extensively in many coastal areas and along the rivers' (page 67). Bodily covering is described in detail and not as being at all uniform, ranging regionally from skin garments made of possum, kangaroo or wallaby skin, cloaks made of rushes, and of bark fibre, to aprons made of twine, belts with shells attached, armbands, necklaces, headbands, and so on; 'no clothing was worn in the central [desert] districts' (page 73), but Reed also warned the reader that 'it is not possible to generalise' (pages 72–3).

Reed's approach to traditional dwellings was also to emphasise regional variation (pages 86–7), ranging from minimal shelter in the central deserts (apart from occasions of rain), to 'solidly constructed' wet-season huts in the north, to regions of more persistent rainfall where people made 'more permanent structures [which] consisted of a frame of saplings covered with overlapping sheets of bark. Round ridgepole and rectangular huts were also built' (page 87). He also described many different kinds of nets, including duck nets and 'very substantial nets' made for trapping emus, wallabies and kangaroos' (page 114).

Reed had an entry under 'WALKABOUT', which he defined as describing 'the nomadic habits of the large numbers of tribes inhabiting the drier parts of Australia' (page 162). And he refuted the 'pure hunter-gatherer' mirage by telling the lay reader:

The Aboriginal was in fact a conservationist, being careful to leave fruiting trees unharmed, and even in some cases to scatter seed on the ground to ensure a future harvest, to leave some yams untouched, and to abandon his fishing while there were still fish to be caught.[20]

Also in the 1960s, an introductory textbook appeared that remained in print for decades afterwards through four successive editions, written by professional anthropologists Ronald and Catherine Berndt. This was *The World of the First Australians*.[21] The couple had carried out extensive and intensive fieldwork at multiple locations in Central Australia, Arnhem Land, Daly River, South Australia and Western Australia over decades since the 1930s and 1940s.

The Berndts warned against using technology and economy to stigmatise some peoples as being 'crude, rudimentary, underdeveloped, mentally backward ...'[22] Theirs was a clear position of cultural relativism and against the kind of social evolutionism unfortunately echoed by *Dark Emu*. They stressed the cultural diversity of Aboriginal peoples: 'What is true for one Aboriginal group, then, does not necessarily hold good for another.'[23] They were warning about making universal generalisations. Pascoe recognises that in regard to firing the country, '[e]ach area had specific requirements' (page 119), but then makes blanket generalisations such as: 'The start of that journey is to allow the knowledge that Aboriginals did build houses, did cultivate and irrigate crops, did sew clothes and were not hapless wanderers across the soil, mere hunter-gatherers' (page 156).

The Berndts said Europeans had judged Aboriginal people 'on the basis of how far they could control the forces of nature, by practical and not by supernatural means: by doing this they neglected the richness and complexity of so many other aspects of Aboriginal life'.[24] Pascoe's almost complete concentration on physical interventions in the food supply similarly downgrades the role of widely practised, complex and highly valued ceremonies and speech acts that constituted spiritual species maintenance (see Chapter 2 of this book).

The Berndts observed that, although 'not a gardening people', Aborigines in specific regions managed food species in the following ways.

At Daly River (Northern Territory), people 'were careful about exhausting certain yam beds and always left a residue well scattered for next season's crop', a practice the Berndts said was 'much more widespread than is often realised'.[25] People realised that 'conservation was essential even in times of plenty'.[26] They were a little coy in saying, 'It has been suggested that because of their hunting and food-collecting methods the Aborigines must, through the ages, have appreciably altered their environment',[27] citing Tindale.[28] One would not be so tentative today. They attacked the myth that Aboriginal people did not store or preserve food, long before Gerritsen did so. They cited specific examples, including: wild plums dried, red-ochred and dried again, along the monsoon-belt north coast; on CYP wild plums stored deep in sand; quandongs dried in the sun and kept for some time in the Great Victoria Desert; in the Bunya Mountains (Queensland) bunya nuts bagged and buried in the gravel of a creek bed for later consumption; zamia nuts in one part of Western Australia stored by being buried; several kinds of fish smoked and dried on the lower River Murray (South Australia) and on the Stirling River (Northern Territory); and at Daly River shark meat preserved for some days by packing the meat in leaves and paperbark and squeezing it completely dry.[29]

The Berndts also published in 1985 a much briefer text aimed at school-age readers, heavily illustrated, written in plain English, and with suggested student exercises. Although their main subject was postcolonial social and political history, they mentioned the skin cloaks of south-west and south-east Australia, and illustrated one type from the south-west (see illustration on page 95 in Chapter 7).[30] They referred to root-plant patches not being completely harvested, and to the firing of country to drive hunted game and encourage plant regrowth.[31]

In an earlier text written to educate the general reader, as is clear from its title (*The Australian Aborigines: How to Understand Them*) and its style, in 1938 anthropologist AP Elkin made a clear corrective to the hapless nomadism model:

> The reference to divisions of the tribal territory amongst local groups reminds us that *the Aborigines are really only semi-nomadic.*[32] They do *not wander any- and everywhere* in search of food, contesting the rights of others who may forestall them, but in visiting the countries of other groups, even of the same tribe, they must observe relationship and visiting rules.[33]

This passage was retained through multiple editions and revisions of this text at least until 1979, and in further printings after that.[34]

Elkin was not simply popularising his own findings. Anthropologist Phyllis Kaberry was one of several who in the 1930s contradicted what she called the 'wandering apparently at random' illusion held by others. On the contrary, 'the Aborigine's knowledge of her environment is an intimate one' and it was this that guided her to resources.[35] Another trained anthropologist, Ursula McConnel, published a detailed account of the finely targeted exploitation of bush foods, integrated with the seasonal calendar, which she observed at first hand in western CYP in the 1920s.[36]

Even the older educational materials prepared for young children could do better than the simple nomadic model of Aboriginal pre-colonial mobility. Fred McCarthy, a museum curator of ethnology, wrote a booklet for children called *Aboriginal Tribes and Customs* that came out in 1950 (see below). Children were encouraged to find small postcards in their packets of Sanitarium cereals, such as Weet-Bix, and paste them in the right spots in the booklet.

In paragraph 7 of his booklet, McCarthy opted for a semi-sedentary model: 'The length of time each camping-place is occupied depends

Front cover of Sanitarium cereal company booklet, 1950.

upon the supply of water and food, and if these are ample *the group may stay in one place for several weeks or months*.' He also explained that people built huts 'when they camp in one place *for a long period*' (paragraph 10), and provided descriptions of a wide range of bodily adornments, from possum and kangaroo skin cloaks, to belts and ornamental items, to complete nudity (paragraph 13). Regional variation permeates this source.

In an essay published first in 1962 and republished in 1979, anthropologist Bill Stanner said, 'The bands could be called "nomadic" but it was *a nomadism of a limited kind, bounded and even land-locked rather than unbounded and free-ranging* ...'[37]

The 1962 edition of *The Australian Encyclopaedia*[38] contained a section on Aboriginal economic life by Fred McCarthy (pages 29–37). The term 'semi-nomadic' occurred in the first line and elsewhere, and he discussed 'increase centres' (page 31).

Also in 1962, the ABC showed a twelve-episode documentary series on Aboriginal traditional life presented by Victorian Aboriginal man Bill Onus (see below), father of the artist Lin Onus whom I met at Maningrida in 1987 and whose work featured in the catalogue of a 1988 New York art exhibition called *Dreamings*.[39] Bill's series was

Bill Onus selecting boomerang wood
from St Kilda Road trees, Melbourne.

called *Alcheringa*[40] and I remember being enthralled by it at the time (I'm a year older than Pascoe). The emphasis was on the old economic life. It was reused extensively for another ABC series in 2001, *Our History*. Since 1962, at least, there have been dozens of TV programs aimed at educating the public about Aboriginal culture and history. Aboriginal classical high culture, especially painting, has been high profile at least since the 1980s.

In 1963 Tindale and Lindsay published a 'simplified summary'[41] of knowledge about Aboriginal people, clearly aimed at the school market, in which they wrote: 'Travel is *never aimless* ... Life was easiest to those who were *able to live as communities in one spot for long periods*, owing to an abundance of food.'[42] No hapless wanderers here.

Donald Thomson was another professional scholar who wrote an account of Aboriginal traditions for children, in the *Australian Junior Encyclopaedia* (1956).[43] I have had my copy since 1957, when I was eleven years old. In it, Thomson largely repeated the nomadic hunter-gatherer model (minus the hapless wandering) even though, as we shall see, he expressed more sophisticated views elsewhere and earlier. In the *Junior Encyclopaedia* he wrote: 'Although the aborigines *were nomadic and lacked any settled village, or even permanent camp life*, this *does not mean that they wandered over the country without restriction*' (page 79). However, referring to the northern monsoon belt, he said:

With the first rains of the wet season, about the end of December, the people move to higher ground ... areas which have long been known as wet-season camp sites. At these places *camps are established of a more permanent nature* than at other seasons of the year.[44]

In the same year, in the popular travel magazine *Walkabout*, Thomson described people of Princess Charlotte Bay in CYP, with whom he had lived as a trained anthropological observer for nearly twelve months in the 1920s:

The aborigines of the eastern seaboard of the Peninsula differ greatly from the natives of the interior ... Because they are largely dependent on the sea and the estuarine reaches of the rivers for their food supply, their movements are *less strongly nomadic*, and for months at a time they live *a more or less sedentary life*, moving their camps little, and then only for short distances.[45]

Another way of putting it was anthropologist Lauriston Sharp's expression 'partially immobilized', when referring to the wet-season camps of people on the lower Coleman and Mitchell rivers of CYP, people among whom he lived in shifting camps for thirteen months in the early 1930s.[46] It is rare for us to have eyewitness descriptions of traditional bush camps where the individual occupants are all identified by name, as they are in Sharp's account.

The Man Molur wet-season camp (see below) consisted of nine huts, used by between one and four people each. The maximum camp population was sixteen, the number of land-owning clans represented in the camp was six, and the number of different languages represented was two (Yir-Yoront and Thaayorre).[47]

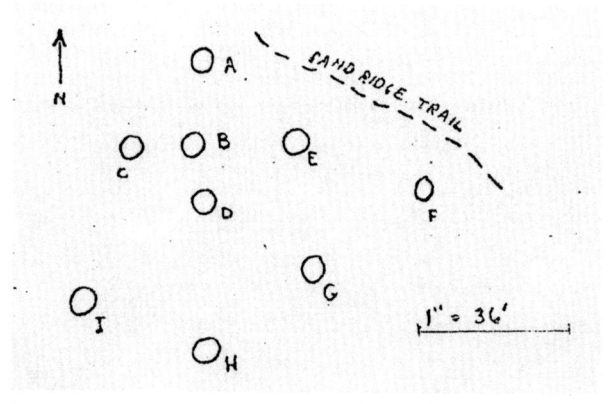

Sharp's sketch of wet-season camp at Man Molur, 1933–34.

The Olwinan wet-season camp (see opposite) consisted of six huts, used by between two and seven people each. The maximum camp population was twenty-two, the number of land-owning clans represented in the camp was ten, and the number of different languages represented was two (Yir-Yoront and Thaayorre). Again, each individual was identified.[48]

The monsoon-belt pattern, with the likely exception of eastern coastal Cape York, was that at the end of the wet season, such semi-sedentary camps would break up and their members disperse to enjoy the resources of the richest season of the year—the post-wet early dry season—and join other bands, until assembling in considerable numbers

Sutton's mentor Isobel Wolmby, Aurukun Mission, Cape York Peninsula, holding Thomas Sutton, 1976: photo by Anne Sutton.

Harry Gertz, teacher of Gugu-Badhun language, at Yangkarrdji, Valley of Lagoons Station, Queensland, 1970: photo by Peter Sutton.

Mary Walmbeng and Dorothy Pootchemunka performing moulting ducks
maintenance rite, upper Knox River, Cape York Peninsula, 1986: photo by David Martin.

Country being fired by Reggie and Cassidy Uluru, Lake Amadeus, 1999:
photo by Peter Sutton.

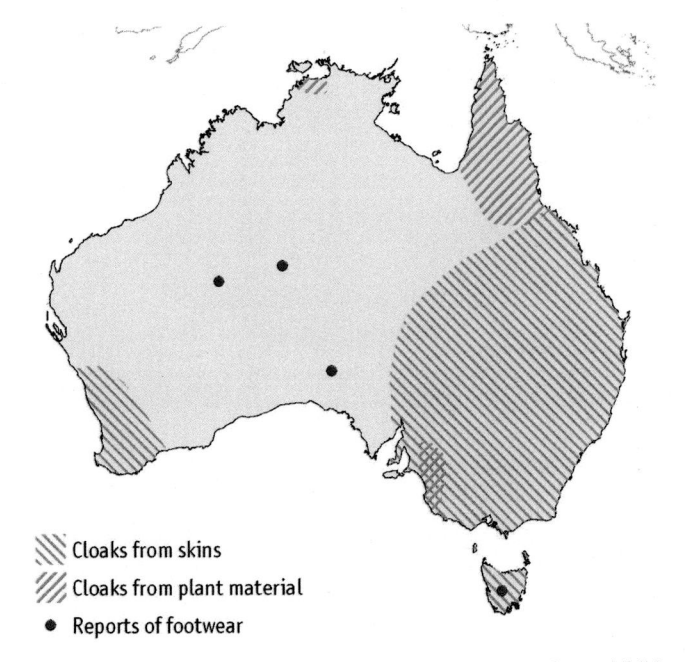

Cloaks and footwear map, *Macquarie Atlas of Indigenous Australia: Second Edition*, 2019.

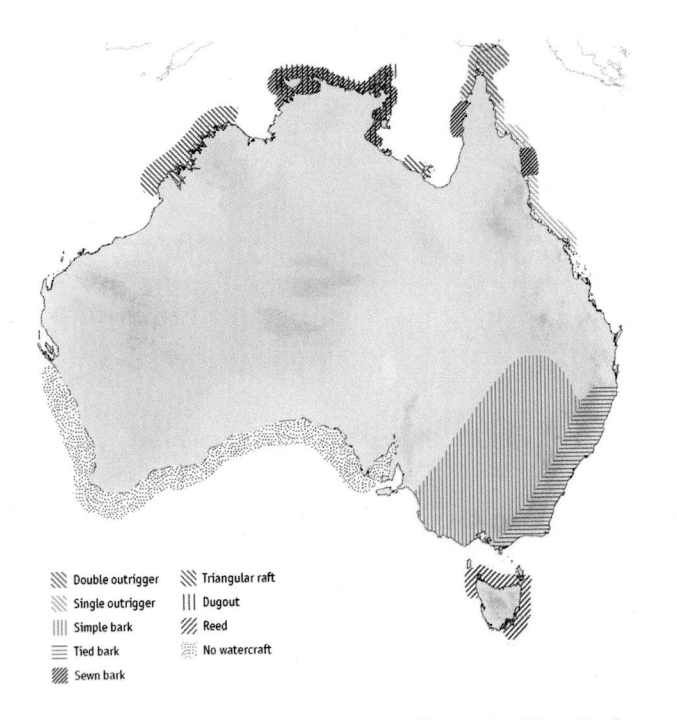

Watercraft in use at the time of European arrival map, *Macquarie Atlas of Indigenous Australia: Second Edition*, 2019.

Reconstruction of traditional dwelling, Lake Condah, 2020: photo by Peter Sutton.

Tree interior alight without external burn, 2020: photographer's name withheld.

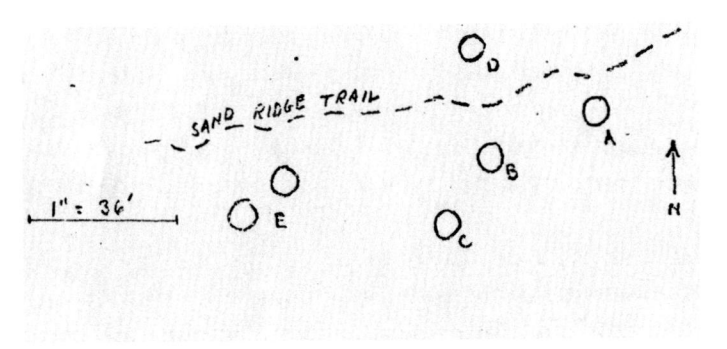

Sharp's sketch of wet-season camp at Olwinan, 1933–34.

for ceremonial events for a few weeks or days. They then redispersed until the next meeting or the next wet.

That is one pattern of Australian 'semi-nomadic' life in bush times but it is not the only one, as we shall see.

In 1969 leading archaeologist John Mulvaney published *The Prehistory of Australia*, a text that became the standard introductory survey of Australian archaeology for many years.[49] He also qualified 'nomadic' with cases of 'near-sedentary' Aboriginal camping:

> Aboriginal life was *nomadic*, while the number, frequency and distance of their shifts depended on local conditions. On the Lower Murray River it seems probable that camps within restricted localities were *semi-permanent*,[50] and this applied also to certain favourable coastal or estuarine situations. Possibly Thomson witnessed the extreme in *near-sedentary* habits on eastern Cape York. He lived for five months during 1928 with the fishing and dugong-hunting 'sandbeachmen' of eastern Cape York. During this period, camp was moved six times but the distance never exceeded about 300 yards [274 metres] on each occasion. But all these localities were exceptionally rich in food supplies ...[51]

Published in 1970 was Aldo Massola's historical sketch of Lake Condah Mission (located in an area discussed in detail in *Dark Emu*). It begins with yet another denial of 'hapless wandering':

> The fact that our Aborigines were nomadic food gatherers *does not mean that they wandered aimlessly* all over their tribal territory in the

hope of finding food. On the contrary; knowing every inch of their country they would spend the different seasons at the most fruitful places. They were mostly located in the vicinity of water, and in some places water fowl, fish, and roots from aquatic plants would be *so abundant as almost to obviate the need to wander to new grounds.*[52]

In 1978 scientists Peter Latz and GF Griffin wrote: 'The whole of Central Australia was not exploited continuously for its plant, animal and water resources. Family groups *did not wander aimlessly* or wherever they pleased in search of food and water.'[53]

The 'hapless wandering' image has also long been corrected in undergraduate student texts. For example, anthropologist Robert Tonkinson wrote in 1991: 'Despite the necessary fluidity of their nomadic life, Aborigines are *not rootless wanderers* who lack territorial attachments.'[54] In his 1988 educational text Bill Edwards wrote: 'The movement of Aboriginal groups was based on detailed knowledge of the environment and the resources and *directed* by a range of economic, social, political and ceremonial purposes.'[55]

Catherine and Ronald Berndt, indefatigable in their attempts to enlighten a wide public, in 1978 published an introductory text that began with a rejection of the idea that Europeans 'discovered' Australia. On the question of mobility, they wrote: 'The Aborigines were *not nomadic* in the sense of wandering fairly freely over a vast region, as the word is often popularly taken to mean. *Semi-nomadic is a better term* for their more circumscribed patterns of movement.'[56]

Another source aimed specifically at the general public and the education market was Bourke, Bourke and Edwards' *Aboriginal Australia* (1994), which was designed also for use by Television Open Learning students (as stated on the back cover blurb). In it, Aboriginal educator Colin Bourke wrote:

> In most cases the people moved around their ancestral lands as hunters and gatherers, so many possessions would have been a hindrance. Their movements around their country *were not haphazard*, but had a purpose. They were part of Aboriginal mastery over the resources of the land.[57]

Writing for a scientific readership in 1939, Thomson said of the Wik people of CYP (in the monsoon belt):

Within the bounds even of a single clan territory a people may spend several months of the year as *nomadic hunters*, in pursuit of bush game, wild honey and small mammals, and exploiting the resources of vegetable food of which a great number are known. A few months later the same people may be found established on the sea coast in camps that have all *the appearance of permanence or at least of semi*-permanence, having apparently abandoned their nomadic habits. They will remain in these camps for months on end ...[58]

Thomson later said of eastern CYP people:

These people are *less nomadic* than the tribes of the interior of the continent; *especially during the northwest monsoon season, they live in settled camps for weeks and months at a time.* Such are the Koko Ya'o and Ompela tribes, and the Yintjingga of Princess Charlotte Bay.[59]

Writing about Yolngu people of north-east Arnhem Land, among whom he spent long periods of fieldwork largely beyond the frontier in 1935–37,[60] Thomson said:

The natives of Arnhem Land are a nomadic people who live by hunting and collecting. They have *no settled village life*, no gardens or agriculture, they know nothing of pottery, and they have no domestic animals other than the half-wild dingo ...[61]

During the wet season ... the people are concentrated in semi-permanent wet season camps in which the population may exceed one hundred. Here they lead *an almost sedentary existence* in contrast with their active nomadic life in the south-east [wind] season.[62]

Thomson was no fool. He was a man of scientific integrity and keen observational skills, and an expert in Australian zoology and anthropology. He was also an active anti-assimilationist and an advocate for respect for Aboriginal people. If Yolngu had been practising horticulture or agriculture he would have reported it in detail. He didn't.

How, then, can Pascoe defend his argument that Aboriginal people in popular imagination subscribe to 'a belief in *the brutish description of Aboriginals that Australian history insists we accept*' (page 100)? Who are these insisting ogres? Isolated pub racists? So-called 'culture warriors'? Australian history writing, including the TV versions of it, moved way beyond that colonial-era delusion long ago. The multiple volumes of historical correctives to colonial frontier 'pioneer' mythology published by Henry Reynolds and other historians since the 1970s are in thousands of households. Their role in correcting the jingoistic settler histories of the past, in which 'brave pioneers' battled against 'a harsh environment' and 'troublesome blacks', was recognised and summarised accurately by Marcia Langton in her prologue to *First Australians* in 2008:

> In the past half century, as a new generation of historians has inter-preted the records, a dazzling view of Australian life has emerged. Instead of the drudges who peopled the pages of the old books, convicts, women, children, African-American slaves, adventurous European aristocrats, artists, con-men, bushrangers and thousands of Indigenous people have assumed more detailed, nuanced and intriguing personas, and their endeavours have become better understood. The ridiculous and audacious, as well as the common or garden, activities of ordinary and extraordinary people have replaced the monotonous tales of the March of Civilisation.[63]

Langton then added that only 'a handful of historians, mostly amateurs, persist in vilifying all the original inhabitants of this continent and their descendants', but she also said their works were very popular with those who 'prefer to imagine the Australia of the old school books'.[64]

Pascoe's information gap as a younger person at school in the 1950s and 1960s is seemingly projected onto the Australian general popula-tion, even onto the whole 'nation' (page 128). He also claims that an assumption of Indigenous inferiority is 'the window through which our nation angles its view of Aboriginal Australia' (page 127), and that what the explorers said they saw is 'a much more complex Aboriginal history than our nation believe(s)' (page 128).

Pascoe in these passages about 'the nation' seems to 'substitute his own autobiographical experience for the national narrative', as histo-rian Patrick Wolfe acutely observed of Robert Manne's late discovery of the Stolen Generations after decades of published work on the sub-ject.[65] People who do not 'know' Pascoe's version of the truth are by definition as ignorant as he claims he used to be. The danger is that some of those who began reading *Dark Emu* in a state of even partially reliable knowledge may have now become enamoured of its sweeping, simplified and distorted mythological history and are thus newly misled.

It is important to be aware of the educational achievements of the Australian Institute of Aboriginal and Torres Strait Islander Studies (AIATSIS) over many decades, something Pascoe might have thought to do. AIATSIS has been an effective disseminator of accurate knowledge, both in print and in audiovisual media, not just to the academy but to the younger educational sector and the wider public. Examples taken from among a vast array are these.

From 1975 to 1977 AIATSIS hosted an education research project supported by the Curriculum Development Centre. One outcome was a carefully assessed teacher's guide and bibliography of knowledge resources on Australia's Indigenous peoples.[66] It covered archaeology, classical cultures and languages, the arts, colonial history, contemporary issues including land rights, and poetry, drama and fiction written by Aboriginal people.

In 1994 AIATSIS published a massive two-volume and highly illustrated *Encyclopaedia of Aboriginal Australia*, edited by David Horton.[67] It was aimed at multiple audiences, but especially both Aboriginal and wider community members—not academics.[68] Among many other subjects, its entries cover food, food preparation, food processing, food production, food sharing, food storage and food taboos.[69] An entry written by ethno-archaeologist Roger Cribb gives a balanced and insightful account of traditional food-procuring economies, including this:

> Complex relationships between plants and people occurred in Australia prior to European contact, but not to the extent of horticulture or agriculture, in which a species' reproduction and future development are fully controlled ...
>
> Relatively high population densities were maintained not by the domestication of food species, but by the intensive use of natural species and extending the range of productive grassland and fire-tolerant habitats.[70]

The AIATSIS *Encyclopaedia* has had wide distribution and its map of Aboriginal language countries has been reproduced frequently, both in print and on television. An example of the map's extended range is its use in the book *First Australians*, edited by Rachel Perkins and Marcia Langton, and in the SBS television series of the same name.

A third example is the work of the AIATSIS Film Unit and film fellowships funded by AIATSIS. The Film Unit operated from 1961 to 1991 and the major filmmakers were Roger Sandall, Kim McKenzie, and David and Judith MacDougall.[71] Many of their films have been shown and reshown on television and in teaching courses for students, and many are available on the market as DVDs or downloads.

Apart from correctives to blinkered history, and to idle notions of hapless hunting and gathering without any environmental management, the decades since the 1960s have also been a time of booming research on the archaeology of Australia. Perhaps the most impactful television documentary conveying many of these recent discoveries was the 2013 ABC series *First Footprints*. Apart from the TV series, there was a study guide and a popular book of the same name by Scott Cane.[72] While such programs are numerically (and unfortunately) swamped by popular archaeological shows about Europe and the Middle East, they are playing their role in educating a broad Australian public.

The Western Desert peoples (see below) have been extensively documented by anthropologists, including some who moved among their bush bands beyond the effective frontier. Thomson was one, Tindale

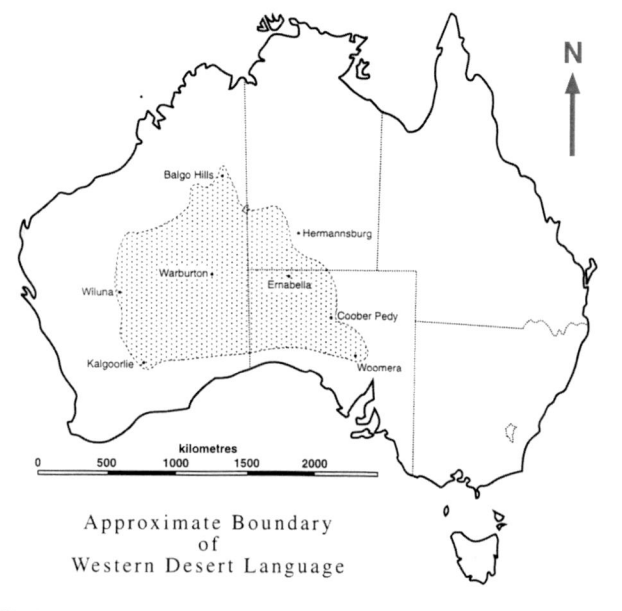

The Western Desert region.

was another, and a number of others have worked with people whose recent memories of lifetimes living in the desert they could record.

Even though these were the most nomadic of the First Australians, reliable descriptions vary between 'nomadic' and 'semi-nomadic'. Ronald Berndt said of Western Desert people of the Balgo (Western Australia) region: 'All these people were/are *semi-nomadic*; they move across limited regions, but *not unrestrictedly so* … During good seasons, they are not obliged to move too far …'[73]

Professor Fred Myers, an authority on the Pintupi people of the Western Desert, wrote:

> Since resources in any one area were quickly exhausted, the daily rhythm of Pintupi life around a camp was part of the larger nomadic pattern of movement from water hole to water hole. *The likely range of a year's movement for a nuclear family was within an area of 3,000 square miles* [c4800 square kilometres]. These movements and the aggregation and dispersal of people into larger and smaller groups depended on seasonal changes.[74]

In 1932 Tindale spent several hours recording the bush travels of a young Warlpiri man, Pariparu, who named 332 desert places he had walked to in the previous eleven months:[75]

> The youth's wanderings have not been plotted out on the map yet, but when they are, probably it will be found they have extended over hundreds of miles, for some of the spots he has named are widely separated. Some of them he has visited three or four times, taking a different course after leaving them each time.[76]

Encampments in western Victoria

Pascoe mentions the fact that William Buckley visited the Lake Condah eel traps in the Western District of Victoria and 'extolled the quantities of fish they captured' (page 58). He sources this to a 2003 article in *The Age* newspaper and surmises that if the stone circles at Lake Condah 'were houses, and if the channels were a fishing system, then around 10,000 people lived a more or less sedentary life in this town' (page 63).

Bill Gammage had written: 'Lake Condah's stone houses could hold about 700 people …'[77] Estimates of the entire pre-colonial population of Victoria range from 5000 to 15,000.[78] The proposition that most of them lived at Lake Condah, leaving the rest of Victoria mainly uninhabited, is untenable. Population estimates for the entire Western District at conquest have varied from 1800 to 3000–4000 to an upper estimate of about 7900.[79] A Western District 'town' of 10,000 people as suggested in *Dark Emu* is therefore a completely insupportable speculation. There is a big difference between seasonal use of a permanent structure and permanent residence in the same location. *Dark Emu* refers to 'permanent housing' and 'permanent occupation' but does not explore the differences between them (pages 19, 73, 95).

Archaeologist Josephine Flood says the Western District eel traps were used in the autumn—that is, in March and April—and people buried some eels in the ground for later consumption.[80] Arthur and Morphy, in the *Macquarie Atlas of Indigenous Australia*, concluded: 'In some well-watered areas people lived in large semipermanent encampments at certain times of the year … The people around Lake Condah built permanent houses with stone walls, *which they occupied during the eeling season*.'[81] Flood adds, in relation to Lake Condah:

> The inhabitants of this fertile region, later known as *Australia Felix*, were more sedentary than most other hunter-gatherers, but still moved camp several times each year. In autumn, several hundred people assembled to exploit eels and each family built itself a temporary hut. Such hut-groups were not permanent and to describe them as some have done as 'villages of stone houses' is an exaggeration. The term 'village' implies permanent residents living in permanent homes in the country.[82]

One of the five references Flood provides in support of this statement is Morgan's life-of-Buckley text. It is appropriate then to tabulate Buckley's eyewitness statements about movement and sedentism of those among whom he lived, which I do in Appendix 2. First, however, we can note the general description of the semi-sedentary occupation pattern Buckley observed in his thirty-two years of living with unconquered Aboriginal people of the Western District:

> We also shifted quarters a short time after, and kept up the old fancy[83] of wandering about; not exactly from 'post to pillar,' but from one hunting ground to another, seeking variety of food, from fish to flesh, from roots to anything available; for the natives are, in truth, a rambling lot, never content …[84]

11
The explorers' records

Archaeologists and anthropologists have typically invested the most time, energy and intellect in scientific studies of classical Aboriginal economic practices and material culture or technology. Scholars who have specialised in Aboriginal economic systems and spent many months living with people who maintained major aspects of their old hunting and gathering activities include Frederick Rose, Betty Meehan, Chris Anderson, Jon Altman and Elizabeth Povinelli. *Dark Emu* does not mention them, except for a brief criticism of Rose[1] for not including fish traps or nets in his book on traditional Aboriginal economics (page 64). None of these specialists in Aboriginal subsistence reported that gardening or agriculture was a traditional economic mode in their study regions, either before their research or during it.

Dark Emu's most frequent and important sources are explorers, those first agents of the spread of Empire. In this chapter I look at how *Dark Emu* has engaged with these old frontier records.

Thomas Mitchell is cited making the familiar observation, using very English categories, of grass that had been pulled and piled into 'hay-ricks': 'we found the ricks or hay-cocks extending for miles'.[2] What Pascoe leaves out, here, is Mitchell's puzzlement.

The grass had evidently been thus laid up by the natives, *but for what purpose we could not imagine* [page 237] … [W]hen we found the ricks, or hay-cocks, extending for miles, *we were quite at a loss to understand* why they had been made … it is probable that the heaps of grass had been pulled here, *for some purpose connected with the allurement of birds or animals* [pages 237–8].

145

The speculation was worth weighing up, but it is not so much left out by Pascoe as converted, by misquotation, and on a distant page, into misleading evidence that Mitchell was talking about agriculture: 'It's true, however, that when Mitchell observed haycocks extending for miles over a stubble paddock where every stalk had been cut he wondered if the heaps of grass had been pulled here, *for some purpose connected with the allurement of agriculture*' (page 31). Mitchell's original 'birds or animals' has been replaced with 'agriculture'. This was corrected in the 2018 edition of *Dark Emu*.

Then Pascoe quotes from Mitchell[3] on some large circular huts he saw in the Grampians of Victoria, suggesting simply that these were Aboriginal houses. Maybe they were, but Mitchell's accompanying words are left out by Pascoe, and should have been quoted also, because they cast doubt on who made these constructions: 'We had this day noticed some of their huts, which were *of a very different construction from those of the aborigines* ... The place seemed to have been *in use for years, as a casual habitation*.'[4] The second sentence contrasts with Pascoe's opinion that in this case the local people 'have used the place for a very long time'; its asserted 'casual' use being left out (page 21).

Pascoe then says of Mitchell: 'He counts the houses and estimates a population of *over one thousand*' (page 21). There is nothing at all resembling this in Mitchell's record of seeing this camp. All Mitchell says is that his party 'noticed some of their huts'; there is no mention of anyone counting anything. Pascoe's 'over one thousand' is pure fiction.

Next Pascoe refers to a member of Mitchell's party, Granville Stapylton, as having recorded that the buildings 'were of very large dimensions, one capable of containing at least 40 persons and of very superior construction' (page 21). It is unfortunate that Pascoe omitted the full context, which says:

> ... passed to day several Guneaks [*sic: guneahs*—that is, *gunyahs* or huts] of very Large dimensions one capable of containing at least 40 persons and of very superior construction and *apparently the work of A White Man* it is A known fact that A runaway Convict has been for years amongst these Tribes He was seen and conversed with lately near Port Philip [*sic*] but nothing could induce him to abandon this wandering life He is represented as being of great statue [that is, stature] with an enormous Beard

and these Guneaks evidently made with no Tomahawks and their superior accomadation [*sic*] I attribute to the influence of this man[5]

This may have been speculation by Stapylton, given that the white man's description fits with William Buckley and the Grampians are just a little to the west of the area Buckley roamed (see Appendix 2), but it is still integral to the record and aligns with Mitchell's comments. If it is rejected, the reasons for the rejection should be given.

A long quotation from George Grey,[6] taken from Gerritsen,[7] comes next (pages 21–2). It relates to the Murchison River region of Western Australia and contains relevant but not overall unusual observations of wells up to 3–4 metres deep, and two groups of huts plastered over with turf and clay, 'evidently intended for fixed places of residence' though uninhabited at the time. However, the 5.6-kilometre-long tract of fertile land perforated with holes where local people had dug for yams is unusual. It suggests a major garnering effort of a size rarely recorded.

Grey referred to these groups of huts as 'villages' and his men called them 'towns'.[8] As only huts are mentioned, this very British vocabulary is perhaps ethnocentrically applied here. Readers unfamiliar with the subject may imagine that these were villages or towns of the kind found in Western or Asian agrarian societies—namely, permanently occupied centres that typically have services such as markets, inns, schools and churches. These were, however, simply groups of huts.

That quotation is followed by Pascoe's comment on a sketch by Andrew Todd made in 1835 of women digging for yam daisy tubers near Indented Head, Victoria (pages 22–3). Pascoe says: 'The area the women were working was *perfectly clear because they have made it so* in order to most effectively harvest their crop' (page 22). No evidence is provided for the assertion that the women had cleared the area.

It is notable that evidence of the extensive digging of *murnong* yams[9] in Victoria, and of *warran* yams in the area north of Perth in Western Australia, is repeatedly relied on, and sometimes in paired fashion, by many writers, including Pascoe (pages 21–2).[10] This seems to be a reflection of the rarity of any comparable observations.

In such conditions, soil becomes loose and friable as a result of the extensive digging and the tubers grow more fulsomely as a result. But, unlike the genetic development of domesticated plant varieties from wild ones, such changes of size and shape (phenotypic changes) are not permanent: 'These phenotypic responses are elastic, they require the maintenance of anthropically [human–made] modified soil environment; once modifications to the soil environment cease, tubers revert to wild type.'[11]

Dark Emu next says: 'Captain John Hunter, captain on the First Fleet, reported in 1788 that the people around Sydney were dependent on their *yam gardens*' (page 23). What Hunter said was:

> The natives here, appear to live chiefly on the roots which they dig from the ground; for these low banks appear to have been ploughed up, as if a vast herd of swine had been living on them. We put on shore, and examined the places which had been dug, and found *the wild yam* in considerable quantities …[12]

A garden by definition is not wild.

Next in *Dark Emu* is a description from Sunbury in Victoria that tells us that 'in 1836 settlers, including Isaac Batey and Edward Page, observed that people had worked their gardens so well and for so long that large earthen mounds were created during the process …' (page 23). However, it is not possible to tell if these are Batey and Page's words or Pascoe's, as the material is unsourced. Isaac Batey was not born until 1839, so the chronology has problems.[13] Pascoe adds: 'The last observation is evidence of *a deliberate farming technique*, one which any modern farmer would recognise as good soil management' (page 24). This is oddly at odds with *Dark Emu*'s quotation from archaeologist David Frankel, who described the uprooting of the soil in Batey's account as, 'to apply the best term, … *accidental gardening*' (Frankel on page 25), even though it was reasonable to assume that the Aboriginal people were aware of the fact that turning the soil over would tend to increase the yam supply. Accidental is the opposite of deliberate.

Thomas Mitchell then reappears. Pascoe quotes him on the Belyando River area of Queensland (page 24). Although he misquotes Mitchell's words several times, what is most problematic here is his omission of statements of Mitchell's that do not favour the assertion of agricultural activity. Compare the *Dark Emu* extract with the original (the words left out of *Dark Emu* are shown here in italics):

Dark Emu	**Mitchell**
We crossed some patches of dry swamp where the clods had been extensively turned up by the natives …	We crossed some patches of dry swamp where the clods had been very extensively turned up by the natives, *but for what purpose Yuranigh [Aboriginal guide from Molong district] could not form any conjecture.*
These clods were so very large and hard that we were obliged to throw them aside, and clear the way for our carts to pass. The whole resembled ground broken with the hoe …	These clods were so very large and hard that we were obliged to throw them aside, and clear a way for our carts to pass. The whole resembled ground broken with the hoe, *the naked surface having been previously so cracked by drought as to render this upturning possible without a hoe.*

A reader who did not check for the missing parts could well entertain the suggestion that this was a hoed field rather than ground upturned 'without a hoe'. The header of the page, 'Ground Tilled by the Natives',[14] probably created by Mitchell's publisher, directly suggests this impression as well. But Mitchell's own text merely indicates the overturning, without a hoe, of heavy platelets of dried mud that were so intact and large they stopped his carts from proceeding. That is not a tilled field. It is consistent with foraging for tubers or for aestivating swamp turtles, for example, but the question of the purpose of turning up the clods remains open.

Certainly it was Mitchell's view only a few years later that Aboriginal people could not be persuaded to till the ground at all. Musing on the inferior physiques, digestive powers, sight, hearing, smelling, tasting, feeling, running, climbing, water and teeth of 'civilised' people, as compared with the superbly fit Aboriginal people he saw in the bush, he wrote:

Such health and exemption from disease; such intensity of existence, in short, must be far beyond the enjoyment of civilised men, with all that art can do for them; and the proof of this is to be found in *the failure of all attempts to persuade* these *free denizens of uncultivated earth to forsake it for the tilled ground. They prefer the land unbroken* and free from the earliest curse pronounced against the first banished and first created man.[15]

This is one of the earliest statements that attributes decision-making and agency to Aboriginal people's shunning of agriculture. It does not, as others falsely did, attribute this shunning to ignorance.

Dark Emu cites explorer Hamilton Hume, who observed people on the Darling River making an edible paste from grinding seeds (page 31). Pascoe cites Charles Sturt on grass set out to dry and ripen near Lake Torrens, then moves from this observation to guess that the people had produced surplus grain—'surplus food production is one of the acknowledged characteristics of sedentary agriculture' (page 31). I have been to Lake Torrens and its vast salt flats with its traditional owners. The suggestion, if that is what Pascoe intends, that anyone could practise 'sedentary agriculture' in that blasted desert environment is simply ill informed.

When Pascoe focuses on surplus production of vegetable food, he relates it to storage and to sedentism, but never to the most common outcomes of surplus food production in the Aboriginal classical world. These were, first, and most frequent in daily occurrence, to fulfil the powerful ethic of sharing and generosity between kin, and the exercising of the right to have food shared with one by one's relatives. This was a two-way street that was essential to the moral system of Aboriginal society, and to its economics.[16] Sharing could be based on accumulation, but it also worked to reduce accumulation.

The second major outcome of surplus resources was the funding of large temporary gatherings of people who assembled for ceremonies. Once again, Pascoe's focus is on a pragmatic, material role of Aboriginal practice, not on its role in facilitating ritual performance, marriage dealing and the settlement of grievances. These were common mingled purposes when groups came together for days or weeks before dispersing again. Natural surpluses, such as cycad and bunya nut ripenings, or bogong moths being in abundance, performed the same role of underpinning large group events but were not forms of storage. The plentiful cycad nuts, processed to leach toxins and made into a paste, were used to form cakes that lasted for some time, and underpinned the diet of groups assembled for ceremonies in Arnhem Land in times past.[17]

Unburned country was also a form of storage. The resources of the grasslands and savannahs were sequentially released, usually in a mosaic burning pattern, during cooperative game drives for which people assembled.

On the lower Kirke River, Cape York, in the early twentieth century, people assembled each year to share the abundance of flying foxes (fruit bats) that had a major colony close to the well called Puunanel. Attendance was highly structured, involving the owners of two local countries inviting members of two neighbouring groups, based on Uthuk and Munpun to their north (Big Lake and Small Lake), to share the bounty. Each sub-camp of the assembled groups was allotted a separate shade area when people were camped at Aayk Lagoon for the duration of the flying fox harvest. Then people dispersed again.[18]

Explorers' observations of surpluses fail to get to the purposes of stored or richly garnered resources. Sturt gives Pascoe the terms 'stubble field' and 'haycocks' to turn into what Pascoe calls a 'major harvest' (page 31), but Sturt made no observations of sowing, only gathering, and presented no information on what such bounty might have been used for. The occasions when the Old People amassed surplus food were investments in nutritional capital for conversion into social capital, not an evolutionary stage on the way to full sedentism, as *Dark Emu* suggests.

Pascoe asserts that 'Another plant, Coopers Clover (*Trigonella sauvissima*), had also been grown and harvested by Aboriginal people' (page 32). He gives no evidence for the 'growing' of this native grass. Mitchell's journal simply describes it as being there.[19]

Pascoe quotes explorer John McKinlay, requoted from Gerritsen, whom he says made this observation on the creek where Burke and Wills died, that is, Cooper Creek: '"The whole country looks as if it had been carefully ploughed, harrowed, and finally rolled". Descriptions like this are common in the first colonial records …' (pages 33–4). By leaving out the rest of McKinlay's original passage, Pascoe misuses the quote, seemingly to fit his agricultural model. What McKinlay originally wrote was:

> There has been a good deal of rain here lately (and from the appearance of the country there has been none for some time previously). Nothing green except in the bed of the creek and the trees. The whole country looks as if it had been carefully ploughed, harrowed, and finally rolled, *the farmer having omitted the seed*.[20]

The description is of the appearance of the bare flat earth in high summer (it was February in the desert). And McKinlay's observation was not made 'on the creek where Burke and Wills starved to death' (page 33), that is, Cooper Creek, but in fact close to Koonchera Waterhole on the Diamantina River, about 180 kilometres from where Burke and Wills perished.[21]

There is no suggestion in *Dark Emu* that Aboriginal people used ploughs, harrows or rollers, although there is a discussion of hoes (pages 27, 34). It is immediately after the McKinlay discussion that Pascoe mentions Robert Etheridge: 'In 1894 he speculated on the use of these "hoes" and concluded that the myth that Aboriginal people had no knowledge of husbandry was a mistake based on prejudice' (page 34). This suggests that Etheridge linked these 'hoes' to agriculture, but he did not. If we go to the original publication by Etheridge, we find a description of 'an Aboriginal implement, believed to be undescribed, and *supposed* to be a hoe'.[22] It was collected on the upper Endeavour River, CYP, from Aboriginal people. What Pascoe does not mention is Etheridge's conclusion about this 'hoe', after discussing the evidence:

> I am of opinion that this hoe *is not of Australian Aboriginal manufacture*, but simply an adoption by the tribe from whom it was obtained of an implement imported from one of the Torres Strait islands in the ordinary way of barter ... That the present *implement is not of Aboriginal manufacture*, is, I think, conclusively proved by the drilling of the hole for the reception of the blade.[23]

That was hardly a speculation, more a final pronouncement. Pascoe is right, however, in citing Etheridge as an early opponent of the view that Aboriginal people had no knowledge of 'husbandry' (page 34). Etheridge said:

> It has been asserted on more than one occasion that the Australian Aborigines were collectively quite devoid of any knowledge of husbandry, even in its most elementary form. This generalisation is, however, a mistake, similar to many other mistakes that have been made by writers with the view of bolstering up the old preconceived and erroneous idea that the Australian Aborigine represents one of the most, if not the most degraded variety of the human race.[24]

But Etheridge's idea of 'husbandry', as is clear from the examples he then gives, consists of people using digging sticks to extract yams.

There is a brief referral to Mitchell on the large dry clods discussed above, and in one case Etheridge cites AC Gregory's observation of people in Western Australia reinserting the head of the yam to ensure a later supply.[25] He left out a highly relevant part of Gregory's original observation: 'In digging up these yams *they invariably re-insert the head of the yams* so as to be sure of a future crop, but *beyond this they do absolutely nothing which may be regarded as a tentative in the direction of cultivating plants* for their use.'[26]

These are examples of extraction and conservation, not of cultivation and sowing. They are not agriculture. Extraction of tubers may, however, loosen and aerate the soil to such an extent that the tubers then develop into larger forms. This is ecological agency, but there is no evidence that the effect was a deliberate strategy of 'tilling'. It is a by-product of digging.

To return to the explorers' journals: Sturt is quoted on his party's discovery of a large well and 'village' of nineteen huts somewhere north of Lake Torrens in South Australia (page 40). Compare Pascoe's elided version with the original passages.[27] Words missing from *Dark Emu* are shown here in italics.

Dark Emu	Sturt
Paths led from this spot to almost every point of the compass, and in walking along one came to a village consisting of nineteen huts …	Paths led from this spot to almost every point of the compass, and in walking along one *to the left*, I came to a village consisting of nineteen huts, *but there were not any signs of recent occupation.*
Troughs and stones for grinding seed were lying about …	Troughs and stones for grinding seed were lying about, *with broken spears and shields, but it was evident that the inhabitants were now dispersed in other places, and only assembled here to collect the box-tree seeds, for small boughs of that tree were lying in heaps on the ground, and the trees themselves bore the marks of having been stripped.*

The omissions here are evidence that this 'village', contrary to Pascoe's model for such places, was not permanently occupied, but—Sturt surmised—used occasionally for collecting box-tree seeds. They also suggest selective quoting to bolster a predetermined assumption of the author.

Pascoe then makes the claim that 'Settlers and explorers from other areas [other than the north-east goldfields of Western Australia] have reported large well systems, miles of stream diversion, and systematic flooding to prepare the ground for sowing seed' (page 44). Unfortunately, these people are left anonymous in his text, their discoveries are not identified or sourced to any writings, and no evidence is brought forward by Pascoe to justify the reference to preparing the ground 'for sowing seed'. It appears to be mere assertion.

On the next page Pascoe tells us that game hunting 'employed a much more reliable procedure than opportunistic kills in the field' (page 42). He supports this very true statement with a few examples of observations, all made in the south-east of Australia in colonial times, in which Aboriginal people used often very large nets to catch birds and kangaroos.

Game nets were in fact used over less than half of classical Aboriginal Australia (see below).[28] It perhaps would follow that Aboriginal people who did not use game nets were only capable of 'opportunistic kills in the field', but this is not the case. There was nothing 'opportunistic' about hunting in any region, whether the people had nets or not. Everywhere, people used their acute knowledge of game habitats,

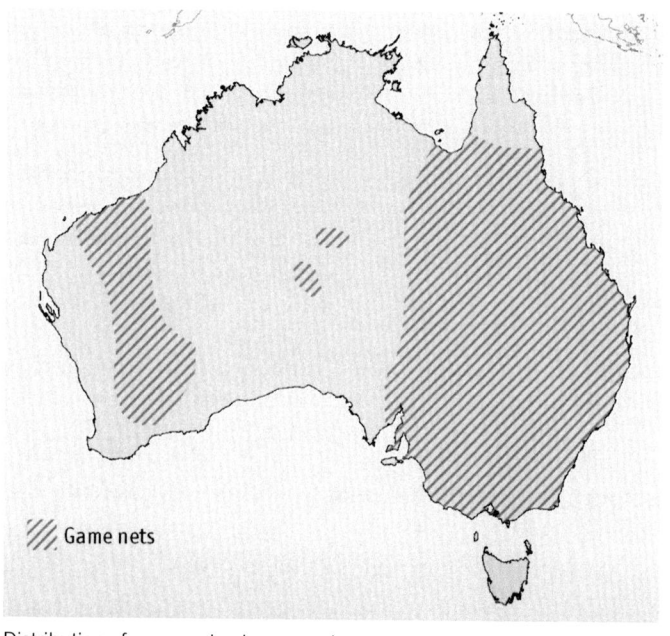

Distribution of game nets at conquest.

animal behaviour, seasonal conditions and hunting magic and tracking skills to take a large amount of chance out of the pursuit of game.

Pascoe cites an unpublished manuscript by Peter Beveridge in which, he says, Beveridge described traditional stories that included, as 'central themes', 'planting, husbandry, harvesting and storage' (page 46). No direct quotation from the source is given. Beveridge is a more readily checkable source for the reader, but the planting of crops does not appear there. There is a harshly dismissive mention of storage: 'When they have a superabundance of food they never try to preserve any for future use, but allow everything which they cannot stuff into themselves to go to waste.'[29]

Pascoe seems unable to provide anything more than sketchy and isolated scraps of evidence of Aboriginal people in the olden days actually sowing crops. Had the sowing of crops been general practice, such evidence would have been abundant. One of the examples Pascoe gives is of a Dreaming being planting nardoo seeds, in the Lake Eyre region (pages 46–7). Dreaming beings, in my experience, are frequently described as putting things into the earth, but this does not mean that living people did the same.

In relying particularly on 'the observations of the first explorers and settlers' (page 70), Pascoe frequently cites explorers who came across substantial groups of dwellings that he, and quite often they, refer to as 'villages'. Given that he does not also cite explorers' observations of smaller camps, this can lead the reader to suppose that large numbers of dwellings, and large populations of hundreds or even thousands—as much as '10,000'—living in them permanently, was the norm in 1788. It was not.

12
'Agricultural' implements and antiquity

Archaeology aims to construct logical and impartial interpretations of sites and provide reliable methods for dating sites and objects. It is a discipline that bridges the sciences and the humanities and, from that bridge, scoops the waters of both to achieve its aims. It is far from easy to be on top of every relevant scientific analytical tool and to source every relevant and accessible document. For these reasons, comparison with other similar sites and/or objects is the ideal situation, alongside the use of multiple lines of testing and recovery of multiple sources of information, to produce a cogent and robust theory.

This chapter looks at the archaeological evidence provided in *Dark Emu* for Aboriginal agriculture and for a much longer occupation of the country by its first human inhabitants than is recognised by the scientific community.

Aboriginal agricultural implements

Pascoe brings together two different types of Australian Aboriginal stone objects and a single bartered object under his category 'Aboriginal agricultural implements'. It is an eclectic and somewhat sensitive selection of types that covers an exotic (non–Australian) hoe, a subset of picks, and the cylindro–conical and cornute (horn–shaped) stones known as 'cylcons'. They are united by being 'large and heavy' (page 37). He writes:

> These implements ['hoes'] have received very little study since ... (1894) ... some commentators decided they were items of penis worship: the researchers assumed Aboriginal people too backward to have cultivated the land, so the stones have to have phallic significance ...

It is these implements ['picks'] that are crucial to our understanding of Aboriginal agricultural history … The few that are labelled are tellingly referred to as Bogan River picks. [pages 36–7]

The first implement that Pascoe puts forward consists of just one example and was discussed here in Chapter 11. In summary, Robert Etheridge published a description of a stone implement traded into north Queensland from the Torres Strait that was described as 'supposed to be a hoe'.[1] Pascoe misquotes Etheridge and implies that the Torres Strait implement is of Australian Aboriginal origin. No other examples of this type have again been reported in Australia, and this one-off find is very interesting in terms of trade but of no further interest here.

Picks and cylcons have been described in a number of publications since the first by anthropologist Walter Harper in 1898.[2] None of these papers classify picks or cylcons as 'agricultural implements'. Pascoe argues that they have been deliberately misinterpreted or left unlabelled in order to avoid revealing their function. In fact, cylcons have been considered for over 100 years to be most likely of ceremonial purpose associated with increase or propagation ceremonies.[3] Cylcons are concentrated in the Darling River valley, which is Barkindji country.

The other stone objects in Pascoe's Aboriginal agricultural group are picks that have, over time, been known under various names, including Bogan River picks, Bogan picks, Bogan types, grooved picks and plain picks. These objects are concentrated in southern and central New South Wales. So far, eleven have been identified and described in museum collections.[4] They are not associated with increase rites or propagation, nor have they been assigned phallic significance or known to have been associated with 'penis worship'. Seven of them were recently displayed as Aboriginal agricultural implements in an exhibition held in South Australia,[5] and photos of two are presented in *Dark Emu*.[6]

Cylindro-conical stones (cylcons)

In 1888 an unusual stone was displayed at a meeting of the Linnean Society of New South Wales. It had been found at a depth of 7 feet (2.1 metres) while sinking a tank at Byrock, and was described as:

… of argillaceous [that is, clayey] sandstone, carrot-shaped, about 11½ × 2¼ inches [29 × 5.7 cm], the broad extremity concave, the surface marked transversely at intervals with lines of which there are five pairs on one side and three pairs on the other. Blackfellows to whom it had been shown could give no information about it; nor had anyone who had yet seen it been able to recognise its import.[7]

A similar object had been displayed during an earlier Linnean Society meeting held in 1884, and Harper decided to investigate the two unusual objects. While doing so, another seven similar stones were offered to him for inclusion in the study. The resulting publication was the first expansive overview of these 'mystery' stones, which were readily recognisable by their shape (cigar or carrot shape), size (25–60 centimetres), weight (2–3 kilograms) and unknown purpose.

Their surface is smooth and the cylindrical form tapers from a broad base to a conical end. The broad base is often concave with flaking, polishing and other abrasions, as if having been used for pounding and stood in sand. A smaller subset of items of 'phacoid' (lentil-like) shape[8] were also called 'stumpy'.[9] But the real fascination lay in the decorative incisions around the body of some cylcons, which took the form of an emu or other bird foot, a boomerang, star shapes or lines.[10]

As to purpose, one theory proposed at the time was seed grinding. Harper dismissed this on the basis of the decorative incisions and the concavity, flaking and polishing visible around the base, all of which he saw as pointless for grinding. He also considered the 'phallic emblem' theory but concluded that:

> This opinion, as far as I know, has nothing to recommend it except the shape of the 'stones' … the element of worship is entirely lacking … unless some better excuse for styling the stones' phallic 'emblems' than that furnished by their shape can be found, we are not justified in considering them as such.[11]

Interestingly, he described one stone in his set of nine as seeming to have been used for 'rubbing or grinding'—so much so that Dr Thomas Cooksey of the Australian Museum suggested that 'the wear looked exactly like that noticeable on stones used for sharpening scythes'.[12] However, Cooksey added that 'probably some European had been using it for such a purpose'.[13]

Harper felt Cooksey's theory to be entirely likely:

> … it is evident the stone was never intended for a sharpening or grinding stone, because wherever the signs of the wear exist there all traces of the decorative marks have disappeared, and the originally smooth and rounded contour of the stone has been in a measure destroyed.[14]

Without evidence for grinding or as a phallic emblem, Harper leant towards ceremonial use (for increasing food production or rainmaking) and added that greater examination was required to settle the question.

Etheridge had access to a far larger collection (105) of 'cylindro-conical and cornute stones' than Harper, but followed a similar line of inquiry by looking at the evidence for their use as a domestic, record-keeping, ceremonial or phallic item. As well as having many more specimens to analyse, he also had access to more information, and concluded that some cylcons were used as a grinder or pounder in domestic settings after the stone had been 'adapted to a more casual purpose'.[15] In regard to it being a record-keeping item, he felt there was 'grave doubt' as 'so large a proportion … are absolutely plain and unincised'.[16] He tentatively accepted two possibilities: 'one indicating a phallic, the other a symbolic, tendency'.[17]

Etheridge's tentative acceptance arose from three separate accounts given voluntarily by Aboriginal men and recorded after Harper's investigations. The first occurred on Cooper Creek near Lake Eyre in 1901, during an expedition led by Professor JW Gregory, who:

> … had with him as guide one 'Emil' … who on arriving in his own 'country' proceeded to dig up 'a conical piece of yellow sandstone … and then presented it to me [Gregory], saying sadly that it would never be wanted again. He explained that it was a Wommagnaragnara, which, being interpreted, is "The heart of the snake". It was used at ceremonies to make the dark olive-brown carpet snake, known to the natives as "Womma", i.e., to increase the supply.'[18]

Etheridge emphasised that in this account, propagation is described 'without in the slightest degree thereby implying any knowledge of phallic worship'.[19] In other words, he echoed Harper's conclusion in 1898 that there is no evidence to support phallic worship. Instead, the stones are suggested as symbolic of or used ritually in increase or propagation, and thereby are phallic in form only, not as an object of 'worship'. In a similar vein, Etheridge cites RH Mathews, who had been told by an (unnamed) Aboriginal man that:

> ... they were 'employed in ceremonial observances connected with the assembling of the people at the time the nardoo seed was ripe ... in incantations for causing the supply of game and other food to increase, for making of rain, and other secret ceremonies ... the stones ... were kept by the headmen, or "doctors" ... on the death of the owner they were hidden in ground near an old camping place of his, or else near his grave.'[20]

The third account considered by Etheridge in reaching his tentative conclusion had been relayed to Edmund Milne by an Aboriginal man named Tom Sullivan. Sullivan had implied that the stones were ceremonial objects belonging to 'doctors' or 'medicine men'.[21]

These three separate accounts converge in suggesting that cylcons were related to increase ceremonies, were used by powerful men and were buried near campgrounds or graves. Etheridge found the cylindro-conical and cornute stones to be 'the most interesting of all the Australian stone implements' and concluded that 'whilst the stones as a whole were almost certainly esoteric their application may have varied amongst different sections of the people using them'.[22]

The next expansive investigation of cylcons took place in the early 1940s and was undertaken by anthropologist Lindsay Black. Black also examined over 100 specimens, and he provided a detailed overview of each. However, he did not find any additional accounts or evidence beyond that previously cited by earlier researchers, and concluded that 'cylcons were of ceremonial significance. Whether they were used at initiation, burial, *Bora*, or other kinds of ceremonies such as increase rites, will never be known'.[23]

Increase rites and their significance were also discussed in Chapter 2 of this book. Accounts provided directly by Aboriginal men all affirm the status of cylcons as an object used in increase rites. Increase is not 'penis worship', as stated by Pascoe (page 36)—a distinction made clear by Harper in 1898 and repeated thereafter.[24]

The specimens examined by Harper, Etheridge and Black are housed in the Australian Museum (AM) in Sydney. These and numerous other cylcons held in major collecting institutions across Australia have been the subject of ongoing inquiry over the past decade or so in order to ensure appropriate classification and access. They have not been on public display for some considerable time due to the sensitivity associated with their perceived functions as shown in the historical context.

Bogan picks

While Black was investigating the 'mystery' stones of the Darling River in the 1940s, anthropologist and museum curator Frederick McCarthy was providing the first clear distinction between cylcons and non-ceremonial stones (picks) of similar shape and weight.[25]

> Bruce Pascoe: 'Jonathon Jones ... asked to examine the stone tool collection at the Australian Museum, and there he found dozens of these implements ... they have received so little study, most have never been displayed and almost all have no labels. The few that are labelled are tellingly referred to as Bogan River picks.' [pages 36–7]

> Jonathon Jones: '... often referred to as Bogan River picks ... which were common along the rich Murray-Darling alluvial plains and are important for understanding Aboriginal agricultural [sic].'[26]

> Lorena Allam: '... the Bogan River picks invite further inquiry: who made them, who wielded them, how and when? Some of the bigger implements are far too heavy to be used by a single person. Were they for cropping? We may never fully know.'[27]

As discussed above, cylcons (ceremonial stones) have been found in large numbers across a wide area of western New South Wales. By contrast, picks are concentrated in southern and central New South Wales with just one find outside of this area—in eastern Victoria.[28] Some were collected off the ground while others were dug up by agricultural machinery. Formal picks held by museums number just eleven, and this appears to be the sum total in the nation's institutional collections. There may of course be others held in private collections; however, it is unlikely that significantly more exist given the very few to have been found over the past 150 years. Two other picks are in the NMA collection, but they have not been expertly verified and no collection details are available.[29]

Picks were initially placed taxonomically with cylcons due to their similar form, weight and uncertain function.[30] However, the absence of incisions, the flat rather than concave bases, and the presence on some of an encircling groove midway along the body kept them alongside, rather than within, the category of cylcons.[31]

McCarthy, with assistance from fellow anthropologist Elsie Bramwell and stone tool specialist Harold Noone, undertook the first systematic study of all known stone tool types in Australia. The resulting publication[32] was built on similar but less expansive studies over the previous twenty years, including McCarthy's own work.[33] The study aimed to cover 'function, shaping processes, form, transverse-section, and aboriginal names as criteria of classification of the Australian implements as a whole'.[34]

With the appearance of the first taxonomic sorting of Aboriginal stone implements, cylcons were placed under 'Ritual implements' while picks were placed within a subset of 'Hunting and domestic', which was itself incorporated under the larger category of 'Miscellaneous implements'. This classification has not been changed in the two revisions of McCarthy and his colleagues' original 1946 publication. Other publications, some more recent, do refer to picks, but the term 'Bogan' falls away.[35]

Under the classification of McCarthy and his colleagues, picks were divided into two groups: plain or Bogan-type, and grooved or conical type.[36] The plain or Bogan type consists of three objects and the grooved or conical type consists of eight objects, thus giving the eleven mentioned earlier. If we add the two undescribed picks in the NMA collection, we have ten grooved (conical) types.

The standard pick is conical and measures about 15.5 centimetres in length, with a 10-millimetre diameter that is, in cross-section, oval or circular; picks can weigh up to 3 kilograms.[37] One end of the conical form is blunt, the other tapering. The blunt end is similar to an adze end and is polished, while the broad end remains quite rough.[38] Bogan picks and their encircling groove often show evidence of preparation by pounding with a hard stone (hammer-dressing) and polishing.[39] The encircling groove is known as a 'waist' and one specimen has two of them, close together.[40] The encircling groove (see opposite, which shows an example of the grooved conical type) was most likely for securing a bent cane, in similar fashion to hafting an axe handle to an axe head.[41] In fact, the similarity to axes is apparent, apart from the adze-shaped end of a pick as opposed to the blunt end of a typical axe. This type of pick can use its weight to split apart dense wood with

Grooved (Bogan style) picks.

the haft positioning the head similarly to a stone axe head—that is, the striking end running parallel to the haft.

Pascoe implies that the groove is the result of wear from binding a handle at right angles to the pick (page 36). This is incorrect given the hammer-dressing, and furthermore, bindings composed of soft materials would take an extraordinary length of time to wear such a groove.

Given the few picks in collections, their history is well known, as presented in Table 9.

Table 9: Bogan picks formally identified and described.

Place	Year of find	Collector	Classification	Institute and accession no.
Gundary, Wollondilly River, Goulburn, NSW	1890	E Milne	Object of unknown significance (in Harper 1898) Doubly grooved conical (Thorpe 1928) Grooved conical (McCarthy 1939) Bogan pick (McCarthy, Bramwell & Noone 1946) Bogan pick (McCarthy 1976)	NMA (Canb.76) 1985.0059

Table 9 (cont.)

Place	Year of find	Collector	Classification	Institute and accession no.
Condobolin, NSW	1905	CJ McMaster	Doubly grooved conical (Thorpe 1928) Grooved conical (McCarthy 1939) Bogan pick (McCarthy, Bramwell & Noone 1946) Bogan pick (McCarthy 1976)	AM E13314
Forest Reefs, Orange, NSW	1907	E Milne	Grooved conical (McCarthy 1939) Bogan pick (McCarthy, Bramwell & Noone 1946) Bogan pick (McCarthy 1976)	NMA (Canb.134) 1985.0059.0767
Daroobalgie, Forbes, NSW	1914	E Milne	Grooved conical (McCarthy 1939) Bogan pick (McCarthy, Bramwell & Noone 1946) Bogan pick (McCarthy 1976)	NMA (Canb.584) 1985.0059
Wulla Wulla, Lachlan River, NSW	1916	W Hall	Grooved conical (McCarthy 1939) Bogan pick (McCarthy, Bramwell & Noone 1946) Bogan pick (McCarthy 1976)	NMA (Canb.383) 1985.0059.0715
Ballan, Vic.	Before 1921	G Horne	Pick (Horne 1921) Grooved conical (McCarthy 1939) Bogan pick (McCarthy, Bramwell & Noone 1946)	Museum of Victoria

Table 9 (cont.)

Place	Year of find	Collector	Classification	Institute and accession no.
Bogan Gate, NSW	1929	HK Rawson	Grooved conical (McCarthy 1939) Bogan pick (McCarthy, Bramwell & Noone 1946) Bogan pick (McCarthy 1976)	AM E32593
Bogan River, NSW	1935	?	Bogan type (McCarthy 1944) Bogan pick (McCarthy, Bramwell & Noone 1946) Bogan pick (McCarthy 1976)	Cast held at AM
Springs Station, Dubbo, NSW	1938	J Baird	Grooved conical (McCarthy 1939) Bogan pick (McCarthy, Bramwell & Noone 1946) Bogan pick (McCarthy 1976)	AM E45300
Hobbys Yards, Lachlan River, NSW	?	E Milne	Bogan type (McCarthy 1944) Bogan pick (McCarthy, Bramwell & Noone 1946) Bogan pick (McCarthy 1976)	NMA (Canb.135) 1985.0059.0770
Grong Grong, NSW	1943	H Wright	Grooved conical (McCarthy 1939) Bogan pick (McCarthy, Bramwell & Noone 1946) Bogan pick (McCarthy 1976)	AM E50909

Having so few specimens (thirteen at most) has restricted (or not inspired) research into the function of this type of pick. The specimen from Ballan, Victoria, was located deep inside a mature gum tree, giving rise to the possibility that it was used to extract possums.[42] This would suggest a similar use to hafted axes, as mentioned above—for splitting dense wood to extract animals or to acquire timber for manufacturing wooden implements. The average weight of a pick (2–3 kilograms) is more than the average stone axe head, and it is possible that the picks were originally designed for splitting particularly dense wood localised to inland New South Wales. Perhaps at some time they were replaced by the lighter and more versatile stone axe.

'Bogan River picks' were a feature of a recent exhibition held at Adelaide's Santos Museum of Economic Botany and the Art Gallery of South Australia. The exhibition was titled *Bunha-bunhanga: Aboriginal Agriculture in the South-east* and was curated by Jonathon Jones in collaboration with Bruce Pascoe and Bill Gammage. *Bunha-bunhanga* is a Wiradjuri word meaning 'abundance of food'.[43] The accompanying catalogue states that the exhibition 'brings us primary evidence of our sophisticated agricultural past … For the first time in public, we see the heaving stone picks and slim shovels used to cultivate the murrnong fields …'[44]

Interestingly, explorer Thomas Mitchell witnessed wooden shovels in use along the Bogan River in 1835:

> There is a small cichoraceous plant with a yellow flower, named Tao by the natives, which grows in the grassy places near the river, and on its root, the children chiefly subsist. As soon almost as they can walk, a little wooden shovel is put into their hands, and they learn thus early to pick about the ground for those roots and a few others, or to dig out larvae of ant-hills.[45]

From this observation, we get a sense of the shovels displayed in the *Bunha-bunhanga* exhibition as a tool for children to dig out tubers.

As discussed in Chapter 11, numerous colonial observations were made of Aboriginal people collecting *murnong*. In each case a wooden digging stick was observed in use rather than a 'heaving stone pick'. Digging sticks are a wonderfully versatile tool, used not only to dig up tubers but also to dig out small mammals from their burrows and keep the camp dogs in order. They were ubiquitous across the country and appear in rock art. At any one point in time, thousands of them would have been in use across the country, such was their usefulness, ease of manufacture, portability and versatility.

In summary, the eight Bogan picks and three plain picks are the only described specimens in institutional collections. With their adze-shaped end and grooved midline for hafting, they were likely used in a similar way to stone axes. A bent cane was hafted along the groove to hold the axe head in place. With the substantial weight and density of stone, the adze end could break through timber to extract animals such as possums, and remove timber for working into wooden implements. Such a scenario was described on the Bogan River itself, by Mitchell in the early 1830s: 'Unlike the natives on the Darling, these inhabitants of the banks of the Bogan subsist more on the opossum, kangaroo, and emu, than on the fish of their river.'[46]

Juan knives

Pascoe persists in claiming that explorer AC Gregory witnessed Aboriginal people harvesting grain with a type of stone tool, which he names as a 'juan' knife:

> ... many northern Australian museums display long, knife-like implements, which usually bear legends such as 'of unknown use' when, in fact, they are juan knives—long, sharp blades of stone with fur-covered handles, which the explorer Gregory described the Aboriginal people using to cut down the grain. [page 38]

> ... including the juan knives, which Gregory saw being used to harvest grain. [page 162]

Long-bladed stone tools, usually called 'knives', were often carried in a paperbark sheath or grip, as shown in the photo overleaf. The sheath worked to protect the edges of the knife from being damaged. McCarthy refers to juan knives 'fitted with fur grips' held in museums in Germany,[47] suggesting an alternative to the more typical paper-bark sheaths. Juan 'knives' have been identified exclusively from a few excavation sites in central and western Queensland;[48] none have been found in Western Australia, where Gregory made his explorations. They are similar to two other blade types, the elouera and the leilira, with all three being described as 'trigonal knives' (that is, they end in

Long-bladed knife and paperbark sheath.

a triangle shape),[49] hafted with gum resin at the butt end in order to create a handle. They are, more simply, a long-bladed stone tool.[50]

As with the geographically limited and rarely found Bogan River pick, Pascoe has selected evidence for harvesting by focusing on a tool that is geographically constrained and rarely reported. The juan knife was first described in 1957 by Norman Tindale in Queensland. The name was derived from the 'Ngaun and kindred tribes' who populated the area west of Charters Towers in western Queensland.[51] An alternative name as suggested by Tindale was the 'joan'. Archaeologist James Knight undertook a comprehensive analysis of a broken juan (or juin, as he prefers) knife found more recently near Charters Towers. At the time of his investigation a mere thirty-seven juan knives had been recorded and published.[52] His analysis of thirty years ago remains the only in-depth investigation for this uncommon and geographically restricted object, and its status has not altered over that time. Based on the rarity of the juan knives, Knight suggests that it was a 'prestige exchange' object,[53] leaving function of little or no regard beyond status.

Stone blades are one of the most common Aboriginal tools. They are used for cutting skin of both humans and animals but according to researchers Casey, Crawford and Wright are 'not specialised in any way, and if found by themselves cannot be recognised, with the exception of those used as women's knives, as having been intended for any particular purpose'.[54] In some locations, blades are attached to spear shafts by use of gum and sinew.[55] Spear blades, or points, survive on archaeological sites but the hafts do not, except in very rare circumstances.

Gregory's original description referred only to 'stone knives', and made no mention of 'juan knives' or of cutting down grain.[56] Gerritsen's speculation that they 'could be the mysterious *juan* knives'[57] has been reimagined by Pascoe into a factual sighting by Gregory of juan knives with fur-covered handles. The fanciful nature of this becomes more notable in view of Gregory's explorations heading far west or north showing the limited geographical distribution for juan knives.

In his attempts to link stone tools with agricultural production, Pascoe mentions another tool without any evidence: 'the increase in production of adzes for sharpening wooden instruments such as digging sticks indicates a shift towards the more intensive cultivation of the yam daisy' (page 162).

Adzes are part of a collection of smaller tools, thought to have increased in style and number about 5000 years ago.[58] They were often hafted with a wooden handle, or set into an existing wooden tool such as a spearthrower, to make them easier to use (see below).

The daily toolkit of Aboriginal people was typically composed of wooden objects: digging sticks, spears, spearthrowers, clubs, hafted axes, hafted adzes, shields and boomerangs. The preparation and finishing of these objects led to countless adzes being discarded across the continent, every day over thousands of years. It is not sensible to build a statistical relationship between numbers of adzes and only one type of wooden tool, such as the digging stick.

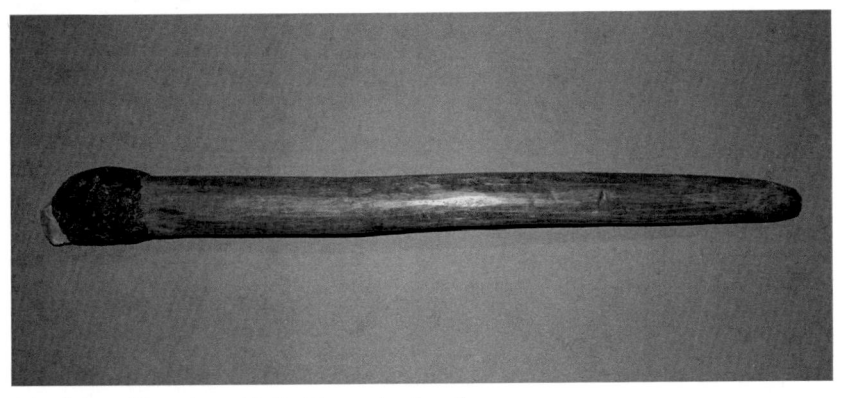

Adze flake set in resin and hafted to wooden handle.

Ancient occupation
The Hopkins River midden

Pascoe suggests that the Hopkins River midden, located on a headland near Warrnambool in western Victoria, provides exceptional evidence for human occupation of Australia that is older by an extra 30,000 years or more than the currently accepted range, which is around 50,000 years (see Appendix 1):[59]

> Western Victorian Aboriginal communities had been trying for thirty years to have an ancient midden on the Hopkins River analysed. It is so old, it has turned into rock. When that examination was finally undertaken, it was found that the midden was as old as 80,000 years, 10,000 years before the Out of Africa theory says humans began to leave Africa ... It's an interesting proposition to investigate for our understanding of all world peoples and their movements across the globe. [pages 40–1]

Middens are accumulations of marine or freshwater shells—essentially shell heaps—and have been a focal point for research in Australian (and global) archaeology for at least 100 years.[60] The challenge for archaeology lies in distinguishing culturally formed shell heaps from naturally formed heaps.[61] Apart from humans, wave action or sea-birds can cause large deposits of shells and the distinction between these and cultural middens is not always clear.[62] This archaeological question has gained greater resolution over time but is by no means completely resolved.

In the late 1970s Warrnambool local Jim Henry noticed a shell scatter near a headland then known as Point Ritchie, now Moyjil. Having an interest in natural history, he sought out Edmund Gill, a renowned scientist and former deputy director of the Museum of Victoria, who had recently retired to the area. Gill, along with Henry and other scientists, commenced investigations into the shell scatter in 1981. The first peer-reviewed paper discussing the site was published in 1988,[63] which puts it at odds with Pascoe's claim that western Victorian Aboriginal communities had been trying for thirty years to have the Hopkins River midden analysed. The paper reported a very ancient date for the midden. Problematically, the methodology used and the definition of the midden as cultural were not considered entirely reliable.[64]

Following the 1988 publication, other papers and postgraduate research theses focused the debate on how the midden was formed. The question remained over the shells being of cultural or natural origin (for example, bird behaviour). Seabirds, particularly the pacific gull, take shellfish from exposed rocks and reefs and break them open by dropping them while on the wing onto a hard beach platform below. Over many generations of seabirds using the same platform, the shells build up into 'bird middens'—dense scatters of broken shell, very similar to middens of humanly discarded shell (for an example, see below).

Distinctions can be found in the narrower range of shellfish species taken by birds compared to those gathered by humans, who are able to forage more widely, use tools to extract shells tightly stuck to rocks, collect from deeper water, and select for size and taste. Looking for evidence of preferential shell size selection in the Moyjil midden, it was found that 'The *Lunella undulata* [wavy periwinkle] shell opercula [feet] show clear evidence of size selection and we believe the deposit

Midden left by seabirds breaking open shells for food.

can be confidently labelled a midden [but] Whether humans or sea-birds were responsible cannot be established confidently from the available evidence.'[65]

With the lack of certainty in identifying birds or humans as the causal agent of the Moyjil midden, the team turned to other evidence. Cultural middens are also likely to contain stone tools, animal bone (particularly fish, reptile and bird) and charcoal from camp fires. The Moyjil midden did not reveal any of these, but it did reveal burned rock. The burned rock was speculated to be the result of wildfire or a camp fire deliberately lit by Aboriginal people—back to a natural versus cultural origin. Eminent geomorphologist Jim Bowler identified the burned rocks as definitively cultural in origin, and they became known as 'feature CBS1'. It is this feature that was dated to far more than 80,000 years old, and, in fact, to a stunning 120,000 years old.[66] However, archaeologist Ian McNiven stated that:

> some evidence exists for CBS1 representing a ~120,000 year old hearth. However, the evidence for CBS1 as a hearth must be definitive and irrefutable for such a substantial claim to be considered credible, given the significant implications that this would have for world history. At this juncture, CBS1 does not meet this high level evidential threshold.[67]

Another scientist working on the site remarked that 'Archaeological scepticism is heightened by the great antiquity of the shelly assemblage—beyond the accepted period of human occupation in Australia at 60–65ka [ka = 1000 years ago].'[68]

There is good reason for scepticism given the increasing number of scholarly reviews and commentaries questioning the dating of northern Australia's ancient sites.[69] In 2016, Wood and others provided solid data for limiting occupation across northern Australia to less than 50,000 years. More recently, investigation into environmental impacts on tropical sites provides good reason for caution while genomic sequencing provides compelling arguments as to why it is not possible for anatomically modern humans to have migrated to Australia any earlier than 50- to 55,000 years ago (see Appendix 1).[70]

The oldest reliably dated shell middens in Australia are about 30,000 years old[71] but most are less than 10,000 years old, coinciding with stabilisation of the current shoreline. Exposed shell also has poor preservation, and it is only in exceptional circumstances that cultural middens are older than 10,000 years.

The six most recent publications devoted to the subject of the Moyjil midden at the time of writing[72] agree that after thirty-plus years of dedicated research the question of the origin of the midden is not straightforward. At this point, we can conclude that shells and burned rock at Moyjil are significantly old—somewhere between 35,000 and 120,000 years—but not that Moyjil is an Indigenous cultural site.

Rottnest Island

In *Dark Emu*, Pascoe writes:

> Rottnest Island, eighteen kilometres off the Western Australian coast from Fremantle, could be reached by land around 12,000 years ago. However, some of the artefacts currently under examination by archaeologists are reputed to be 60,000 years old. Ocean voyages must have been undertaken to reach the island under the lure of the enormous seafood resources. [pages 93–4]

In his more recent publication *Salt: Selected Essays and Stories,* the same sentences appear, except that '12,000 years ago' has become '120,000 years ago'.[73] Unfortunately, in both publications the comments are unreferenced, making it difficult to verify the source(s).

The reference to 60,000-year-old stone artefacts that are apparently still under examination by archaeologists appears to arise from two papers published more than two decades ago.[74] In the early 1990s, three small stones, thought to be stone tools, were found in a deflation bowl (a hollow made by wind erosion) on the coastal margin of Rottnest Island.[75] Two of the stones displayed typical features for small tools, but the third was less convincing—although because of its close spatial association with the other two, it was included in the final assessment.

These cultural items, the first ever identified on Rottnest Island, were hypothesised to be considerably old given their association with ancient soils revealed through wind erosion. No dateable material, such as charcoal, was found with the stones, but some years later a land snail shell, collected at the time, was dated. It provided what is a proxy date of 60,000 years:

> The prehistoric artefacts and finds (3 stone tools in total) ... do not provide absolute evidence for a human presence on Rottnest

Island during the Late Pleistocene ... these sites provide a significant addition to the archaeological and potential archaeological record for Rottnest Island and for Australia as a whole. They provide additional provisional evidence for Aboriginal occupation of Australia during the Late Pleistocene (>50 ka) ...[76]

Although the paper in which this quote appears was published twenty years ago, the date of the snail shell remains provisional. Certifying an association between a proxy and an archaeological object or feature is not possible if no further or alternative evidence emerges. It is yet to be conclusively demonstrated that the land snail has anything to do with the three stones, and, in all, there is no evidence to argue for ancient ocean voyages between the mainland and Rottnest Island. Like many offshore islands around southern Australia, it was cut off from the mainland due to the sea-level rise following the end of the last glacial era—that is, 10,000–12,000 years ago.[77]

Apart from this residual uncertainty, the Rottnest Island stone tools themselves need to be reconsidered in light of other research into historic Aboriginal presence on offshore islands.[78] After 1800, many Australian Aboriginal women involved in sealing and whaling operations off eastern and southern Australia left evidence of their presence on offshore islands, including Flinders and Kangaroo islands off South Australia.[79] Kangaroo Island in particular has revealed numerous stone tools left by those working in the 1800s sealing industry, and many of these tools are associated with exposed, older soils.[80] It is possible that the tools from Rottnest Island were left by Aboriginal people involved with the sealing and whaling industry.

When *Dark Emu* presents evidence from archaeological sites and objects, it is the caveats that go missing. As with any scientific reporting, caveats are critical for understanding the whole site context. When caveats are excluded from the discussion, the reader is grossly misled.

'Farming' wildlife
Other examples, such as *Dark Emu*'s claims for 'kangaroo battues' and 'emu harvesting', lack archaeological and archival evidence and are simply implausible. Archaeologist David Horton remarked some twenty years ago that 'the concept of kangaroo farming keeps re-emerging at intervals ...'[81] He posed the question for himself in regard to the absence of such farming: 'Given the Aboriginal practice of driving

mobs of wallabies into enclosures in order to kill them, the step to permanently enclosing and maintaining such animals was, on the face of it, not a big one.'[82] But in the end, he knew that:

> There are some things about both the animals themselves and Aboriginal interaction that make this unlikely. Early stages of domestication probably involved keeping and raising young animals whose mothers were killed while hunting. This seems not to have happened in Australia. One reason may have been that the need for mobility meant that you didn't want the added burden of carrying or being slowed down by young animals. Another reason may be that it is only worthwhile raising young animals if the effort results in a bigger return when they are mature. This is not intuitively obvious (and may indeed not be the case in Aboriginal circumstances), and in a hunting society you would be better off trying for a bigger animal the next day.[83]

Horton also raises an interesting question in regard to the absence of farming and agriculture in pre-colonial Australia. He presents farming as 'addictive behaviour',[84] meaning that plants and animals become as reliant on humans as humans become on the few plants and animals that are domesticated: 'Aborigines knew instinctively that there was no point in "conserving" individual animals: you had to conserve ecosystems. Farming wildlife was a process that a system established to maintain the Australian environment didn't permit.'[85]

Dedicated, long-term and resilient conservation of ecosystems by Aboriginal hunter-gatherers for thousands of years has been discussed in Chapter 4 of this book. This is why Australia was in such good shape when Europeans arrived, and why it is has since undergone radical eco-instability.

13
Stone circles and 'smoking' trees

A conference titled 'Man the Hunter' was held in 1966 in the United States and generated enormous interest for its challenge to orthodox views on hunter-gatherers. It inspired new methodologies as well as revisionist feminist responses,[1] and the proceedings, published in 1968, were soon followed by an impactful work titled *Stone Age Economics*.[2] Fieldwork on hunter-gatherers during the 1960s and 1970s gathered a range of case studies sufficient to upset the social evolutionary view of hunter-gatherer life as in all ways inferior to that of the farmer. Scholars could no longer unquestioningly perpetuate the view that the emergence of agriculture had involved 'progression from the hardship of the hunter's lonely, nomadic and hungry life to one of security and sociability'.[3]

With the release of *Man the Hunter* and *Stone Age Economics*, farming as a progressive and inevitable step up from hunter-gathering was no longer immutable. Slightly earlier in Australia, anthropologist and Museum of Victoria curator Aldo Massola had voiced similar sentiments:

> The fact that ... Aborigines were nomadic food gatherers does not mean that they wandered aimlessly all over their tribal territory in the hope of finding food. On the contrary, knowing every inch of their country they would spend the different seasons at the most fruitful places. These would mostly be located in the vicinity of water, and in some places water fowl, fish and roots from aquatic plants would be so abundant as almost to obviate the need to wander to new grounds. Such a place was Lake Condah.[4]

Of some importance to Pascoe is Lake Condah in the Western District of Victoria, which has been studied geologically, hydrologically, ecologically and archaeologically. It is via the latter discipline that Pascoe finds evidence for high populations of people living in large aggregations of stone houses in order to harvest, smoke and cache thousands of eels annually in that location.

This chapter focuses on the archaeological evidence for settlement and aquaculture at Lake Condah—that is, the aggregations of stone houses and smoking and caching of eels—prior to European arrival. Important to this discussion is an understanding of the naturally formed lava-flow plain that provides the context for the Budj Bim fish trap complex (see below).

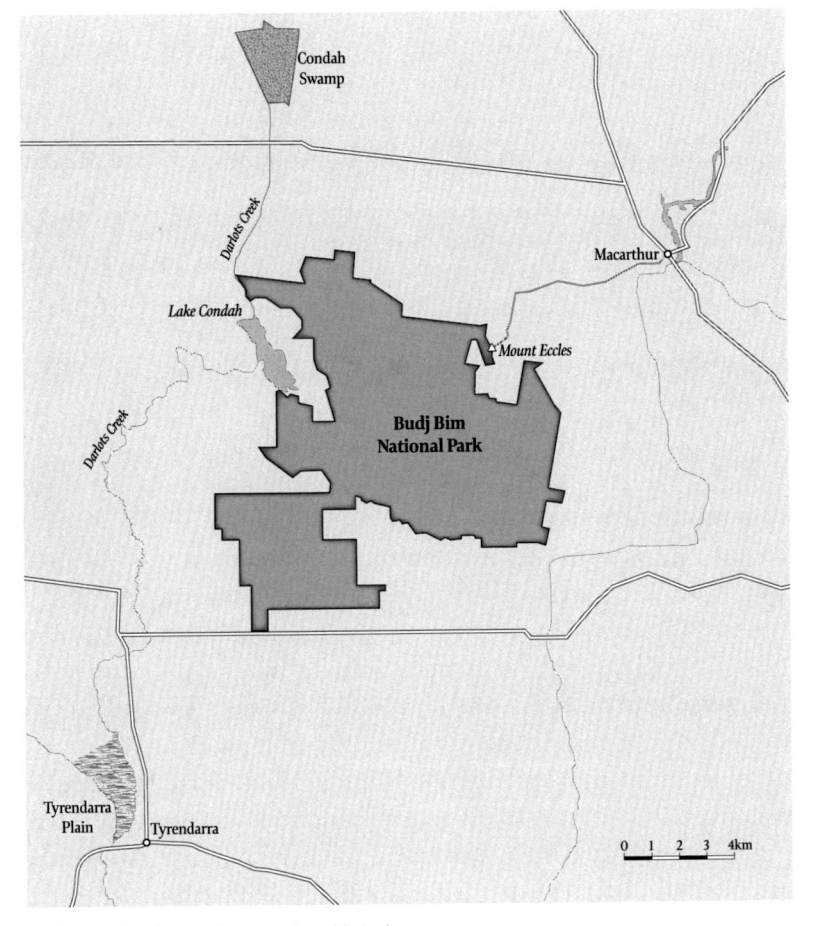

Map of Lake Condah region, western Victoria.

Detail of part of Lake Condah fish and eel trap.

The natural flow

Budj Bim (Mount Eccles) is the principal volcanic vent amid a series of numerous minor vents in western Victoria. This volcanic system was last active about 9000 years ago, with a major eruption much earlier, about 37,000 years ago,[5] causing a massive lava flow across the pre-existing drainage plain.[6] As the lava cooled, a series of swamps, shallow lakes and narrow channels formed on a very flat plain.[7]

This flat plain was further eroded by wind and rain over the ensuing millennia. However, a slight tilt to the south-west enabled water to flow along naturally formed ancient river channels to reach the Southern Ocean.[8] This complex hydrological system of swamps, lakes, creeks, rivers and the ocean provides the perfect conditions for migratory fish to achieve maturation and cyclical spawning by alternating between fresh and salt water.[9] In other words, fish can spend time in or away from the ocean by migrating along naturally formed channels, according to their physiological needs.

The most common species of migratory fish known to exist in western Victoria are short-finned eels (*Anguilla australis*) and mountain trout (*Galaxia* spp.).[10] Lake Condah and Condah Swamp are significant places along this complex hydrological system. In times of low rainfall, they are reduced to a series of muddy-bottomed puddles and waterholes. At these times, short-finned eels survive by burying themselves in the mud or traversing open ground to find a more tolerable refuge. In contrast, heavy rainfall initiates currents in streams, creeks and rivers, and the current in turn initiates migration for both short-finned eels and mountain trout.

Eels and trout inhabiting the naturally formed system of connected swamps, lakes, creeks and rivers on the lava plain of Budj Bim annually reach or leave the Southern Ocean. As Massola observed in the 1950s and 1960s,[11] Aboriginal people advantageously used their deep ecological knowledge of a vast array of natural and cyclical events in order to maximise their fish catch. Since at least 6000 years ago this naturally formed system has been deliberately modified by Aboriginal people building stone structures replete with brush fencing and woven baskets in order to trap migratory fish.[12] The trapping activity was closely observed and in most cases documented in the 1800s by explorers, missionaries, settlers and wanderers alike. These records have since been much referred to by archaeologists and anthropologists.[13]

Cultural modification of the natural system

Aldo Massola's public address to the Royal Historical Society of Victoria in June 1962 referred to observations and sketches from the mid to late 1800s of Aboriginal people operating fish traps in western Victoria.[14] In 1973, Harry Lourandos relocated a fish trap at Toolondo (in western Victoria) by referring to the 1800s journals of George Augustus Robinson and James Dawson.[15] Peter Coutts was investigating Aboriginal mound sites in the area at that time[16] and, inspired by Lourandos' success in using the early journals, he headed to Lake Condah. During 1975 Coutts, along with Rudy Frank and Philip Hughes, located and undertook an extensive survey of the Lake Condah system.

Of the system, Pascoe wrote: 'The channels *looked* like human-made structures, but experts couldn't believe they would work hydrologically' (page 83) and 'Local Aboriginal people were not credited with sufficient knowledge of engineering or energy to have created them' (page 84).

In fact, Coutts and his team were impressed by the scale of the trap, which was clearly designed by Aboriginal people to capitalise on migratory fish as they moved between fresh and saline waters:

> Our surveys suggest that there are four major systems of fishtraps, each of which comprises several stone races, canals, traps and walls which are articulated, either by accident or by design. The route of each stone race and canal has been carefully chosen to take full advantage of the natural topography, generally following drainage lines.[17]

Coutts was also, at that time, the director of the Victoria Archaeological Survey (VAS), and over the next decade or so he led numerous archaeological surveys in the Lake Condah environs. Archaeological surveys across western Victoria from 1973 onwards resulted in hundreds of cultural sites being placed on the record. Pascoe takes a dim view of this survey work on fish-trap sites, referring to 'the rather desultory examination of them by the Victorian Archaeological Survey' (page 78) and remarking that 'many [of the sites] have been destroyed by agriculture and rock collection for fencing, commercial purposes, and home gardens …' (page 78).[18]

Certainly, many heritage features across western Victoria have been impacted or destroyed by the activities named here by Pascoe. The same destructive activities were identified in the late 1980s during a regional cultural heritage survey and conservation assessment instigated by VAS.[19] This assessment also identified drainage works as a major destructive activity. Such works commenced on a minor scale with the establishment of Lake Condah Mission in the 1860s, but were dramatically scaled up in the early 1900s to appease local pastoralists complaining of seasonal flooding in Condah Swamp. The natural ecology of the lake and adjoining swamps, as well as heritage features, were significantly impacted by the drainage works.

Stone circles

Regardless of the destructive activities operating in the first half of the twentieth century, by 1990 over 200 stone circles, and numerous fish-trap arrangements, had populated the heritage database for the region.[20] The stone circles are roughly circular in shape, as their name suggests; they are 1–2 metres in diameter and each has one or two courses (layers) of stone.[21] Coutts recorded them 'scattered throughout the area, in groups, individually and adjacent to fish traps' and interpreted them as the base for a 'stone house'.[22] Pascoe suggests that construction was allotted to fabled others: 'The structures … looked like small round houses, but all sorts of speculation on their origins abounded, including conjecture that survivors of the fabled Mahogany ship … had built the systems' (pages 83–4).

As depicted in the various ethnographies, the frame posts for huts in this region could not be positioned directly in the ground due to the hardness of the lava plain. Instead, timber frames were held in place using stones. The ethnographic depictions were a powerful influence and Coutts saw no alternative for the stone circles other than being the bases for dwellings.

Western Victoria is pivotal to Pascoe's argument for large sedentary populations aggregated into villages. Stone circles are critical to population estimates and to interpreting housing arrangements. Coutts and, later, Pascoe used them to estimate the population of western Victoria: 'So, if they were houses, and if the channels were a fishing system, then around 10,000 people lived a more or less sedentary life in this town' (page 84).

By the late 1970s, Coutts thought that perhaps 200 people aggregated temporarily around Lake Condah:

> Certain areas may have been temporarily occupied by large aggregations of Aboriginals (for example up to 200 or more people) for the purpose of eeling. During other times of the year, group sizes were almost certainly smaller and of a semi-sedentary nature, as the Aboriginals exploited other food sources including freshwater fish, daisy yam and marine resources.[23]

A few years later and perhaps for the benefit of an interested news media, Coutts offered a village scenario with a far larger population:

> Living in a small stone house in a village of similar houses … It's a far cry from the traditional picture of the Australian Aborigine as a nomadic hunter and food gatherer with his spear … There

are more than 140 house sites and we keep discovering more …
They are situated in an area rich in food resources—and they are
associated with bird hunting and fishing … In one paddock there
are 146 houses. If most of them were occupied by one family that
makes a population of 700—in one paddock alone.[24]

This unusual scenario of prolonged settlement and intensive subsistence in a particular area had been hypothesised a little earlier by Harry
Lourandos,[25] who twenty years later summarised his thinking as 'high
population density, semi-sedentism and complex economy and social
relations … could be explained not only by the high bioproductivity of
the area but also by the development of these features through time …'[26]

Both Lourandos and Coutts recognised that the unique natural
endowments of western Victoria's lava plain provided a premium
habitat for migratory fish and that in response, Aboriginal people
developed elaborate trapping systems that were built in the knowledge
of the natural flow regime and migratory fish habits. For this reason,
hunter-gatherers were able to remain for unusually long periods in the
region. Archaeologically, this was expressed in high numbers and types
of cultural stone features.

Coutts estimated at least 700 people around Lake Condah, based on
the number of recorded dwellings and using an average of five people
per dwelling. Pascoe estimates 10,000 people by presumably applying
an average of fifty or more people per dwelling:[27]

> Early reports from settlers and colonial administrators such as [GA]
> Robinson refer to buildings where over fifty people gathered, but
> the most common size was a dome three to five metres across and
> two metres high. As a family had more children extra rooms were
> added or the larger structures underwent subdivision by internal
> walls. [pages 128–9]

With an average diameter of 1–2 metres per base, fifty people is quite
a crowd. However, the important point is not how many people can
occupy a small rounded dwelling but the interpretation of stone circles.
The trend set by Coutts in the 1980s meant that every stone circle was
indiscriminately recorded as a 'stone house'.

By 1990, it was recognised that possible overenthusiasm (in the form
of archaeology summer schools), rather than 'desultoriness', had led to

a lack of rigour in site recording. In response, VAS engaged an independent archaeologist to undertake 'collation and field checking of all known sites and the documentation of previously unrecorded sites ... as an essential contribution to the future planning and management of the Study Area'.[28]

The study area was principally Lake Condah and the archaeologist was Anne Clarke. She found that terms such as 'stone house', 'hut' and 'village' had been loosely applied without a clear and consistent definition.[29] The vision of 'hundreds of people living in villages' had gone unquestioned and become all-pervasive, as witnessed in a former diorama at the Museum of Victoria that depicted a scene at Lake Condah with the caption: 'The Kerrup-Jmara did not need to move house, and their villages of stone were probably permanent. Several hundred people lived in some villages.'[30] This exhibit was complemented by educational resources designed by VAS, conveying the same image of permanent stone houses set out in villages.[31]

In order to truly appreciate the complexity and diversity of the Lake Condah stone arrangements, it is critical to distinguish between different site types. If some stone circles were not house bases, then additional functions and purposes for stone features at Lake Condah were being overlooked. Clarke spent four months in the study area, inspecting and confirming the location of every recorded stone circle and logging stone circles not previously recorded. She was assisted in the field by Linda Saunders and Christina Saunders, Aboriginal traditional owners from Portland, and by archaeologist Giles Hamm. The final report was completed in conjunction with the Kerrup Jmara Elders Aboriginal Corporation.[32] Kerrup Jmara is a subgroup of the Gunditjmara people. It was therefore mistaken of Pascoe to refer to 'the local Gundidjmara people, who knew all along what the structures represented, but whose opinion had never been sought' (page 85).[33]

Clarke focused on establishing robust criteria for distinguishing natural from cultural processes that result in stone circles. Distinguishing natural from cultural phenomena is very familiar ground for archaeologists, and fundamental in generating reliable and robust heritage registers. In regard to possible processes leading to the formation of stone circles, Clarke listed geological and post-lava-flow landscape processes as natural, and Aboriginal construction and European landscape modification as cultural.[34] Examples of natural formations included the edges of sinkholes and lava tubes; cultural examples included such things as hunting hides, blinds and windbreaks. Any of these processes can make stone circles out of the basalt rock that was left strewn about by various volcanic events. There can also be some degree of overlap between, or mimicking of, cultural and natural processes, and Lake Condah proved no exception.

Geologist Neville Rosengren was engaged by VAS to provide further assistance in the field surveys. He identified natural processes capable of forming stone circles indistinguishable from cultural circles—such as 'pahoehoe', or lava that 'is also a process capable of forming circular accumulations.[35] The greater mobility of lava that forms pahoehoe surfaces gives rise therefore to several mechanisms by which circular stone accumulation may occur',[36] and 'given the nature of the volcanism at Mount Eccles that provided the lava for Lake Condah, it is possible to develop hypotheses that would explain circular structures developing and persisting there'.[37] But in the end, he felt there was a degree of uncertainty in making definitive statements: 'Although there is no strong evidence of volcanic or other "natural" origin of the rock piles, more precise evaluation can be determined by further field research …'[38]

Rosengren went on to list five essential points for further field research, emphasising morphological analysis, particularly the relationship of the stone circles to the underlying lava surface. In other words, it was imperative to know if the stones forming the circles were clearly separate from the ground surface. But the continuity or attachment of the upper layer of fractured basalt blocks to the fissured lava field could not be adequately inspected due to dense vegetation cover.[39] This was also apparent to Clarke, who commented that 'The problem of trying to establish clear criteria for distinguishing Aboriginal stone circles was never satisfactorily resolved during the field season.'[40]

Another phenomenon identified by Clarke, and one that also forms a stone circle, is a tree falling over. Trees growing on the basaltic plain have their roots intermeshed with basalt stones, and on heaving over, pull up the stones held tightly in the root mass (see opposite). Clarke examined a place where a tree had recently heaved over, leaving a stone circle that she described as 'one or two courses high, with the basalt blocks resting at a range of different angles, mimicking the pattern expected if people were collecting blocks and making circular shelters. If the tree falls over this also creates a break in the circle making an "entrance".'[41] Living trees can also bring up stones from around the base as their girth expands. Once the tree dies and rots away this, too, leaves a circle of stones.

Rocks held in root mass of fallen tree.

At the end of the fieldwork, Clarke had field-checked 173 previously recorded stone circles and recorded 92 new stone circles, resulting in:

a resource inventory comprising accurate mapping of the sites on aerial photographs and maps, preparation of a record form for each site, a site gazetteer and a report. The project also posed new questions about the way some site types may have been formed, and made preliminary comments on the integrity and management requirements for the sites.[42]

The VAS database, having commenced with 226 Aboriginal cultural sites in 1990, rose to 318 with the 92 new records, before dropping to 265 with the removal of 53 records that could not be verified as cultural sites.[43] The result was a more reliable database, reflecting greater site integrity. It was also larger than it had been prior to the 1990–91 survey commencing. Yet *Dark Emu* erroneously claims that 'The Victorian Archaeological Survey examined stone arrangements at Lake Condah in the late 1990s, and declared that they couldn't be house sites' (page 83).

If the cultural stone circles had revealed cultural artefacts, such as stone tools, shell, animal bone, ash or charcoal, and the natural stone circles were sterile, then it would have simplified matters. Instead, and interestingly, of the 318 cultural and natural stone features recorded in the region, only one circle was recorded with artefacts. It was excavated, and its charcoal samples returned a date of less than 200 years old, which was fitting with the glass identified on the same site.[44] Speculation arose that some stone circles represented huts built by Indigenous people post-European settlement in order to avoid direct conflict. A second stone circle was recently identified with stone and glass artefacts and also returned a modern date, of circa 1950s.[45]

Archaeology in Australia has witnessed many drawn-out debates over nature versus culture, and the stone circles at Lake Condah was one debate that has rolled on into the twenty-first century and brought with it a new level of interpretation.

Measuring the circles

Heather Builth commenced fieldwork south of Lake Condah in the late 1990s to find evidence for the premise that 'complex fisher-hunter-gatherers' (as she termed Aboriginal people in western Victoria) became sedentary by virtue of evolving a highly specialised techno-logical innovation around food supply, storage and distribution.[46] This, she believed, led in turn to hereditary chiefdoms,[47] which denied the 'prevailing anthropological perspectives of Aboriginal primitivism, [and] resulted in the acceptance of pre-contact Aboriginal people as struggling to survive within a hostile environment'.[48]

In other words, Builth believed that at the end of the twentieth century, the prevailing anthropological view of Aboriginal people was still that of a population locked in a perennial battle with a hostile environment over which they had no agency. The falsehood of this view has been discussed earlier in this chapter, and in Chapter 3, where clearly it was very much taken to task from the 1960s onwards by anthropologists, and long before Builth began her research.

Identifying hereditary chiefdoms is a popular theme in anthro-pology, but it is outside of what is intrinsic to the archaeological exploration here. Instead, the prime interest here is that Builth links highly specialised technology (food supply, storage and distribution) with human emancipation from natural whimsies—that is, she equates personal agency with having control over nature. Finding technological evidence for controlling the supply, storage and distribution of food became the key focus of her research. Pascoe writes:

> Builth … knew that only science could convince the doubters … and found that human agency was the only thing that could have produced such complexity. So, if they were houses, and if the channels were a fishing system, then around 10,000 people lived a more or less sedentary life in this town … If, she wondered, such a large population lived there, the demand for food would be extreme. There had to be some form of food preservation associated with this town.[49] [page 84]

As Pascoe states, Builth was keen to demonstrate complexity in food preservation as this would provide evidence for large, sedentary populations and thus set the scene for those hereditary chiefdoms. At first she focused on the stone circles; later she included mature trees in her field surveys. Inevitably she had to revisit the natural-versus-cultural stone circle origin debate, including the work of Rosengren. She wrote: 'Rosengren concluded that geological processes do not account for an obvious misidentification of natural features of [sic: or] cultural features.'[50] This comment by Builth is not particularly clear, but a comment by Rosengren is:

> The lava thus developed a highly irregular outline in plan and a rough and broken surface. Some of the stone arrangements which are the subject of archaeological interest could possibly be natural features resulting from this period of lava surface formation.[51]

Rosengren had also commented in his report that the lack of excavation or disturbance of any stone features prevented 'the opportunity to evaluate the relationship of stone blocks with the underlying lava surface and [made] it impossible to confidently assert as to the nature of the arrangement or movement of the overlying material'.[52] However, convinced that there was no geological interpretation for stone circles having formed, Builth claimed just two possible origins—humans or tree heaves (falls).

Pascoe wrote: 'She weighed and measured each stone in the house-like structures …' (page 84). Not exactly. Builth elected to weigh and measure stones from one stone circle and the visible stones from around one tree heave.[53] The metrical analysis revealed that stones taken from the stone circle fell within 'a relatively limited range which are relatively easy for an individual to move'.[54] In contrast, stones from the tree heave did not conform to a narrow range for size and volume. Based on the analytical results for one example of each of the two formation processes, Builth reported that cultural-versus-natural origin could be easily determined. If the average diagonal measurement across the base of a set of stones is less than 200–350 millimetres, the formation is cultural. Anything outside of this range results from a natural event—which could only be a tree heave.

These results need to be interpreted against their methodological limitations, which are that sample size is limited to one in each case; geological processes were erroneously eliminated as a causative factor; and no allowance was made for change over time. There is also a degree of uncertainty around how stones were selected for analysis. It seems that not every stone was collected from within arbitrarily defined collecting areas. This point is important given that many stone circles were found very close to one another.[55]

There is also the emphasis on absence of wood as evidence for a cultural circle:

> In the study areas, wherever trees had grown through the basalt and died, there was evidence of this effect in the form of dead wood and roots, remaining even though the tree had been long dead. However, these are areas where bushfires have not occurred for possibly hundreds of years.[56]

Here Builth is stating that a fallen tree will be recognisable by the dead wood and roots for a very long time as no bushfires have been present for hundreds of years to destroy the evidence. This in itself would suggest that there is no reason even to measure, because if there is no wood or root debris then formation can only be due to human action, as she reasoned earlier. However, in regard to bushfires, Massola refers to particularly severe fires in 1874 and 1901 in the region.[57] This is supported by newspaper reports from the 1800s. For example:

> ... the southern portion of this locality has also suffered through the fire which started in the vicinity of Lake Condah Mission Station on Saturday last [but] does not seem to have claimed much attention, simply, I suppose because it is looked upon as a necessary evil to have a fire on this part of the country known as the 'Stones' every

year to eradicate the wild dogs and other vermin … Saturday as will be remembered was both hot and windy and the fire gained ground rapidly. On Sunday and Monday, it was still burning, although all the male inhabitants of the Mission Station and the people who had somewhat checked further progress in the southern direction, which caused it, aided by the wind, to travel towards Lake Condah and Mount Eccles …[58]

Clearly, the absence of associated wood and roots inside a stone circle is not evidence alone for classifying a circle as cultural. The metrical results presented by Builth are measures of partial, single events resulting from an uncertain cause. This outcome could potentially have been offset by introducing a control group and perhaps more importantly by increasing the sample size. Geological processes and bushfire impact also need to be acknowledged.

Mapping the circles

The construction of archaeological classifications has long been recognised as a high-risk area for introducing bias.[59] Clarke highlighted this very problem at Lake Condah:

> Implicit in the recording of these sites are our own culturally based interpretations of how we think these sites would have operated as traps, channels and so on. This is one of the problems with the terminology adopted by Coutts et al. (1978). They have used terms that carry with them a whole spectrum of meanings that extend beyond the structural and morphological traits of the sites, and imply by such association a range of attributes and functions that have not been demonstrated or argued from the archaeological evidence.[60]

As discussed in the previous section, Builth's classification of a cultural circle was based on two fundamental errors: that both geological processes and bushfires are irrelevant to classifying stone circles. This bias was inevitably transported into the next step: spatial mapping.

Builth followed up her metrical analysis with a geographical information system (GIS) approach, which she used to generate an impressive simulation of an operating fish-trap complex on the lava plain. The data were also run through various software in order to specify spatial relationships between heritage features—that is, fish traps and stone circles—and revealed a close spatial relationship between these features, thus confirming the findings of Coutts, Frank and Hughes forty years earlier. Was this meaningful? Yes, if the stone circles were reliably classified, but, as presented here, they were not. As with the Moyjil midden, discussed in Chapter 12, we have a named feature but no evidence for a robust cultural feature.

As it was in the mid-1990s, we are still no closer to distinguishing a naturally formed circle of basalt rocks from a culturally formed one. For this reason alone, it is not possible to reliably estimate human populations from the numbers of stone circles. It is then worthwhile to consider the remainder of Builth's innovative research into evidence for complexity in food supply, storage and distribution, in view of its contribution to Pascoe's theories of sedentism and aquaculture.

'Smoking' trees and eel caching

Builth inspected the mature trees in her survey area and noticed that some had been hollowed out by burning. She wondered if the burning had been caused by deliberately heating the interior to smoke eels as a means of preserving them.[61] She also noticed holes in the upper branches of some trees and suggested that these were chimneys for the internal fire.

The idea of smoking eels as a preservative was a novel hypothesis but lacked ethnographic or ethnohistorical support, as Builth noted: 'to my knowledge, no local oral histories exist of manna gums being modified and used for eel smoking (personal communication, Gunditjmara Elders Keith Saunders and Johnny Lovett, 2001)'.[62]

James Dawson recorded numerous and detailed observations of various Indigenous activities at Lake Condah in the mid to late 1800s. He relates the spearing of eels by day and night, baiting freshwater fish, using baskets as a drag-net, damming rivulets with small stones, driving fish downstream into baskets, building stone barriers across rapid streams, diverting currents by use of a funnel-mouthed basket placed in a small opening, and building clay embankments across streams when the marshes were flooded. In fact, he described every activity for which archaeological evidence exists. He did not describe smoking eels inside mature trees but he did remark that 'fish ... are quickly cooked by spreading them on hot embers raked out of the fire and are lifted with slips of bark and eaten hot'.[63] There are a few accounts from elsewhere in Australia of fish being dried and thus preserved for a few days or possibly a few months, and, for some, to add flavour.[64]

At Lake Condah, Dawson also mentions that:

Each tribe has allotted to it a portion of a stream, now known as Salt Creek; and the usual stone barrier is built by each family, with the eel basket in the opening. Large numbers are caught during the fishing season. For a month or two the banks of the Salt Creek presented the appearance of a village ... No other tribe can catch them without permission, which is generally granted, except to unfriendly tribes from a distance, whose attempts to take eels by force have often led to quarrels and bloodshed.[65]

This portrays a regulated system of permission and entitlement practised among tribes during seasonal abundance. However, Builth considered the ethnographic and ethnohistoric observations to be unreliable[66] and pushed ahead with finding evidence for 'smoking trees'. She noticed that 'Most of the trees had been burnt inside and yet showed no evidence of external burning—thus dismissing the cause of burning as bush fire related'[67] and believed this to be key evidence for fires being deliberately contained inside the trees and managed in order to smoke eels.

During recent bushfires in southern Australia this very phenomenon was recorded, as shown in the photo in page 4 of the photo section. Here, the tree is well alight internally but shows no burning externally. Given the number and intensity of fires recorded since European settlement in western Victoria, as mentioned earlier, 'chimney trees' or 'smoking trees' require additional evidence.

Mature large trees with hollowed-out interiors (see overleaf) were more plentiful in the 1800s before large-scale land clearance, which was relatively common across south-eastern Australia.[68] River red gums with large openings at the base were known to be used as 'shelter' trees by Aboriginal people.[69] Small cooking or warming fires were often lit at the entrance of the tree, or, if the internal space was large enough, a small fire was maintained inside; these fires caused internal blackening from smoke, extending up into the trunk. Fires were also lit inside trees to smoke out possums.[70]

Builth did not accept that any of these activities were relevant at Lake Condah, and pursued the notion that eels could be cured inside trees. She reasoned that oil might be present in the soil due to 'domestic family baking on the stones'[71]—'stones' in this case being heated stones placed

Mature 'shelter type' tree, Canberra.

in the tree or heated inside the tree,[72] and 'family baking' being, presumably, eels. However, unhelpfully, no stone of any description or other archaeological material—such as stone tools, shell or animal bone—was found inside any of the fifty-two mature trees inspected by Builth.

In the absence of any actual archaeological evidence, traces of eel oil remained the only way of providing support for the 'smoking trees' theory. Four trees were selected for sampling sediment from the internal floor. The samples were sent for biochemical analysis (gas chromatography) and found to be generally degraded, but two were deemed sufficiently viable. The degraded but apparently viable samples revealed the presence of unsaturated long-chain fatty acids (those classified as 16:1, 18:1, 18:2, 20:4 and 20:5). Builth focused on fatty acids 20:4 and 20:5, which she said are:

> commonly found in aquatic animals in relatively high levels and are rare in plants. Given the large amounts of long chain fatty acids, an aquatic source is most likely ... Given the context of the samples the most likely source of the residues is eel processing.[73]

Fatty acid 20:4 is arachidonic acid, a polyunsaturated fatty acid actually found in a range of mammals, including humans, as well as in fish; while 20:5 is timnodonic acid, a polyunsaturated fatty acid found in fish as well as other animals.[74] Biochemically, the presence of a range of long-chain degraded fatty acids appeared to support Builth's theory that the lipids were more likely to be of fish origin than mammal. However, at Lake Condah eight fish species have been identified[75] and timnodonic acid is not a unique signature for eels.

Builth then compared the biochemical results with those from a sample of recently cooked eel flesh and a sample of recently smoked and cooked eel flesh. She found a good fit for the chromatograms for both sets of samples (tree-extracted and recently cooked/smoked), but, as with all scientific testing, it is necessary to scrutinise the sampling methodology. The age of the tree samples is unknown, leaving it impossible to estimate oxidation and microbial activity in altering the composition and integrity of soil lipids over time. Further, as with the stone circles, this analysis involved just two archaeological samples and two recent samples. No controls were introduced as a measure of confidence, and no blanks were used to check for contamination. No samples were taken from elsewhere inside the tree—for example, higher up on the inside of the trunk, where volatile acids may have been trapped—or, as remarked by Ian Keen, from soil outside of the trees,[76] as a marker of comparison. Sampling from trees of different ages would also have made sense in terms of identifying standards and baselines, in that soil communities vary significantly with the level of maturity of a tree.

Establishing baselines and standards by introducing a control group, blanks and test runs larger than one or two samples is a basic scientific principle. Further, reliance on multiple lines of inquiry is far preferable. Builth's two sediment samples were the only line of evidence presented to argue for a tradition of smoking eels inside mature trees for possibly thousands of years.

As before, rather than focus on quality control and lack of supporting evidence, an obvious and yet highly important question was not posed during the research into smoking of eels inside mature trees: by what other means might phospholipids (fish oil) get into sediments inside a tree cavity?

Lake Condah, Condah Swamp and the surrounding savannah woodland, prior to the introduction of European water and land management, was a 'pretty gem of a place'[77] and a haven for a wide range of fish, birds, mammals, reptiles and insects. Even after drainage works, a surprisingly high number of birds were reported for the Western District in the mid-1970s.[78] Of these, a number of the listed birds are known to consume fish and to perch in nearby trees to eat their catch, the darter bird being an obvious example.

Tiger quolls and eastern quolls, although now locally extinct or rare, were once prevalent in western Victoria.[79] They are carnivorous hunters but will also scavenge fish remains, for example, from fishing expeditions.[80] They also prefer cavities in mature trees for sleeping and making latrine areas. Another competent scavenger is the brush-tailed possum, which behaves similarly by sleeping and defecating in tree cavities. Dingoes are also prime scavengers and defecate and urinate in or around trees.[81] The very mature tree from which a sample was taken was photographed without a scale but was obviously quite a large cavity, easily accessible by larger mammals.[82]

Apart from faeces and urine being deposited inside tree cavities, natural mortality takes place. And, as mentioned earlier, Indigenous people are also well known to have made a small fire while sheltering inside mature trees. At Lake Condah it is reasonable to consider that eels would be consumed at these times.

Given the wide range of possible agents and activities leading to traces of fish oil in sediments inside mature trees, it would have been valuable for Builth to sample sediments from trees known to be used by mammals and roosting birds, and also trees where an animal had died. The absence of testing across a range of environmental conditions and scenarios undermines confidence in the tested samples as being biomarkers unique to eels.

Left with, at best, tenuous evidence for smoking eels inside trees, the only unexplored avenue to possibly provide evidence is feasibility.

The hypothetical method of domestic baking on rocks to smoke eels inside a confined tree hollow was not described in detail by Builth. Nor were details of this activity given by Gunditjmara elder Eileen Alberts, when fifteen years later recalling that her family had used trees for this purpose.[83] Instead, Builth focused more broadly on the very real difficulty of digging pit ovens into the soil-deficient basalt lava plain—which, she suggested, was overcome by burying heated rocks inside hollowed-out trees.[84] This would of course generate heat rather than smoke, but could perhaps dry the fish. The absence of heat-retaining rocks inside the inspected mature trees has been noted previously.

Most backyard eel curing today makes use of a barrel-shaped oven (similar to a hollow tree trunk), either electric or wood-heated. The eels are hung inside and exposed to a temperature of 60°C for some three hours and then 80°C for a further four hours.[85] The trees recorded by Builth do not have evidence for an internal rack on which eels could be laid or from which they could be hung. Perhaps the eels were impaled on wooden sticks and stood upright inside the tree and exposed to smoke or heat. Maintaining 60°C for three hours and then 80°C for four hours would necessitate heated rocks or fire to be introduced periodically into the tree. The average internal diameter of the trees was measured at 1–1.5 metres, which is about the same length as an average adult eel. Juggling eels and heated rocks inside a confined space seems a complicated manoeuvre to undertake for possibly hundreds or even thousands of eels during peak season. It would seem far easier, in all ways, to cook the eels in the open, as detailed elsewhere for smoking fish.[86]

The logistics of abundant eels being dried or smoked inside confined spaces would have required hundreds of trees operating simultaneously and continuously over a season. It would have presented quite a sight on the lava-flow plain, and yet not a single person remarked on it— although Builth refers to an illustration by William Blandowski, which she describes as Aboriginal people with 'food prepared for cooking or smoking in a tree—feasibly eels'.[87] This illustration is, however, a cropped image of Aboriginal people 'smoking possums out of trees and preparing possum skins for cloaks'.[88]

There is no reliable or convincing archaeological or ethnographic evidence for thousands of eels being smoke-dried and stored in the Lake Condah district before or at colonisation. The temporary caching of live eels may well have taken place, however, in view of another account by Dawson:

> The small fish 'tarropatt' and others of a similar description, are caught in a rivulet which runs into Lake Colungulac, near Camperdown, by damming it up with stones, and placing a basket in a gap of the dam. The women and children go up the stream and drive the fish down; and when the basket is full, it is emptied into holes dug in the ground to prevent them from escaping.[89]

Logically these holes would be close to the trap system, and some might be given a low stone rim to heighten water levels. Perhaps some of the stone circles were used to cache live fish for a day or two.

A remarkable fish-trap system

Archaeological investigations over many decades in western Victoria have confirmed the existence of a complex and long-established fish-trap system, as described and depicted by early explorers, settlers and others. Archaeology has not provided convincing evidence for the preservation and storage of fish in order to generate a trade item.

Stone circles have been well recorded around Lake Condah but remain in an unknown ratio of cultural to natural formations. In view of the nineteenth-century ethnographies and illustrations and the excavation of two circles,[90] there is no doubt that some circles represent the base for constructing a dwelling. Other circles close to the fish-trap complex may have been used for caching live eels or to serve some other purpose related to the ponding and channelling of fish within the system. Still others may be due to a range of natural phenomena, such as geological processes and tree falls.

Pascoe's estimate of 10,000 people in the Western District prior to European settlement is without archaeological support. It also defies census records. Census estimates for 1836 indicate about 5000 Aboriginal people for the whole of Victoria,[91] and the entire population of Australia prior to 1788 is estimated at less than one million.[92]

Pascoe is some fifty years behind the scholarly discussions that have traversed Australia, Papua New Guinea, Polynesia and more widely across the Pacific ethnographically. Archaeologists and anthropologists have not conspired to 'hide' evidence of agriculture or aquaculture but, instead, have systematically and objectively recorded Aboriginal subsistence practices. As demonstrated in earlier chapters, fieldwork has led to a wealth of detail describing complex ecological sustainability achieved via personal and social agency within a natural and spiritual world order. It is Pascoe who adds pejoratives such as 'primitive', 'simple' and 'mere' (pages 2, 86, 183) to the term hunter-gatherer, and it is he who argues for a very different scenario—that of agriculture and aquaculture.

The fish-trap complex of Budj Bim has been the focus of attention from admiring Europeans since the mid-1800s and of archaeologists since the 1970s; all of the latter have referred to the ethnographic records. Much of the earlier work was undertaken with Indigenous collaboration, resulting in recorded sites, management plans and ongoing research.

This collaborative and investigatory trend has continued into the twenty-first century with the huge efforts undertaken by archaeologists such as Builth and McNiven. Each has consulted and engaged with communities across all aspects of their work.

All archaeological investigations are vulnerable when applying so many different methods and complicated analytical tools. But this is what also achieves remarkable results. In the end, the total archaeological effort in the Western District has been sophisticated and comprehensive. If some methods have been less reliable than others, it has been due to the difficult, complex and diverse environmental conditions of the region rather than individual failings.

Recommendations arising from the comprehensive heritage management plan instigated by VAS in the early 1990s[93] resulted in national-significance listing of the complex. Successful World Heritage nomination of the Budj Bim cultural site in 2019[94] is an extraordinary achievement, built from years of dedication by many Indigenous and non-Indigenous people. As with all investigations, mistakes, setbacks, disagreements and misfortunes underlie the good outcomes. At Lake Condah, there is no disputing the high significance and heritage value of Budj Bim.

Conclusion

If non-Aboriginal Australians become enamoured of works like *Dark Emu* in a search for forgiveness, or reconciliation, or the undoing of the colonial crimes of their forebears, this is understandable. In the case of the crimes, most of them cannot now be undone, although recognition of native title has been and will continue to be a welcome reversal of at least some of the dispossession the Old People suffered during colonisation.

But the stains of blood are permanent. No number of apologies—valuable, just and cathartic as they have been—can change what happened, yet they have been imperative nonetheless. There remains the need for the future to be better than the past, both practically and symbolically. Constitutional recognition of Australia's First People is one important pathway of unfinished business.

Another outstanding issue is Australia Day. Australians are divided over changing the date to something other than that of the beginning of the British invasion of New South Wales in 1788 (26 January), or keeping it. A prime alternative is the day when the colonies united for the first time to form the nation-state of Australia, Federation Day. Federation occurred on 1 January 1901. Shifting the date to 1 January would be a useful move away from effectively celebrating the beginning of the destruction of much of Aboriginal society to a date that settler descendants, and Australians generally, might recognise as the beginning of their nation-state.

Australian governments at several different levels (local, state, federal) have apologised formally for the wrongs of the past, but the government that remains missing in action, and that should have been the very first to say something in apology, is that of Great Britain. Whitehall has not yet moved. The British Government, under the Crown, was the key engine on whose watch a mob of prisoners, accompanied by civilians, armed redcoats and bureaucrats, marched uninvited into New South Wales in the low thousands in 1788 and kick-started the land theft, conquest, physical attrition and emotional trauma of the original Australians generally, and the widespread degradation of the environment—all of which is now our indelible legacy, together.

The settling of land claims over large sections of the Australian map has been a partial but positive turning-back of some of the crimes of history. This is a massive if patchy process that has been going on since the 1970s. Perhaps the most reckless assertion in *Dark Emu*, one easily falsifiable by anyone with a library card or a computer, is this:

Every Land Rights application hinges on the idea that Aboriginal and Torres Strait Islander people did nothing more than collect available resources and therefore had no managed interaction with the land; that is, *the Indigenous population did not own or use the land.* [page 129]

I have a slight vested interest here, having acted as an expert anthropologist in various roles for some eighty-seven Aboriginal land claims during a period of over forty years (1979–2021), and having published numerous articles and two books on the subject, with a third on the way.[1] I have never held a permanent university job and have spent most of my working life at the coalface of applied anthropology, with land claims research, heritage surveys and expert court witness work being the lion's share of that history.

Pascoe here has the facts completely inverted. Australian land claim applications are based on evidence of traditional land tenure systems and managed resource use systems and their modern descendants. These were and are systems of considerable complexity, and constitute one of the main pillars of Aboriginal Law. Native title and other land rights regimes are an attempt to respect that Law, albeit too late for some applicants to have their wishes met. Native title is a pre-existing title, continuous since before effective British sovereignty in each region—not a grant of title.

Pascoe shows no respect for this process. He also claims that categorising Aboriginal people as 'hunter-gatherers' 'is prejudicial to the rights of Aboriginal people to land' (page 103). It certainly was in the colonial era, but in present-day Australia this claim is simply obsolete and untrue, because Aboriginal land tenure, and the primary requirements for proof of it under legislation, was not and is not based on economic use of the country: it is founded on a perpetual spiritual belonging to country that is based, usually, on descent from preceding landowners, plus some other factors, depending on the legal jurisdiction.[2] The classifying of Aboriginal people as wandering hunting-and-gathering people who did not use the land the way Europeans did, and were therefore not owners of it, is a colonial-era fiction long expunged from Australian law, with the Northern Territory Aboriginal Land Rights Act of 1976, the Queensland Aboriginal Land Act of 1991, the Mabo High Court decision of 1992, and the Native Title Act of 1993. It has been expunged for much longer than that from the minds of all those with an active grasp of the subject.

There is no better condition for relationships than truthfulness. We have tried here to set part of the record straighter than it has become through the popularised mythology of history of the kind found in *Dark Emu*. We have done so in a positive spirit, but also a corrective one. The Old People—the First Australians—and all of us deserve better than a history that does not respect or do justice to the societies whose economic and spiritual adjustment to their environment lasted so well and so vigorously until the advent of the colonies and the subsequent degradation of much of that environment through land clearing, pastoral stocking, and the spread of feral animals and plants.

Pascoe, by consistently gilding a lily that needs no gilding, suggests that he sees a foraging way of life as inferior. Its own practitioners saw it as the Law, sanctioned by the ancients. Unlike agricultural farmers, they worked *with* the biota rather than overweening it and subjugating it to the god of surplus material production. They left a far better Australian environment than we have now, given that so many native species are now extinct, so many feral introduced species are creating havoc, and huge regions have been domesticated under monoculture cropping and thereby degraded in ecological richness.

In this book we have grappled with *Dark Emu*'s mixture of positive factual information and its tendency to trim the evidence to fit the author's model, its lack of true scholarship, its ignoring of Aboriginal elders' knowledge, its disturbing social evolutionist philosophy, and its overwhelming attention to the material aspects of Aboriginal food production to the exclusion of the rich spiritual propagation philosophy of the Old People's culture.

People keep telling us, even those who are aware of *Dark Emu's* many flaws, that at least it has got people thinking about an important subject. We hope their interest continues, and that the tens of thousands who have read the book go beyond it and keep learning more from other sources. So long as *Dark Emu* is not the agent of their entrenchment in a dogmatic view, that is good. So long as we remain open to debate and a respectful exchange of views, in a shared space and not from behind walls, it is more than good. It is in that spirit that we offer this book to the reader.

Appendix 1: When did Indigenous people arrive in Australia?

Keryn Walshe

There are relatively few archaeology sites in Australia that have been dated between 45- to 50,000 years old by more than a single line of evidence.[1] By arriving at the same dates via different methods allows greater confidence in the age of a site. Well beyond this 'safe' time frame, is Madjedbebe in northern Australia, claimed to be between 65,000 and 80,000 years old.[2] Madjedbebe is truly an outlier.

Amongst the many difficulties in dating sites and objects are the fragmentary nature of finds, disturbed geological contexts (bioturbation) and insufficient data to arrive at statistical confidence. Controversial reports such as 65,000 years plus for Madjedbebe has led scientists to look carefully at environmental factors that may have affected the dating. In northern Australia the impact of termite activity[3] on sediments in caves has come into focus. Convincing evidence has recently been put forward to demonstrate that termite activity in particular, has caused stone tools in Madjedbebe to have been pushed downward and thus become associated with much older sediments.[4] This is extremely relevant because it is the sediments that are dated in ancient sites and a correlation made with stone tools. Based on this and other evidence the reported age of Madjedbebe cannot be conclusively accepted.

The use of molecular data to date key events in the recent history of anatomically modern humans (AMH) is a highly valuable addition to dating sediments. These can be used to estimate the timing of the movement of modern humans out of Africa and into Europe and Asia. For example, the genomic sequence of an AMH dated to 45,000 years old from western Siberia (Ust'Ishim) has revealed introgressed (hybridised) Neandertal genetic material.[5] The size of this Neandertal genetic material can be used to conservatively constrain the timing of the ancestors of modern AMH out of Africa at 50- to 60,000 years ago.

Other DNA studies have provided almost identical estimates and for Australia, the appearance and strength of Neandertal and Denisovan genetic signals in the genomes of Australian Indigenous people confirm they were part of this initial diaspora. Molecular and archaeological evidence provides strong support that AMH reached Australia around 50,000 years ago or very slightly before.[6] This also matches fossil and sedimentary evidence in southern Asia and is reflected in the most reliably dated sites across northern Australia.

In fact it is claimed that DNA and direct dating of carbon in skeletal remains (rather than relying on associated sediments) are essential for reliability and accuracy.[7]

As others have remarked, if there are sites older than 65,000 years in Australia, then these can only have been occupied by an earlier AMH population.[8] This hypothetical population has left no DNA traces and would be in direct conflict with Indigenous connection to and knowledge of sites.

Appendix 2: Band movements recorded by William Buckley

Note that Buckley's distances were given in miles. Where he gives a specific number of miles, they have here been converted to kilometres. Page numbers are from John Morgan, *The Life and Adventures of William Buckley: Thirty-two years a Wanderer Amongst the Aborigines of the then Unexplored Country around Port Phillip, now the Province of Victoria* (Hobart: Archibald MacDougall, 1852 / London: William Heinemann, 1967).

Pages	Stasis/Movement	Destination (current name)	Distance travelled	Length of stay at destination
20–2	Group went from Maamart, a swamp west of Barwon Heads, to a lagoon near 'the Barwin'	Barwon River area	'some miles'	a few days
25	from Barwon River area	not named	'a few miles'	'a few weeks'
28	from the latter location	'the place my friends chiefly inhabited'	not stated	'there we lived for a very long time unmolested'
29	from the latter location	not stated; meeting place	'two or three days'	probably a few days

Pages	Stasis/Movement	Destination (current name)	Distance travelled	Length of stay at destination
30	'We next joined the Bengali tribe, and went with them to their hunting ground, a place surrounded by the sea and the Barwin River'	Bellarine Peninsula, Barwon Heads, Indented Head area[1]	not stated	'some months' on hunting ground[2]
35	'We ... then proceeded to the borders of another large lake, which they call Yawangcontes, in the centre of an extensive plain'	not named	not stated	'many months; perhaps for a year or two, for I had lost all recollection of time'
36	'After this very long stay, we received a message to visit another very large lake, many miles round, which they call Kongiadgillock'	Lake Corangamite	not stated	not stated
37–8	'We next went about forty miles, I should think, to a place they call Kironamaat'; 'It took us several days to accomplish this march ...'	Lake Gerangamete near present-day Colac	about 64 km	'many months'
38	'... then went to the borders of another lake, called Moodewarri'	Lake Modewarre	not stated	not stated
38	Exchange visit (eels for roots) from Lake Modewarre to 'Bermongo, on the Barwin River'	On Barwon River	'The time stated for this march would be fourteen days ...'	'a short time'

Pages	Stasis/Movement	Destination (current name)	Distance travelled	Length of stay at destination
38–9	From last place went to Beangala	Indented Head	not stated	'some months'
39	exchange visit (kangaroo for roots) to Liblib near a large lake called Bangeballa	'Apparently places north-east of Colac' (p. 39)	not stated	not stated
42	'… having crossed the Barwin, had gone as far as a spot called Biarhoo, where we halted'	'Probably north-east of Lake Colac' (p. 52)	not stated	'awhile'
42–3	… after awhile we all moved on to a place they call Godocut, near the sea side, where we pitched our bark huts …'	Point Addis (p. 52)	at least 60 km	'At this spot, however, nothing was to be had to eat but shell fish; so we soon left for another …'
43	'… so we soon left for another about eight miles distant …	not stated	about 13 km	'Here we settled down for a few days …'
43	'Our next journey was to Palac Palac …'	'Paraparap, farming centre in the Barrabool Shire' (p. 52) [west of Barwon Heads; now part of Surf Coast Shire]	not stated	'… we remained many months'
43–4, 46	Invitation to share eels came from another group, so 'we accepted the invitation and joined them that day'	a lagoon unnamed	short (same day)	'many months' (p. 46)

Pages	Stasis/Movement	Destination (current name)	Distance travelled	Length of stay at destination
46	'Getting tired at length of the sameness of food, we all left and travelled about twenty miles [about 32 km] …'	Boordek; 'Possibly in the hills west of Colac' (p. 52)	not stated	not stated
47	left the above and went to Morriock	'Mount Moriac, a township in and headquarters of Barrabool Shire' (p. 52)	not stated	not stated
48	'The next place we went to was called Ballackillock …'	'Ballark' (p. 52)	not stated	not stated
48	'… then we shifted again, and for some time kept moving about …'	not stated	not stated	not stated
49	'… we reached the appointed place, which the natives call Monwak …'	'Airey's River' (p. 52) [Airey's Inlet]	two days	not stated
50	'The next day we moved on to another fresh water lake of considerable extent …'	not stated	not stated	one night
50, 63	'The day following we therefore left the spot, and kept wandering about for some time after, until we came again to our old quarters at Moodewari …'	'Lake Modewarre' (p. 52)	not stated	'… we remained several months'

Pages	Stasis/Movement	Destination (current name)	Distance travelled	Length of stay at destination
53–5, 56	'... let us now return to our halting place at Moodiwiri, when, after a long time another tribe joined us ... A short time after this affair we shifted our quarters ... After this affair, we continued wandering about in a similar way, from place to place, joining one tribe, then leaving it for another, and so on, nothing particular occurring. At length we pitched our huts upon the borders of a lake or lagoon ... it being called Koodgingmurrah ...'	lagoon not identified	not stated	'many months' ... 'until the approach of spring'
57, 63	'... we shifted our quarters ...', moved to 'near a river they called Booneawillock'	Barwon River near Buckley Falls, Geelong; also spelled Boonea Yalloak	not stated	waited until floodwaters subsided then crossed over to other side of river
66, 74	'After a time [at Buckley's solo camp] they persuaded me to accompany them to a salt lake, called Nellemengobeet ...'	'A lagoon at the mouth of the Barwon River'	about 8 km	a month or less
66, 67	'When the moon was again at the full we returned to the Karaaf [River]—my old fishing quarters ...'	Bream Creek (Kaarof, Karaaf; now Breamlea)	about 10 km	'some time'

Pages	Stasis/Movement	Destination (current name)	Distance travelled	Length of stay at destination
67, 69	'After some time, we all went away together in search of the kangaroo …'	not stated	not stated	'a very long time'
70, 74	'We now took up our quarters at a place they called Nullemungobeed …'	'Murgheboluc Flat … near Bannockburn' [c35 km west of Geelong]	not stated	not stated
70–1	Buckley returned to solitary camp for 'many months' and was then joined by 'a friendly party'	not stated	not stated	'several months' (after friendly party joined Buckley)
72, 74	went to Bearrock	'Swamps near Gerangamete'	not stated	'a long time'
73, 74	moved off to a more concealed place called Banor	'One of several sugarloaf hills along the southern coast near Cinema Point'	about 18 km	not stated
73–4	returned to Karaaf River	Bream Creek (now Breamlea)	about 40 km	'many months'
75	'… our small party broke up, and left the Karaaf on a short hunting excursion'	not stated	not stated	not stated
83	'we proceeded together to a lake called Jerringot—one of a chain of that name—which supplies the Barwin River'	Waurn Ponds [about 8 km south-west of the centre of Geelong]	not stated	not stated

Acknowledgements

Acknowledgements by Peter Sutton

I owe a vast debt to senior Aboriginal cultural mentors and bushcraft teachers who, since 1970, have educated me about traditional living on their lands and waters, and about their engagement with resources of the Australian bush. Many have also been my language teachers. Of particular relevance here is that a good number taught me a great deal about the spiritual propagation of species and about plant classification, garnering and use in the rich non-agricultural economy that was their common heritage. The main people in these various regards, although there have been hundreds more who played smaller roles, are:

Dick Hoolihan and Harry Gertz (Gugu-Badhun, north Queensland); Johnny Flinders and Maryanne Mundy (Flinders Island group, Cape York Peninsula (CYP)); Alec Niger (Kaanju, CYP); Alec Sandy, Michael Sandy, Sandy Yella and Johnson Butcher (Sandbeach people, eastern CYP); Isobel Wolmby, Victor Wolmby, Noel Peemuggina, Ray Wolmby, Dan Gothachalkenin, Billy Landis Gothachalkenin, Johnny Lak Lak Ampeybegan, Silas Wolmby, Bruce Yunkaporta, Alan Wolmby, Rex Walmbeng, Paddy Yantumba, Jack Sleep Yunkaporta, Clive Yunkaporta, George Sydney Yunkaporta, Jack Spear Karntin, Tarchee Ngakapoorgum, Archiewald Otomorathin, Dugal Tarpencha, Clara Tarpencha and Ron Yunkaporta (Wik people, western CYP); Pompey Raymond (Jingulu, NT); Pharlap Dixon Jalyirri (Mudburra, NT); Dick Ngulayngulay Murrumurru (Kunwinjku/Dangbon, NT); Jimmy Tapnguk and Lofty Smith (Malak Malak, NT); Long Harry (Madngele, NT); Engineer Jack Japaljarri, Charlie Charles Jakamarra and Dolly Granites (Warlpiri, NT); Arthur Warren, Brian Marks and Glen Hull (Arabana, SA); David Malangi (Djinang, NT); Jimmy Wululu (Gupapuyngu, NT); Linda Crombie (Wangkangurru, SA); Windlass Aluritja, Nellie Armunta, Johnny Jango, Milly Okai, Dora Walkabout, Nguyunguyu Donald, Tony Tjamiwa, Donald Frazer, Reggie Uluru and Cassidy Uluru (Yankunytjatjara, NT/SA); Barbara Nipper (Pitjantjatjara, SA/WA/NT); Malya Teamay (Luritji/Arrernte, NT); Clancy MacKellar and Malcolm Ebsworth (Wangkumara, south-west Queensland).

A special thanks as well to colleagues the late Athol Chase and John von Sturmer, who included botanical studies and plant-specimen collecting in our site and country mapping of eastern Cape York Peninsula, under instruction by traditional owners and Athol's leadership, right through the wet season of 1975–76, where I was engaged to concentrate on plant linguistic identifications and use, and environmental language. Ethnobotanist Philip Clarke has assisted me greatly with literature sources.

Similarly, I thank Dermot Smyth, then an ecologist and botanist, who collaborated with Wik seniors and me to carry out two fairly arduous bush plant use studies in 1978 and 1979 between the Archer and Holroyd rivers, western Cape York. The specimens collected on all these trips are in the Queensland Herbarium. Zoologist Glen Ingram did field work with us on Wik zoology, especially birds, in 1979.

Special thanks go also to Lea Gardam of the South Australian Museum Archives for assistance with images from that collection.

Acknowledgements by Keryn Walshe

Acknowledgment is made to the following Aboriginal land or heritage councils, associations and committees with whom I have had the privilege to collaborate on archaeological research projects, repatriation or consultancy contracts 1990–2018:
ACT Aboriginal Heritage Corporation, 1990s: Ngunnawal
NSW Aboriginal Land Councils, 1990s: Barkindji, Birpai, Bunyah, Purfleet-Taree
SA, 1990s–2018 Aboriginal Heritage Council/Association/Committee for: Adnyamathanha, Barngarla, Boandik, Dieri, Far West Coast, First People of the River Murray, Kaurna, Kokatha, Koonibba, Kungari, Kuyani, Mirning, Narungga, Nauo, Ngadjuri, Ngarrindjeri, Nukunu, Peramangk, Ramindjeri, Tatiara, United Yuras, Wirangu, Yalata.

Joint acknowledgements

We are both grateful to the following colleagues who commented on draft sections of this book or who supplied specific information upon inquiry: Barry Alpher, Robert Amery, Val Attenbrow, Geoffrey Bagshaw, Caitlin Bonham Smith, Maggie Brady, John Carty, Athol Chase, Philip Clarke, Alan Cooper, Christophe Darmangeat, Bob Ellis, Tom Gara, Lily Gurambara, Nathan Hollier, Paul Irish, Philip Jones, Ian Keen, Judith Littleton, Alan Magnusson, Chris Majewski, Betty Meehan, Paul Memmott, Francesca Merlan, John Morton, David Nash, Christine Nicholls, Noel Pearson, Nicolas Peterson, Nick Piper, Ruth Singer, Mike Smith, Dermot Smyth, Clara Stockigt, Jared Thomas, Petronella Vaarzon-Morel, Leslie Van Gelder, Jean-Christophe Verstraete, J Peter White, Ray Wood, Stephen Zagala, and three anonymous manuscript referees.

Thank you to our meticulous editor, Katie Purvis, and Louise Stirling and the team at Melbourne University Publishing.

Image credits

Map of places mentioned in the text: Guy Holt

Chapter 1

The British Empire and its 'races' in 1937: John A Hammerton, *For King and Empire: Pictorial Souvenir of the Coronation* (Amalgamated Press, 1937), pp. 34–5.

Bruce Yunkaporta spearing a stingray, Wooentoent, Kirke River, Cape York Peninsula, 1976: photo by Peter Sutton.

Three gypsum mourning caps: Harry Allen, 'Aborigines of the western plains of New South Wales', in Christine Haigh & Wendy Goldstein (eds), *The Aborigines of New South Wales* (NSW National Parks & Wildlife Service, 1980), p. 35; photo by Sharon Sullivan.

Brewarrina fish traps: Allen, p. 39; photo by Thomas Dick.

Duck net, Murrumbidgee River, 1880s: *Augustus Baker Peirce, Knocking About: Being some Adventures of Augustus Baker Peirce in Australia* (Yale University Press, 1924), sketch by Augustus Baker Peirce, p. 156.

Remnant stakes used to divert fish to nets, Lake Eyre region: George Horne & George Aiston, *Savage Life in Central Australia* (Macmillan, 1924), Figure 48.

Diversion fence with wicker fish trap, Arnhem Land, 1952: Roslyn Poignant & Axel Poignant, *Encounter at Nagalarramba* (National Library of Australia, 1996), p. 105; photo by Axel Poignant.

Noel Peemuggina and his student Peter Sutton, Ti Tree Outstation, Cape York Peninsula, 1977: photo by David Martin.

Chapter 2

Long yam carving for house-opening ceremony, near Aurukun, 1976. Francis Yunkaporta (holding yam), Peter Peemuggina and James Kalkeeyorta: photo by Peter Sutton.

Totemic centres, Wik region: Ursula H McConnel, *Myths of the Muŋkan* (Melbourne University Press, 1957), p. xviii.

Barramundi maintenance site Moenchenh-nhiin, Wik region, 1977: photo by Peter Sutton.

Magpie goose egg maintenance site, Yaad, Wik region, 1976: photo by Peter Sutton.

Johnny Lak Lak Ampeybegan cuts a blaze in a tree at a goose egg maintenance site, Wik region, 1976: photo by Peter Sutton.

Gypsum emu eggs sung to start emus nesting, Simpson Desert, South Australia: Tom McCourt, *Aboriginal Artefacts* (Rigby, 1975), p. 125.

'Increase ceremony' for *yarrinyarri* (nutgrass), north-west Australia: Ralph Piddington, 'Totemic system of the Karadjeri tribe', *Oceania* 4, 1932, pp. 376–93, Plate II.

Chapter 4

Wik people firing the country, middle Kirke River, Cape York Peninsula, 1977: photo by Peter Sutton.

Field worker Ursula McConnel writing for the *Sydney Morning Herald*: Ursula H McConnel, 'Science—but not from an armchair: Adventures in anthropology', *Sydney Morning Herald Women's Supplement*, 8 March 1934, p. 17.

Catholic missionaries: Sisters of the Order of Our Lady of the Sacred Heart of Darwin: Francis Xavier Gsell, *'"The Bishop with 150 Wives": Fifty Years as a Missionary* (Angus & Robertson, 1955), facing p. 48.

Chapter 6

Tindale's 'Grassland areas exploited by aborigines [*sic*] as important sources of grain food with some of the names of tribes': Norman B Tindale, *Aboriginal Tribes of Australia: Their Terrain, Environmental Controls, Distribution, Limits, and Proper Names* (University of California Press, 1974), p. 99.

Pascoe's 'Aboriginal grain belt': Bruce Pascoe, *Dark Emu: Black Seeds: Agriculture or Accident?* (Magabala Books, 2014), p. 29.

Davidson and McCarthy's seed-grinding area: DS Davidson & FD McCarthy, 'The distribution of stone implements in Western Australia', *Anthropos* 52, 1957, p. 440.

The distribution of large millstones (Smith): Mike Smith, *The Archaeology of Australia's Deserts* (Cambridge University Press, 2013), p. 190, Figure 6.9c.

Radcliffe-Brown's 'Estimated number and distribution of Aboriginals in 1788': *Macquarie Atlas of Indigenous Australia: Second Edition*, General Editors Bill Arthur & Frances Morphy, © Macquarie Dictionary Publishers, Pan Macmillan Australia Pty Ltd 2019, Map 6.3 compiled by the Archaeological Computing Laboratory (ACL), University of Sydney.

The seven case studies of Ian Keen: Ian Keen, *Aboriginal Economy and Society: Australia at the Threshold of Colonisation* (Oxford University Press, 2004).

Distribution of *iga* (native orange) in the Flinders Ranges region: Bob Ellis, 'Iga: The tree that walked', *South Australian Geographical Journal* 112, 2013, p. 8.

Rex Walmbeng with shell midden at Punth-Kuunteng, near Love River, Cape York Peninsula, 1985: photo by Peter Sutton.

Cecil Walmbeng at Waathem, Wik country, Cape York Peninsula, 1985: photo by Peter Sutton.

Chapter 7

Men of south-west Western Australia, 1870s–1880s period: Daisy M Bates, *Aboriginal Perth and Bibbulmun Biographies and Legends* (Hesperian Press, 1992), p. 27.

Mitchell's 'Female and child of Australia Felix': Thomas L Mitchell, *Three Expeditions into the Interior of Eastern Australia; with Descriptions of the Recently Explored Region of Australia Felix, and of the Present Colony of New South Wales* (T & W Boone, 1839), vol. 2, Plate 39.

Tiwi women and girls wearing traditional paperbark aprons, Bathurst Island, 1913: Nicolas Peterson, 'The use of Spencer's photographic imagery', in P Batty, L Allen & J Morton (eds), *The Photographs of Baldwin Spencer* (Melbourne University Press at The Miegunyah Press, 2005), p. 174.

Man with two wives and children, Tomkinson Ranges, 1903: Herbert Basedow (comp. & ed. David M Welch), *Notes on Some Native Tribes of Central Australia* (David M Welch, 2008), p. 42; photo by Herbert Basedow, from Mitchell Library PiccAcc 5669, Box 5, p. 13, Sp8-1.

Wik girl on plains south of Aurukun, western Cape York Peninsula, 1927: photo by Ursula McConnel, South Australian Museum Archives AA191/22/1/9/2.

Wik women performing mourning dance, western Cape York Peninsula, 1927: photo by Ursula McConnel, South Australian Museum Archives AA191/22/4/28L.

Wik men in ceremony, western Cape York Peninsula, 1927: photo by Ursula McConnel, South Australian Museum Archives AA191/22/4/21D.

Chapter 8

Aboriginal watercraft distribution at conquest: Australian National Maritime Museum.

Chapter 9

Woodcut of shelters at Careening Bay, Kimberley, in 1820: Phillip Parker King, *Narrative of a Survey of the Intertropical and Western Coasts of Australia Performed between the Years 1818 and 1822*, vol. 1 (John Murray, 1827), p. 431.

Dry-season shelter, western Cape York Peninsula: photo by Ursula McConnel, South Australian Museum Archives, AA191/24/49.

Firewood collector, Wik region, Cape York Peninsula, 1927: photo by Ursula McConnel, South Australian Museum Archives AA191/22/1/24/1.

Punga-style hut, Lake Eyre region: photo by George Aiston, image supplied by South Australian Museum AA3-2-3-8.

Cape York Peninsula dwelling types, illustrated by Donald Thomson: Donald F Thomson, 'The fishermen and dugong hunters of Princess Charlotte Bay', *Walkabout* 22(11), 1956, p. 93.

Chapter 10

Front cover of Sanitarium cereal company booklet, 1950: Frederick D McCarthy, *Aboriginal Tribes and Customs* (Sanitarium Health Food Co., 1950).

Bill Onus selecting boomerang wood from St Kilda Road trees, Melbourne: from 'Boomerangs are booming', *Australasian Post*, 16 July 1964, pp. 16–17.

Sharp's sketch of wet-season camp at Man Molur, 1933–34: R Lauriston Sharp, *The Social Anthropology of a Totemic System in North Queensland, Australia*, PhD dissertation, Harvard University, 1937, p. 319.

Sharp's sketch of wet-season camp at Olwinan, 1933–34: Sharp, p. 321.

The Western Desert region: Illustration from Amee Dorothy Glass, *Cohesion in Ngaanyatjarra Discourse* (Summer Institute of Linguistics, 1997), p. 1.

Chapter 11

Distribution of game nets at conquest: *Macquarie Atlas of Indigenous Australia: Second Edition*, General Editors Bill Arthur & Frances Morphy, © Macquarie Dictionary Publishers, Pan Macmillan Australia Pty Ltd 2019, Map 5.13 compiled by the Archaeological Computing Laboratory, University of Sydney.

Chapter 12

Grooved (Bogan style) picks: photo by Malcolm Davidson.

Long-bladed knife and paperbark sheath: photo by Greg Carver.

Adze flake set in resin and hafted to wooden handle: photo by Greg Carver.

Midden left by seabirds breaking open shells for food: photo by Keryn Walshe.

Chapter 13

Map of Lake Condah region, western Victoria: Guy Holt

Detail of part of Lake Condah fish and eel trap: original map by Alexander Ingram, 1883, South Australian Museum Archives AA298/18/1_p95_Ingram.

Rocks held in root mass of fallen tree: photo by Keryn Walshe.

Mature 'shelter type' tree, Canberra: photo by Keryn Walshe.

Picture Section

Sutton's mentor Isobel Wolmby, Aurukun Mission, Cape York Peninsula, holding Thomas Sutton, 1976: photo by Anne Sutton.

Harry Gertz, teacher of Gugu-Badhun language, at Yangkarrdji, Valley of Lagoons Station, Queensland, 1970: photo by Peter Sutton.

Mary Walmbeng and Dorothy Pootchemunka performing moulting ducks maintenance rite, upper Knox River, Cape York Peninsula, 1986: photo by David Martin.

Country being fired by Reggie and Cassidy Uluru, Lake Amadeus, 1999: photo by Peter Sutton.

Cloaks and footwear: *Macquarie Atlas of Indigenous Australia: Second Edition*, General Editors Bill Arthur & Frances Morphy, © Macquarie Dictionary Publishers, Pan Macmillan Australia Pty Ltd 2019, Map 5.33 compiled by the Archaeological Computing Laboratory (ACL), University of Sydney.

Watercraft in use at the time of European arrival: *Macquarie Atlas of Indigenous Australia: Second Edition*, General Editors Bill Arthur & Frances Morphy, © Macquarie Dictionary Publishers, Pan Macmillan Australia Pty Ltd 2019, Map 5.19 compiled by the Archaeological Computing Laboratory, University of Sydney.

Reconstruction of traditional dwelling, Lake Condah, 2020: photo by Peter Sutton.

Tree interior alight without external burn, 2020: photographer's name withheld.

Notes

Chapter 1: The *Dark Emu* debate

1 Bruce Pascoe, *Dark Emu: Black Seeds: Agriculture or Accident?* (Magabala Books, 2014); and *Dark Emu: Aboriginal Australia and the Birth of Agriculture*, 2nd edn (Magabala Books, 2018). Note that in this book we rely principally on sources of information that were available before *Dark Emu* appeared in 2014. Some highly relevant works have appeared since. For example, on traditional south-eastern Australian economy and domestic technology and clothing, see Fred Cahir, Ian D Clark & Philip A Clarke, *Aboriginal Biocultural Knowledge in South-Eastern Australia: Perspectives of Early Colonists* (CSIRO Publishing, 2018).

2 Bill Gammage, *The Biggest Estate on Earth: How Aborigines Made Australia* (Allen & Unwin, 2011).

3 Rupert Gerritsen, *Australia and the Origins of Agriculture* (British Archaeological Reports, 2008).

4 Although the absence of agriculture in Australia was used as an excuse for dispossession by colonists, the presence of agriculture on other continents was no barrier to conquest and appropriation of land by the British: 'The fact that the Aborigines were to a very large extent hunter-gatherers probably provided a convenient pretext for their dispossession by the Westerners. But, as far as is known, the existence of agriculture never stopped any colonisation in the world, on any continent whatsoever. To take just one example, North America was, at the time of contact, populated, depending on the area, by hunter-gatherer or farming societies, the latter sometimes being very dense. As for Africa, it was almost entirely agricultural, and moreover organized in States. In what way did this protect the populations from the greed of the conquerors?'—Christophe Darmangeat, '*Dark Emu: Aboriginal Australia and the Birth of Agriculture* (Bruce Pascoe)', *La Hutte des Classes*, 4 January 2020, https://cdarmangeat.blogspot.com/2020/01/dark-emu-bruce-pascoe.html (accessed 17 July 2020).

5 Gerritsen's book lacks an index so it is very hard to use as a reference work.

6 Paul Memmott, *Gunyah, Goondie + Wurley: The Aboriginal Architecture of Australia* (University of Queensland Press, 2007).

7 R Lauriston Sharp, *The Social Anthropology of a Totemic System in North Queensland, Australia*, PhD dissertation, Harvard University, 1937, pp. 27–8.

In the typed copy of this dissertation, Sharp did not mention the exceptional nonda plum. He later inserted it thus in a handwritten addition on the copy I have used: 'Only the nonda' (p. 28).

8 Philip A Clarke, *Aboriginal People and Their Plants* (Rosenberg, 2007), pp. 76–7.

9 Peter Sutton & Dermot Smyth, 'Ethnobotanical data from Aurukun Shire, Queensland' (mainframe computer printout, 1980).

10 Peter Sutton, 'Material culture traditions of the Wik people, Cape York Peninsula', *Records of the South Australian Museum* 27, 1994, p. 45. Similarly, for Central Australia, Latz and Griffin wrote: 'Foraging parties gathered sufficient food for their immediate requirements and only rarely stored food for later use' —Peter Latz & GF Griffin, 'Changes in Aboriginal land management in relation to fire and to food plants in Central Australia'. In BS Hetzel & HJ Frith (eds), *The Nutrition of Aborigines in Relation to the Ecosystem of Central Australia* (CSIRO, 1978), p. 79.

11 Bruce Pascoe, 'A real history of Aboriginal Australians, the first agriculturalists' [video], TEDxSydney, *TEDx Talks*, YouTube, 24 July 2018, https://youtu.be/ fqgrSSz7Htw (accessed 11 January 2020).

12 The fishing-hunting-gathering-gardening people of Torres Strait were different (see Chapter 6).

13 Yangzi and Yellow rivers about 9000 years ago (BP), New Guinea 9000–6000 BP, Sub-Saharan Africa 5000–4000 BP, Central Mexico and north-west South America 5000–4000 BP, and eastern USA 4000–3000 BP: see Peter Bellwood, *First Farmers: The Origins of Agricultural Societies* (Blackwell, 2005), p. 7. (BP means 'before present' and is used in archaeology to specify when events occurred before the advent of radiocarbon dating; the standard start date is 1 January 1950.)

14 Bellwood, p. 7.

15 Thomas Barfield (ed.), *The Dictionary of Anthropology* (Blackwell, 1997).

16 Barfield, p. 202.

17 Barfield, p. 244. This refers to an animal-drawn plough, not a hand-plough, we surmise.

18 Jeremy Beckett, *Torres Strait Islanders: Custom and Colonialism* (Cambridge University Press, 1987), pp. 28–9, 114; 'Torres Strait Islanders: Economy', *Countries and Their Cultures*, n.d., https://www.everyculture.com/Oceania/ Torres-Strait-Islanders-Economy.html (accessed 19 February 2020).

19 Barfield, p. 9.

20 Susie Beattie (ed.), *Collins German Dictionary and Grammar* (HarperCollins, 2014); DR Harris & GC Hillman (eds), *Foraging and Farming: The Evolution of Plant Exploitation* (Unwin Hyman, 1989), p. 19.

21 Bellwood, p. 13.

22 For further details, see chapters 4, 9, and 10 of this book.

23 Harry Lourandos, 'Review of *Australia and the Origins of Agriculture* by Rupert Gerritsen'. Australian Archaeological Association, 1 June 2010, https:// australianarchaeologicalassociation.com.au/journal/review-of-australia-and- the-origins-of-agriculture/ (accessed 27 February 2020).

24 Bellwood, p. 12.

25 AMT Moore, 'The transition from foraging to farming in Southwest Asia: Present problems and future directions'. In Harris & Hillman (eds), p. 628.

26 Ofer Bar-Yosef & Mordechai E Kislev, 'Early farming communities in the Jordan Valley'. In Harris & Hillman (eds), p. 632.

27 See Peter White, 'New Guinea and Australian prehistory: The "Neolithic" problem'. In DJ Mulvaney & J Golson (eds), *Aboriginal Man and Environment in Australia* (ANU Press, 1971), p. 187.

28 Clarke, 2007, pp. 127–32.

29 Harriet V Hunt, Hannah M Moots & Peter J Matthews, 'Genetic data confirms field evidence for natural breeding in a wild taro population (*Colocasia esculenta*) in northern Queensland, Australia', *Genetic Resources and Crop Evolution* 60, 2013, pp. 1695–707.

30 Ray Wood pers. comm., 13 July 2020. For other evidence of ancient east Papuan contact with the wider Cooktown area, see Ray Wood, '*Wangga*: The linguistic and typological evidence for the sources of the outrigger canoes of Torres Strait and Cape York Peninsula', *Oceania* 88, 2018, pp. 202–31.

31 Rhys Jones & Betty Meehan, 'Plant foods of the Gidjingali: Ethnographic and archaeological perspectives from northern Australia on tuber and seed exploitation', in Harris & Hillman (eds), p. 132; Tim Denham, Mark Donohue & Sara Booth, 'Horticultural experimentation on northern Australia reconsidered', *Antiquity* 83, 2009, pp. 643–5.

32 Bronislaw Malinowski, *Coral Gardens and Their Magic: A Study of the Methods of Tilling the Soil and of Agricultural Rites in the Trobriand Islands* (Allen & Unwin, 1935).

33 In a refereed paper, scholars in Western Australia have provided detailed evidence from the Kimberley of plants represented in ancient rock art. They concluded in part that there '[W]e have a society in which people actively chose not to pursue orthodox agriculture while according plants a central place in their lives' (Peter Veth et al., 'Plants before farming: The deep history of plant-use and representation in the rock art of Australia's Kimberley region', *Quaternary International* 30, 2016, p. 1).

34 Gammage, p. 301.

35 Gammage, p. 300.

36 Gammage, p. 301.

37 Fiona Jane Walsh, 'Review of R Gerritsen, *Australia and the Origins of Agriculture* (2008)', *GeoJournal* 74, 2009, p. 500.

38 Gammage's book has a large index but the following items are not among its entries: agriculture, cultivation, horticulture, sowing, planting; there are entries for farming, and for land management. Another method Gammage and Pascoe share is the preferencing of early explorer and settler accounts over the studies of anthropologists and archaeologists, and the reconstruction of vegetation history. This point was made by Professor of Archaeology Peter Hiscock in his review of Gammage (see Peter Hiscock, 'Creators or destroyers? The burning questions of human impact in ancient Aboriginal Australia', *Humanities Australia* 5, 2014, p. 45).

39 Clearly a journalist's error, given the limited range of palm trees. The commonest materials were bark, boughs, posts and grass.

40 Barbara McMahon, 'Scientist debunks nomadic Aborigine "myth"', *The Guardian*, 9 October 2007, https://www.theguardian.com/world/2007/oct/09/australia.barbaramcmahon (accessed 20 December 2019).

41 Helen Clemens, 'The Aborigines: Hunter-gatherers: Why not agriculturists?' In Christine Haigh & Wendy Goldstein (eds), *The Aborigines of New South Wales* (NSW National Parks & Wildlife Service, 1980), pp. 52–3. Archaeologists John Mulvaney and Johan Kamminga expressed a similar view in their *Prehistory of Australia* (Allen & Unwin, 1999), p. 87.

42 Philip Clarke, *Where the Ancestors Walked: Australia as an Aboriginal Landscape* (Allen & Unwin, 2003).

43 Other texts for the general reader that cover most if not all of the same topics have been the bestseller by Geoffrey Blainey, *Triumph of the Nomads: A History of Ancient Australia* (Macmillan, 1983; 1st edn 1975), and Josephine Flood's *Archaeology of the Dreamtime: The Story of Prehistoric Australia and Its People* (JB Publishing, 2006).

44 Thomas Worsnop, *The Prehistoric Arts, Manufactures, Works, Weapons, etc., of the Aborigines of Australia* (CE Bristow, Government Printer, 1897), p. 102.

45 George Horne and George Aiston in *Savage Life in Central Australia* (Macmillan, 1924) describe a wall of stakes being used to divert fish into nets (p. 64). Altman in *Hunter-Gatherers Today: An Aboriginal Economy in North Australia* (AIAS, 1987) provides photos of the making of a conical fish trap and the related creek-trapping fence inland from Maningrida in the period 1979–81 (pp. 124–5).

46 The rest of the fence can be seen in another photo in Roslyn Poignant & Axel Poignant, *Encounter at Nagalarramba* (National Library of Australia, 1996), on p. 63.

47 A similar limitation applies to Peter O'Brien's *Bitter Harvest: The Illusion of Aboriginal Agriculture in Bruce Pascoe's* Dark Emu (2nd edn, Quadrant Books, 2020), a pugnacious polemical assessment of *Dark Emu*. While O'Brien relies on Mitchell, Sturt, Grey, Davis, McKinlay, Giles, King and other explorers, and on colonial lay observers such as Tench, Hunter, Beveridge, Robinson and Kirby, extremely few anthropologists or archaeologists other than self-taught ethnographers Howitt, Dawson and Basedow manage to make an appearance.

48 Ian Keen, *Aboriginal Economy and Society: Australia at the Threshold of Colonisation* (Oxford University Press, 2004).

49 See Bruce Pascoe, *Young Dark Emu: A Truer History* (Magabala Books, 2019) and Simone Barlow & Ashlee Horyniak, *Dark Emu in the Classroom: Teacher Resources for High School Geography* (Magabala Books, 2019).

50 Sometimes a work is mentioned in the text but is missing from the references, such as Rhys Jones's paper 'Fire-stick farming' (in Australian *Natural History* 16(7), 1969, pp. 224–8), a seminal contribution to Pascoe's core subject: the pre-colonial Aboriginal management of country and its resources.

Chapter 2: Spiritual propagation

1 Kenneth Maddock, *The Australian Aborigines: A Portrait of Their Society* (Allen Lane / The Penguin Press, 1972), p. 25.

2 Athol Chase, 'Belonging to country: Territory, identity and environment in Cape York Peninsula, northern Australia'. In LR Hiatt (ed.), *Aboriginal Landowners* (Oceania, 1984), p. 114.

3 Elizabeth Povinelli, *Labor's Lot: The Power, History, and Culture of Aboriginal Action* (Chicago University Press, 1993)—for example, p. 153.

4 R Lauriston Sharp, 'Ritual life and economics of the Yir-Yoront tribe of Cape York Peninsula', *Oceania* 5, 1934b, pp. 30–1.

5 R Lauriston Sharp, 'The social organization of the Yir-Yoront tribe, Cape York Peninsula', *Oceania* 4, 1934a, p. 409.

6 Ursula H McConnel, *Myths of the Muŋkan* (Melbourne University Press, 1957), pp. 2–11.

7 McConnel, 1957, p. 2.

8 Ursula H McConnel, 'The Wik-Munkan tribe, Part 2: Totemism', *Oceania* 1, 1930b, p. 187.

9 In the Cape York Peninsula language Umpithamu, the word for 'to activate' an increase site is *uympan*, otherwise used for 'to wake someone up' or 'to herd fish into a drag net by frightening them' (J-C Verstraete pers. comm., 31 May 2020).

10 Peter Sutton et al., *Aak: Aboriginal Estates and Clans between the Embley and Edward Rivers, Cape York Peninsula* (unpublished report; South Australian Museum, 1990); Peter Sutton, David Martin & John von Sturmer, 'Supplementary site report', Appendix 3 of *The Wik Peoples Native Title Determination Application QC94/3* (unpublished report; Cape York Land Council, 1997).

11 On demand-sharing among the living, see Nicolas Peterson, 'Demand sharing: Reciprocity and the pressure for generosity among foragers', *American Anthropologist* 95, 1993, pp. 860–74.

12 Sutton et al., 1990, pp. 283–4.

13 Sutton et al., 1990, pp. 562–3 and photo facing p. 562.

14 David Martin's record is in Sutton et al., 1990, p. 418 and photo of ritual facing p. 416.

15 Sutton et al., 1990, p. 555.

16 Peter Sutton, *Wik-Ngathan Dictionary* (Caitlin Press, 1995), p. 19.

17 Ursula McConnel, 'Native arts and industries on the Archer, Kendall and Holroyd rivers, Cape York Peninsula, north Queensland', *Records of the South Australian Museum* 11, 1953, pp. 1–42, plates I–XVII.

18 Peter Sutton, 'Material culture traditions of the Wik people, Cape York Peninsula', *Records of the South Australian Museum* 27, 1994, pp. 31–52.

19 Caroline Tennant Kelly, 'Tribes on Cherburg [*sic*] settlement, Queensland', *Oceania* 5, 1935, pp. 461–73.

20 Lindsey Page Winterbotham, 'The Gaiarbau story: Some native customs and beliefs of the Jinibara tribe as well as those of some of their neighbours in south-east Queensland'. In G Langevad (ed.), *Queensland Ethnohistorical Transcripts* 1(1), 1982, p. 129.

21 Winterbotham, p. 82.

22 AR Radcliffe-Brown, 'Notes on totemism in eastern Australia', *Journal of the Royal Anthropological Institute* 59, 1929, pp. 401, 406.

23 Radcliffe-Brown, 1929, pp. 401–7.

24 Peter Sutton, 'Aboriginal ceremonial sites of New South Wales', unpublished report for National Parks and Wildlife Service of New South Wales, 1985.

25 AW Howitt, *The Native Tribes of South-east Australia* (Macmillan, 1904), p. 399.

26 Ian Keen, *Aboriginal Economy and Society: Australia at the Threshold of Colonisation* (Oxford University Press, 2004), pp. 219–20, 225, 227–8 and 232 respectively.

27 Ronald M Berndt, *Australian Aboriginal Religion* (EJ Brill, 1974), Fascicle 1, p. 26.

28 Robert Tonkinson, *The Mardu Aborigines: Living the Dream in Australia's Desert* (Fort Worth, TX: Holt, Rinehart & Winston, 1991), p. 37.

29 Lorraine Mortimer, *Roger Sandall's Films and Contemporary Anthropology: Explorations in the Aesthetic, the Existential, and the Possible* (Bloomington, IN: Indiana University Press, 2019), p. 70.

30 Ronald M Berndt & Catherine H Berndt, *The World of the First Australians: Aboriginal Traditional Life, Past and Present*, 4th rev. edn with additions (Aboriginal Studies Press, 1988), pp. 269–73.

31 AP Elkin, 'Cult-totemism and mythology in northern South Australia', *Oceania* 5, 1934, p. 177.

32 Elkin, 1934, p. 186.

33 Elkin, 1934, p. 189.

34 G Horne & G Aiston, *Savage Life in Central Australia* (Macmillan, 1924), pp. 133–4.

35 Horne & Aiston, p. 134.

36 Mervyn Meggitt, *Desert People: A Study of the Walbiri Aborigines of Central Australia* (Angus & Robertson, 1962), p. 220.

37 Meggitt, p. 221.

38 David Nash pers. comm., 14 January 2020.

39 Brian Geytenbeek & Helen Geytenbeek, *Gidabal Grammar and Dictionary* (AIAS, 1971), p. 53. Their spelling is *biřbanj*.

40 Peter Latz, *Bushfires & Bushtucker: Aboriginal Plant Use in Central Australia* (IAD Press, 1995), p. 69. About 200 plants are discussed in the book.

41 Norman B Tindale, 'The Pitjandjara'. In MG Bicchieri (ed.), *Hunters and Gatherers Today: A Socioeconomic Study of Eleven Such Cultures in the Twentieth Century* (Holt, Rinehart & Winston, 1972), p. 234.

42 Baldwin Spencer & FJ Gillen, *The Native Tribes of Central Australia* (Macmillan, 1899), pp. 167–211. See also John Morton, 'The effectiveness of totemism: "Increase ritual" and resource control in Central Australia', *Man* (New Series) 22, 1987, pp. 453–74.

43 Morton, p. 456.

44 Petronella Vaarzon-Morel pers. comm., 15 January 2020.

45 The writing on one of the eggs in the photo on p. 36 says: 20 M Nth WEST OF / YALKAWARDALINA / WATER HOLE SA / SIMPSON DESERT—66.

46 Tom McCourt, *Aboriginal Artefacts* (Rigby, 1975), p. 125.

47 TGH Strehlow, 'Culture, social structure, and environment in Aboriginal Central Australia'. In RM Berndt & CH Berndt (eds), *Aboriginal Man in Australia: Essays in Honour of Emeritus Professor AP Elkin* (Angus & Robertson, 1965), p. 144.

48 Strehlow, p. 144.
49 Isobel White in Daisy M Bates (ed. Isobel White), *The Native Tribes of Western Australia* (National Library of Australia, 1985), p. 89.
50 Bates, pp. 199–200.
51 Bates, p. 202.
52 Bates, p. 212.
53 Bates, p. 203.
54 Phyllis Kaberry, *Aboriginal Woman, Sacred and Profane* (George Routledge & Sons, 1939), pp. 203–7.
55 Kaberry, p. 203.
56 Kaberry, p. 177.
57 Kim Akerman, *From the Bukarikara: The Lore of the Southwest Kimberley through the Art of Butcher Joe Nangan* (UWA Publishing, 2020), p. 11.
58 Radcliffe-Brown, 1929, p. 399.
59 Ralph Piddington, 'Totemic system of the Karadjeri tribe', *Oceania* 4, 1932, pp. 376–93; AP Elkin, 'Totemism in north-western Australia (the Kimberley division)', *Oceania* 3, 1933, pp. 284–96.
60 A common name originating in the Pilbara, not a Karajarri name. In Karajarri it is *yarrinyarri* (KR McKelson, *Studies in Karajarri*, unpublished ms, Australian Institute of Aboriginal and Torres Strait Islander Studies, Canberra, 1989, p. 10). *Yarrinyarri* is *Cyperus bulbosis*, known also as nutgrass and onion-grass or yelka; Philip A Clarke, *Aboriginal People and Their Plants* (Rosenberg, 2007), pp. 24, 39, 41, 74.
61 Pebbles ('magic stones') were also scattered by people in the Lake Eyre region in order to make the yelka grow (Horne & Aiston, p. 53).
62 Piddington, p. 391.
63 Clarke, p. 74.
64 AR Radcliffe-Brown, 'Three tribes of Western Australia', *Journal of the Royal Anthropological Institute* 43, 1913, p. 160.
65 Radcliffe-Brown, 1913, p. 167.
66 WEH Stanner, *On Aboriginal Religion* (Oceania Monograph No. 11, 1963), p. 31 also said 'increase' sites 'were not developed to any extent in the region', referring to the region just to the west of Daly River in the area of Port Keats.
67 Photographs and description in Peter Sutton & Arthur Palmer, *Daly River (Malak Malak) Land Claim* (Northern Land Council, 1980), pp. 70–2.
68 Ronald M Berndt & Catherine H Berndt, *Man, Land and Myth in North Australia: The Gunwinggu People* (Ure Smith, 1970), pp. 147, 216.
69 Francesca Merlan, *Caging the Rainbow: Places, Politics, and Aborigines in a North Australian Town* (University of Hawai'i Press, 1998), pp. 95–6.
70 Jon C Altman, *Hunter-Gatherers Today: An Aboriginal Economy in North Australia* (AIAS, 1987), p. 219.
71 Geoffrey Bagshaw pers. comm., 20 January 2020. Lily Gurambara gave this information to Bagshaw, an anthropologist with long and deep experience of the Maningrida region, who translated it for me from Burarra.
72 Jeffrey Heath, *Nunggubuyu Dictionary* (AIAS, 1982), p. 43.
73 Jeffrey Heath, *Nunggubuyu Myths and Ethnographic Texts* (AIAS, 1980), p. 283.

74 Translated by Heath, a professional linguist who made a detailed study of the
     language. Other texts by a senior man called Ma:di on increase ceremonies are
     at Heath, 1980, pp. 279–83. Biographical notes on Yurumura and Ma:di are at
     Heath, 1980, pp. 8–9.
75 Heath, 1980, pp. 278–9.
76 Heath, 1980, pp. 284–90.
77 W Lloyd Warner, *A Black Civilization: A Social Study of an Australian Tribe*
     (Harper & Brothers, 1937), pp. 39–51.
78 Warner, p. 410.
79 But see Warner, p. 311.
80 Ian Keen, *Knowledge and Secrecy in an Aboriginal Religion* (Clarendon Press,
     1994), p. 267.
81 Berndt, 1974, Fascicle 4, p. 9.
82 Berndt, 1974, Fascicle 4, p. 26. Readers are warned that this publication con-
     tains religious material restricted to adult men only.
83 John Bradley, 'The social, economic and historical construction of cycad palms
     among the Yanyuwa'. In B David, B Barker & IJ McNiven (eds), *The Social
     Archaeology of Australian Indigenous Societies* (Aboriginal Studies Press, 2006),
     p. 177. 'Too many' in Aboriginal Kriol does not mean an excess, but merely
     plenty or many.
84 Bradley, pp. 163–4.
85 Bradley, p. 168.
86 Geoffrey Bagshaw pers. comm., 15 January 2020.
87 Sutton, 1995, p. 48.
88 From my own fieldwork in the area 1999–2000.
89 Cf. L Head, D D'Costa & P Edney, 'Pleistocene dates for volcanic activ-
     ity in Western Victoria and implications for Aboriginal occupation'. In
     MAJ Williams, P de Deckker & AP Kershaw (eds), *The Cainozoic in Australia:
     A Reappraisal of the Evidence* (Geological Society of Australia, 1991), pp. 302–8.
90 Paul Memmott & Robyn Horsman, *A Changing Culture: The Lardil Aborigines
     of Mornington Island* (Social Science Press, 1991), p. 163.
91 Paul Memmott et al., 'Fission, fusion and syncretism: Linguistic and environmen-
     tal changes amongst the Tangkic people of the southern Gulf of Carpentaria,
     northern Australia'. In J-C Verstraete & D Hafner (eds), *Land and Language in
     Cape York Peninsula and the Gulf Country* (John Benjamins, 2016), p. 128.
92 Nicolas Peterson pers. comm., 13 January 2020.

Chapter 3: The language question

 1 Peter Austin, 'Diyari language postcards and Diyari literacy', *Aboriginal
     History* 10(2), 1986, p. 176; Peter Austin, *A Grammar of Diyari, South Australia*
     (Cambridge University Press, 1981).
 2 David R Moore, 'Cape York Aborigines and Islanders of western Torres
     Strait', in D Walker (ed.), *Bridge and Barrier: The Natural and Cultural History
     of Torres Strait* (Australian National University, 1972), pp. 327–43; David R
     Moore, *Islanders and Aborigines at Cape York* (AIAS, 1979), pp. 268–85; David
     R Harris, 'Subsistence strategies across Torres Strait', in J Allen, J Golson &

R Jones (eds), *Sunda and Sahul: Prehistoric Studies in Southeast Asia, Melanesia and Australia* (Academic Press, 1977), pp. 441–8; Jeremy Beckett, *Torres Strait Islanders: Custom and Colonialism* (Cambridge University Press, 1987), pp. 28–9, 114; Athol Chase, 'Domestication and domiculture in northern Australia: A social perspective', in DR Harris & GC Hillman (eds), *Foraging and Farming: The Evolution of Plant Exploitation* (Unwin Hyman, 1989), p. 45.

3 Nicholas Thieberger & William McGregor, *Macquarie Aboriginal Words: A Dictionary of Words from Australian Aboriginal and Torres Strait Islander Languages* (The Macquarie Library, 1994), p. 613.

4 Thieberger & McGregor, pp. 344, 630.

5 RMW Dixon, *Australian Languages: Their Nature and Development* (Cambridge University Press, 2002), pp. xxx–xxxi.

6 Dixon, p. xxx.

7 In volume 2 of his classic work on the horticultural Trobriand Islanders of New Guinea, a volume called *The Language of Magic and Gardening*, Malinowski laid great stress on language as a pathway into the culture, including presenting a detailed vocabulary of plant cultivation that included terms for 'garden under cultivation', 'garden plot' and 'land intended for cultivation'—see Bronislaw Malinowski, *Coral Gardens and Their Magic: A Study of the Methods of Tilling the Soil and of Agricultural Rites in the Trobriand Islands* (Allen & Unwin, 1935), vol. 2, pp. 86–7.

8 Page numbers in tables 1 and 2 refer to Sidney H Ray, *Reports of the Cambridge Anthropological Expedition to Torres Straits. Vol. III: Linguistics* (Cambridge University Press, 1907). In line 1, 'M' indicates the Muralag dialect; in line 2, 'K' indicates Kiwai, a New Guinea language.

9 Nick Piper pers. comm., 29 January 2020 adds *memeg barki*, 'fallow land, empty of food'.

10 Piper pers. comm., 29 January 2020: *kar-iruk*.

11 Piper pers. comm., 29 January 2020 says verb for 'to clear land' is *igeb*.

12 Piper pers. comm., 29 January 2020 says 'not so much an object as keeping quiet about your planting time'.

13 Piper pers. comm., 29 January 2020: probably the word *wez*, 'croton plant, to mark your garden and ownership'.

14 Donald F Thomson, 'The hero cult, initiation and totemism on Cape York', *Journal of the Royal Anthropological Institute* 63, 1933, pp. 453–537.

15 Ray Wood, '*Wangga*: The linguistic and typological evidence for the sources of the outrigger canoes of Torres Strait and Cape York Peninsula', *Oceania* 88, 2018, pp. 202–31.

16 Barry J Blake, Ian Clark & Sharnthi H Krishna-Pillay, 'Wathawurrung: The language of the Geelong-Ballarat area'. In BJ Blake (ed.), *Wathawurrung and the Colac Language of Southern Victoria* (Pacific Linguistics, 1998), p. 110. Blake (pers. comm., 28 January 2020) does not know the etymology for this expression.

17 The languages are Adnyamathanha, Alawa, Alyawarr, Anmatyerr, Arabana, Arrernte (East and Central), Awabakal, Bandjalang, Bardi, Barngarla, Bunganditj, Burarra, Flinders Island language, Gathang, Githabal, Guugu-Yimidhirr, Jingulu, Kayardild, Kaytetye, Martu Wangka, Morrobolam,

Mudburra, Muruwari, Ngaanyatjarra/Ngaatjatjarra, Ngarinyman, Ngarrindjeri, Noongar (Nyungar), Nunggubuyu (Wubuy), Nyulnyul, Pintupi/Luritja, Tiwi, Umpithamu, Warrnambool language, Wathawurrung, Western Desert (Balgo), Western Desert (Warburton), Western Kulin, Wik-Mungkan, Wik-Ngathan, Wiradjuri, Yawuru, Yaygir, Yidiny, Yintyingka, Yir-Yoront.

18 Rose Whitehurst, *Noongar Dictionary: Noongar to English and English to Noongar* (Noongar Language and Culture Centre, 1992), p. 22.

19 Kathleen Glasgow, *Burarra–Gun-nartpa Dictionary with English Finder List* (Summer Institute of Linguistics, 1994), p. 447.

20 Lily Gurambara via Geoffrey Bagshaw pers. comm., 15 January 2020. CC Macknight, *The Voyage to Marege': Macassan Trepangers in Northern Australia* (Melbourne University Press, 1976), pp. 59, 157 (endnote 54).

21 Jenny Green, *Central & Eastern Anmatyerr to English Dictionary* (IAD Press, 2010), p. 50.

22 Rob Pensalfini, *Jingulu Texts and Dictionary* (Pacific Linguistics, 2011), p. 129.

23 Pensalfini, p. 120.

24 Myfany Turpin & Alison Ross, *Kaytetye to English Dictionary* (IAD Press, 2012), pp. 300–1.

25 Jennifer R Lee, *Ngawurranungurumagi Nginingawila Ngapangiraga: Tiwi–English Dictionary* (Nguiu Nginingawila Literature Production Centre, 1993), pp. 292, 346; Stan Grant (Snr) & John Rudder, *A New Wiradjuri Dictionary* (Restoration House, 2010), p. 152.

26 Grant & Rudder, p. 307.

27 Grant & Rudder, p. 286.

28 Grant & Rudder, p. 387.

29 Grant & Rudder, p. 219.

30 Grant & Rudder, p. 234.

31 Robert Amery pers. comm., 27 January 2020.

Chapter 4: Ecological agents and 'firestick farming'

1 Rhys Jones, 'Fire-stick farming', *Australian Natural History* 16(7), 1969, pp. 226, 228.

2 Norman B Tindale, 'Ecology of primitive aboriginal man in Australia'. In A Keast, RL Crocker & CS Christian (eds), *Biogeography and Ecology in Australia* (Junk, 1959), pp. 42–3.

3 Frederick D McCarthy, 'Ecology, equipment, economy and trade'. In Helen Sheils (ed.), *Australian Aboriginal Studies: A Symposium of Papers Presented at the 1961 Research Conference* (Oxford University Press, 1963), pp. 171–91.

4 Ronald M Berndt & Catherine H Berndt, *The World of the First Australians: An Introduction to the Traditional Life of the Australian Aborigines*, 1st edn (Ure Smith, 1964), p. 95.

5 Ronald M Berndt & Catherine H Berndt, *The World of the First Australians: Aboriginal Traditional Life, Past and Present*, 4th rev. edn with additions (Aboriginal Studies Press, 1988), p. 110.

6 Bill Gammage, *The Biggest Estate on Earth: How Aborigines Made Australia* (Allen & Unwin, 2011), p. 284.

7 Gammage, p. 3.

8 Tindale, 1959, p. 43.

9 Rhys Jones, 'The Neolithic, Palaeolithic and the hunting gardeners: Man and land in the antipodes'. In RP Suggate & MM Creswell (eds), *Quaternary Studies* (Royal Society of New Zealand, 1975), p. 25.

10 Jones, 1969, p. 226.

11 Jones, 1969, p. 227.

12 Jones, 1975, p. 28.

13 Rhys Jones, 'Mindjongork: Legacy of the firestick'. In DB Rose (ed.), *Country in Flames: Proceedings of the 1994 Symposium on Biodiversity and Fire in North Australia* (Department of the Environment, Sport and Territories / North Australia Research Unit, Australian National University, 1995), p. 14.

14 Jones, 1995, p. 15. As Marcia Langton observed, 'The disputes over garden plot boundaries played a significant role both in their status under colonial and post-Federation Australia and in their land tenure traditions which were recognised partially under the Torres Strait Islander Land Act 1993, and at common law with respect to Mer or Murray Island following the Mabo No 2 case decided by the High Court. It was this extensive court record of land disputes that provided a wealth of evidence supporting their claim to native title heard first by the Queensland Supreme Court.' See Marcia Langton, *An Aboriginal Ontology of Being and Place: The Performance of Aboriginal Property Relations in the Princess Charlotte Bay Area of Eastern Cape York Peninsula, Australia*, PhD thesis, Macquarie University, 2005, p. 147.

15 Silas Wolmby on the left, Morrison Wolmby on the right, children possibly Perry and Ursula Yunkaporta. The raised clod of clay was where Noel Peemuggina had checked for the presence of red ochre.

16 Petronella Vaarzon-Morel & Kasia Gabrys, 'Fire on the horizon: Contemporary Aboriginal burning issues in the Tanami Desert, Central Australia', *GeoJournal* 74, 2009, pp. 469–70.

17 Peter Latz & GF Griffin, 'Changes in Aboriginal land management in relation to fire and to food plants in Central Australia'. In BS Hetzel & HJ Frith (eds), *The Nutrition of Aborigines in Relation to the Ecosystem of Central Australia* (CSIRO, 1978), p. 78.

18 Dean Yibarbuk, 'Introductory essay: Notes on traditional use of fire on upper Cadell River'. In Marcia Langton, *Burning Questions: Emerging Environmental Issues for Indigenous Peoples in Northern Australia* (Northern Territory University, 1998), pp. 1–6.

19 Vaarzon-Morel & Gabrys.

20 Philip A Clarke, *Aboriginal People and Their Plants* (Rosenberg, 2007), pp. 60–71.

21 Nancy M Williams & Eugene S Hunn, *Resource Managers: North American and Australian Hunter-Gatherers* (Westview Press, 1982), p. 1.

22 Langton, 1998, p. 39.

23 Marcia Langton, 'Earth, wind, fire, water: The social and spiritual construction of water in Aboriginal societies'. In B David, B Barker & IJ McNiven (eds), *The Social Archaeology of Australian Indigenous Societies* (Aboriginal Studies Press, 2006), p. 140.

24 Marcia Langton, 'Botanists, Aborigines and native plants on the Queensland frontier'. In J-C Verstraete & D Hafner (eds), *Land and Language in Cape York Peninsula and the Gulf Country* (John Benjamins, 2016), p. 221.

25 Langton, 2005.

26 Norman B Tindale, *Aboriginal Tribes of Australia: Their Terrain, Environmental Controls, Distribution, Limits, and Proper Names* (University of California Press, 1974), pp. 94, 95.

27 Phyllis Kaberry, *Aboriginal Woman, Sacred and Profane* (George Routledge & Sons, 1939), pp. 20, 24.

28 Quoted in Stephanie Anderson, *Pelletier: The Forgotten Castaway of Cape York* (Melbourne Books, 2009), p. 163.

29 Anderson, p. 317.

30 Anderson, p. 312.

31 Anderson, p. 272. On p. 273 Anderson provides a note by Athol Chase, citing Chase and Peter Sutton ('Hunter-gatherers in a rich environment: Aboriginal coastal exploitation in Cape York Peninsula', in A Keast (ed.), *Ecological Biogeography of Australia*, W Junk, 1981, pp. 1817–52), who describe a different management practice in relation to yams, namely removing the tuber but leaving the stem and vine in place to encourage a continuing supply.

32 Tindale, 1974, pp. 94–109, 126, 145.

33 Tindale, 1974, p. 104.

34 Cf. Frederick GG Rose, *The Traditional Mode of Production of the Australian Aborigines* (Angus & Robertson, 1987), p. 58.

35 Peter Bellwood, *First Farmers: The Origins of Agricultural Societies* (Blackwell, 2005), pp. 16–17.

36 Robert Layton, Robert Foley & Elizabeth Williams, 'The transition between hunting and gathering and specialized husbandry of resources', *Current Anthropology* 32, 1991, p. 262.

37 Layton, Foley & Williams, p. 261.

38 Layton, Foley & Williams, p. 261.

39 Transhumance is the seasonal movement of livestock between lowlands and adjacent mountains.

40 Ian Keen, *Aboriginal Economy and Society: Australia at the Threshold of Colonisation* (Oxford University Press, 2004), p. 97.

41 Ian Keen pers. comm., 6 July 2020. He details his reasons in Keen, 'Foragers or farmers: *Dark Emu* and the debate over Aboriginal agriculture', *Anthropological Forum*, 2021, DOI: 10.1080/00664677.2020.1861538.

42 See especially Keen, 2004, pp. 30–44.

43 WEH Stanner, *After the Dreaming: The 1968 Boyer Lectures* (ABC, 1969), p. 36.

44 Peter Sutton, 'Australian anthropologists and political action 1925–1960', *Oceania* 79, 2009, pp. 202–17.

45 Athol Chase, 'Domestication and domiculture in northern Australia: A social perspective'. In DR Harris & GC Hillman (eds), *Foraging and Farming: The Evolution of Plant Exploitation* (Unwin Hyman, 1989), p. 52.

46 Rev. Amos Brazier, 'Report on Lake Condah Mission', quoted in Aldo Massola, *Aboriginal Mission Stations in Victoria* (Hawthorn Press, 1970), p. 100.

47 Francis Xavier Gsell, *'"The Bishop with 150 Wives": Fifty Years as a Missionary* (Angus & Robertson, 1955), p. 54.

48 Wilbur S Chaseling, *Yulengor: Nomads of Arnhem Land* (Epworth Press, 1957), p. 17.

49 IG (Ella) Shepherdson, *Half a Century in Arnhem Land* (One Tree Hill, SA: Ella & Harold Shepherdson, 1981), p. 91.

50 Berndt & Berndt, 1988, p. 108.

51 Berndt & Berndt, 1988, pp. 108–9.

52 Berndt & Berndt, 1988, p. 109.

53 Christopher Anderson pers. comm., 8 February 2020.

54 Ann E Wells, *Milingimbi: Ten Years in the Crocodile Islands of Arnhem Land* (Angus & Robertson, 1963), p. 41.

55 Lazarus Lamilami, *Lamilami Speaks: The Cry Went Up: A Story of the People of Goulburn Islands, North Australia* (Ure Smith, 1974), p. 93. There are in my memory also cases where people took up private farming after learning it on missions, in the cases of Coranderrk, Poonindie and Point McLeay, but I have been unable to locate written evidence in time for this book.

Chapter 5: Social evolutionism rebirthed

1 Tom Griffiths, 'Reading Bruce Pascoe', *Inside Story*, 26 November 2019, https://insidestory.org.au/reading-bruce-pascoe/ (accessed 20 January 2020).

2 Apart from pubic tassels, various adornments and belts, perhaps the most common body covering was fat, animal grease retrieved from game—often mixed with pigments as decoration. This functioned as protection against chill conditions and biting insects, and was also an enhancement of one's appearance.

3 W Lloyd Warner, *A Black Civilization: A Social Study of an Australian Tribe* (Harper & Brothers, 1937), p. 475.

4 Warner, p. 477.

5 Rupert Gerritsen, *Australia and the Origins of Agriculture* (British Archaeological Reports, 2008), p. 71.

6 Ken Maddock notably wrote a chapter called 'The defensibility of Aboriginal society' in his *The Australian Aborigines: A Portrait of Their Society* (Allen Lane / The Penguin Press, 1972, pp. 177–94), in which he compared the freedoms of the old society with the lack of it in modern states. The argument might have been extended to economics.

7 Layton, Foley and Williams wrote of 'the usefulness of treating hunting and gathering, herding, and [plant] cultivation as alternative strategies which are, singly or in combination, appropriate to social or natural environments' (Robert Layton, Robert Foley & Elizabeth Williams, 'The transition between hunting and gathering and specialized husbandry of resources', *Current Anthropology* 32, 1991, p. 255).

8 Heather Builth, *Ancient Aboriginal Aquaculture Rediscovered* (Lambert Academic Publishing, 2014), p. 514.

9 Griffiths.

10 'Brewarrina Aboriginal fish traps: Creation story' (n.d.), in *Wikipedia*, https://en.wikipedia.org/wiki/Brewarrina_Aboriginal_Fish_Traps#Creation_story (accessed 14 February 2020).

11 Roger Cribb et al., 'Landscape as cultural artefact: Shell mounds and plants in Aurukun, Cape York Peninsula', *Australian Aboriginal Studies* 2, 1988, pp. 60–73.

12 R Lauriston Sharp, 'Steel axes for stone-age Australians'. In TG Harding & BJ Wallace (eds), *Cultures of the Pacific: Selected Readings* (The Free Press, 1970), pp. 394–5.

13 Harry Allen, 'The Bagundji of the Darling Basin: Cereal gatherers in an uncertain environment', *World Archaeology* 5, 1974, p. 317.

14 Donald F Thomson, *Economic Structure and the Ceremonial Exchange Cycle in Arnhem Land* (Macmillan, 1949), p. 7.

15 Mike Smith, *The Archaeology of Australia's Deserts* (Cambridge University Press, 2013), pp. 202, 210–11, 287.

16 Luise Hercus & Peter Clarke, 'Nine Simpson Desert wells', *Archaeology in Oceania* 21, 1986, p. 58.

17 Eric Rolls, *Epic Rolls* (unpublished manuscript, 2009), Chapter 7, p. 7. [Further details unknown. Citation after Pascoe, 2014, p. 169.]

18 Smith, p. 85.

19 Bruce Pascoe, *Young Dark Emu: A Truer History* (Magabala Books, 2019a), p. 16.

20 Pascoe, 2019a, p. 16.

21 Federation of Bakers, *Factsheet no. 9: The History of Bread*, Federation of Bakers Ltd, London, 2011, https://www.fob.uk.com/wp-content/uploads/2017/01/FS-9-History-of-Bread.pdf (accessed 6 August 2020); Peter Bellwood, *First Farmers: The Origins of Agricultural Societies* (Blackwell, 2005), p. 101.

22 Matthew Connellan, '"Clearly wrong": Bruce Pascoe on what people get wrong about Australian Indigenous history', *NITV Radio*, 5 July 2019, https://www.sbs.com.au/language/english/clearly-wrong-bruce-pascoe-on-what-people-get-wrong-about-australian-indigenous-history (accessed 7 July 2020).

Chapter 6: The agriculture debate

1 Ian Keen, *Aboriginal Economy and Society: Australia at the Threshold of Colonisation* (Oxford University Press, 2004), p. 97; Ian Keen, 'Foragers or farmers: *Dark Emu* and the debate over Aboriginal agriculture', *Anthropological Forum*, 2021, DOI: 10.1080/00664677.2020.1861538.

2 For example, Elizabeth Williams, *Complex Hunter-Gatherers: A Late Holocene Example from Temperate Australia* (British Archaeological Reports, 1988).

3 Eleanor Leacock & Richard Lee, *Politics and History in Band Societies* (Cambridge University Press, 1982).

4 Lesley Head, *Second Nature: The History and Implications of Australia as Aboriginal Landscape* (Syracuse University Press, 2000), p. 40.

5 Rhys Jones, 'The Neolithic, Palaeolithic and the hunting gardeners: Man and land in the antipodes'. In RP Suggate & MM Creswell (eds), *Quaternary Studies* (Royal Society of New Zealand, 1975), p. 24.

6 Norman B Tindale, *Aboriginal Tribes of Australia: Their Terrain, Environmental Controls, Distribution, Limits, and Proper Names* (University of California Press, 1974), p. 99.

7 DS Davidson & FD McCarthy, 'The distribution of stone implements in Western Australia', *Anthropos* 52, 1957, p. 440. Tindale's 1974 grasslands map and the Davidson and McCarthy millstones map were combined to form a composite map in Mike Smith, *The Archaeology of Australia's Deserts* (Cambridge University Press, 2013), p. 190, Figure 6.9c; see the map on p. 77.

8 Harry Allen, 'The Bagundji of the Darling Basin: Cereal gatherers in an uncertain environment', *World Archaeology* 5, 1974, pp. 312–14.

9 Allen, pp. 316–18.

10 Roger Lawrence, *Aboriginal Habitat and Economy* (Department of Geography, ANU, 1968).

11 Norman B Tindale & HA Lindsay, *Aboriginal Australians* (Jacaranda Press, 1963), p. 121.

12 Jones, p. 23.

13 Ursula McConnel, 'Native arts and industries on the Archer, Kendall and Holroyd rivers, Cape York Peninsula, north Queensland', *Records of the South Australian Museum* 11, 1953, p. 7.

14 McConnel, p. 1.

15 See Peter Sutton, 'Ursula McConnel's tin trunk: A remarkable recovery', *Transactions of the Royal Society of South Australia* 134, 2010c, pp. 101–14.

16 Peter Sutton & Dermot Smyth, 'Ethnobotanical data from Aurukun Shire, Queensland' (mainframe computer printout, 1980); Peter Sutton, 'Linguistic aspects of ethnobotanical research', in B Rigsby & P Sutton (eds), *Contributions to Australian Linguistics* (Pacific Linguistics, 1980), pp. 303–14; Peter Sutton, *Wik-Ngathan Dictionary* (Caitlin Press, 1995); Athol Chase & Peter Sutton, 'Hunter-gatherers in a rich environment: Aboriginal coastal exploitation in Cape York Peninsula', in A Keast (ed.), *Ecological Biogeography of Australia* (The Hague: W Junk, 1981), pp. 1817–52.

17 *Dioscorea transversa* and *D. bulbifera*. Plant ecologist Dr Len Webb relayed Aurukun missionary William MacKenzie's information on the subject to Alastair Campbell. MacKenzie wrote: 'I made careful enquiries from the old folk but was told that only those two roots were replanted'; see Alastair H Campbell, 'Elementary food production by the Australian Aborigines', *Mankind* 6, 1965, p. 208.

18 Edward Palmer, 'On plants used by the natives of north Queensland, Flinders and Mitchell Rivers, for food, medicine, &c., &c.', *Journal and Proceedings of the Royal Society of New South Wales* 17, 1883, p. 93.

19 JH Maiden, *The Useful Plants of Australia (including Tasmania)* (Turner & Henderson, 1889).

20 Leonard J Webb, *Guide to the Medicinal and Poisonous Plants of Queensland* (Commonwealth of Australia: Council for Scientific and Industrial Research Bulletin No. 232. Melbourne: JJ Gourley, Government Printer, 1948).

21 Dulcie Levitt, *Plants and People: Aboriginal Uses of Plants on Groote Eylandt* (AIAS, 1981); Julie Waddy, *Classification of Plants & Animals from a Groote*

Eylandt Aboriginal Point of View (ANU North Australia Research Unit, 1988).

22 Levitt, p. 137.

23 The Australia-wide record of Aboriginal people translocating or dispersing plants is reviewed in JL Silcock, 'Aboriginal translocations: The intentional propagation and dispersal of plants in Aboriginal Australia', *Journal of Ethnobiology* 38(3), 2018, pp. 390–405. Silcock found the ethnographic evidence useful but 'sparse' (p. 390). The 'isolated historic reports of deliberate planting are difficult to verify and were ranked as having low reliability, as they are made within generalized works and no sources are provided' (p. 395).

24 Mary Gilmore, *Old Days, Old Ways: A Book of Recollections* (Angus & Robertson, 1986), p. 138.

25 Lazarus Lamilami, *Lamilami Speaks: The Cry Went Up: A Story of the People of Goulburn Islands, North Australia* (Ure Smith, 1974), pp. 9–10.

26 Lamilami also recorded the myth of Naganmara, an ancestral being who named and created trees and grass (Lamilami, pp. 15–19).

27 WEH Stanner, *On Aboriginal Religion* (Oceania Monograph No. 11, 1963), p. 88.

28 Jeff Hardwick, *Wadeye Kardu Murntak Warra: Old People Before: Plant Food Collecting and Processing*. Book 3 of *Traditional Knowledge, Language and Skills of the Aboriginal People from the Wadeye Region, NT, Australia* (The author, 2019).

29 WEH Stanner, 'Caliban discovered'. In WEH Stanner, *White Man Got No Dreaming: Essays 1938–1973* (ANU Press, 1979 (1962)), p. 163.

30 David R Harris, 'Subsistence strategies across Torres Strait'. In J Allen, J Golson & R Jones (eds), *Sunda and Sahul: Prehistoric Studies in Southeast Asia, Melanesia and Australia* (Academic Press, 1977), p. 437.

31 Harris, p. 434.

32 In Adnyamathanha *iga*, scientific name *Capparis mitchellii*.

33 Bob Ellis, 'Iga: The tree that walked', *South Australian Geographical Journal* 112, 2013, p. 11.

34 Ross Hynes & Athol Chase, 'Plants, sites and domiculture: Aboriginal influence upon plant communities in Cape York Peninsula', *Archaeology in Oceania* 17, 1982, pp. 38–50.

35 *Sic: Syzygium*, wild cherry.

36 Rhys Jones, 'Ordering the landscape'. In I Donaldson & T Donaldson (eds), *Seeing the First Australians* (George Allen & Unwin, 1985), p. 204. In Aboriginal and Torres Strait Islander kriol, *olisem* or *olsem* (from English 'all the same') usually means 'resembling', not 'the same as'—for example, see Anna Shnukal, *Broken: An Introduction to the Creole Language of Torres Strait* (Pacific Linguistics, 1988), p. 174. 'Gardeni' or *katini* is the English word 'garden' pronounced in an Aboriginal sound system.

37 Rex Walmbeng, 'Mythological affinities of shell mounds'. Appendix B in Roger Cribb et al., 'Landscape as cultural artefact: Shell mounds and plants in Aurukun, Cape York Peninsula', *Australian Aboriginal Studies* 2, 1988, pp. 60–73 (72–3).

38 Hynes & Chase; Athol Chase, 'Domestication and domiculture in northern Australia: A social perspective', in DR Harris & GC Hillman (eds), *Foraging and Farming: The Evolution of Plant Exploitation* (Unwin Hyman, 1989), pp. 42–78.

39 Cliff Goddard & Arpad Kalotas (comps & eds), *Puṉu:Yankunytjatjara Plant Use: Traditional Methods of Preparing Foods, Medicines, Utensils and Weapons from Native Plants* (Angus & Robertson, 1985).

40 Peter Latz, *Bushfires & Bushtucker: Aboriginal Plant Use in Central Australia* (IAD Press, 1995), p. 63.

41 FR Irvine, 'Evidence of change in the vegetable diet of Australian Aborigines'. In AR Pilling & RA Waterman (eds), *Diprotodon to Detribalization: Studies of Change among Australian Aborigines* (Michigan State University Press, 1970), p. 279.

42 Rupert Gerritsen, *Australia and the Origins of Agriculture* (British Archaeological Reports, 2008), pp. 39–41, 62.

43 Gerritsen, p. 41.

44 Campbell, p. 209.

45 Campbell, p. 209; see also Gilmore, pp. 186–8.

46 Gilmore, p. 134.

47 RG Kimber, 'Resource use and management in Central Australia', *Australian Aboriginal Studies* 2, 1984, p. 16.

48 Kimber, p. 16.

49 Kimber, p. 17.

50 Gerritsen, p. 59.

51 Gerritsen, p. 63.

52 Warwick Dix & Mance E Lofgren, 'Kurumi: Possible Aboriginal incipient agriculture associated with a stone arrangement', *Records of the Western Australian Museum* 3, 1974, pp. 73–7.

53 Dix & Lofgren, p. 77.

54 Dix & Lofgren, pp. 74, 77.

55 Tindale does not identify the 'two situations' but they are likely to be the sole examples of damming provided in Campbell (pp. 206–7): Roper River and the Grampians.

56 In this paper (Norman B Tindale, 'Adaptive significance of the Panara or grass seed culture of Australia', in RVS Wright (ed.), *Stone Tools as Cultural Markers*, AIAS, 1977, pp. 345–7), Tindale referred to the dependence of the grain-zone peoples on '*natural* grain crops' (p. 347; emphasis added).

57 Tindale, 1977, p. 345.

58 Alice Monckton Duncan-Kemp, *Our Sandhill Country: Nature and Man in South-western Queensland* (Angus & Robertson, 1934), p. 30.

59 Duncan-Kemp, pp. 146–7.

60 Duncan-Kemp, pp. 188–9.

61 DE Yen, 'The domestication of environment'. In Harris & Hillman (eds), p. 59.

62 Yen, p. 62.

63 Campbell, p. 208.

64 Campbell, p. 207.
65 Campbell, p. 208.
66 Barry Alpher pers. comm., 15 January 2020.

Chapter 7: Patterns of apparel

1 William Arthur & Frances Morphy (eds), *Macquarie Atlas of Indigenous Australia: Culture and Society through Space and Time* (Macquarie Library, 2005), p. 62. The footwear distribution may be added to from my own work with Wik people: sandals were used in very hot seasonal conditions in the area on the coast between the Archer and Edward rivers on western CYP. They were called *tha'-morrok* (Wik–Ngathan) and *tha'-murruk* (Wik–Mungkan).

2 Edmund Gregory, *Sketch of the Residence of James Morrill among the Aboriginals of Northern Queensland for Seventeen Years* ('Courier' General Printing Office, 1866), http://handle.slv.vic.gov.au/10381/114510 (accessed 22 December 2019).

3 Thomas L Mitchell, *Three Expeditions into the Interior of Eastern Australia; with Descriptions of the Recently Explored Region of Australia Felix, and of the Present Colony of New South Wales* (T & W Boone, 1839), vol. 1, p. 249.

4 James Dawson, *Australian Aborigines: The Languages and Customs of Several Tribes of Aborigines in the Western District of Victoria, Australia* (George Robertson, 1881), p. 8.

5 John Morgan, *The Life and Adventures of William Buckley: Thirty-two Years a Wanderer Amongst the Aborigines of the then Unexplored Country around Port Phillip, now the Province of Victoria* (William Heinemann, 1967), pp. 34, 37.

6 Buckley said of the Victorian people among whom he lived: 'In the winter months they are often very much distressed for fire, and suffer greatly from hunger and cold; their only covering being skin rugs sown [*sic*] together with sinews …' (Morgan, p. 68). See also Morgan, pp. 55–6.

7 Stephanie Anderson, *Pelletier: The Forgotten Castaway of Cape York* (Melbourne Books, 2009), p. 151.

8 Anderson, p. 219.

9 DS Davidson, 'Footwear of the Australian Aborigines: Environmental vs cultural determination', *Southwest Journal of Anthropology* 3, 1947, pp. 114–23. Davidson's map of footwear (p. 115) indicates a larger area of use than that implied in the map presented here on p. 3 of the picture section.

10 Ronald M Berndt & Catherine H Berndt, *The World of the First Australians: An Introduction to the Traditional Life of the Australian Aborigines*, 1st edn (Ure Smith, 1964), pp. 103–4.

11 Anthropologist Jane Goodale, who worked intensively with Tiwi people, wrote: 'Tiwi males wore no clothing, while females usually held a sheet of paperbark covering themselves in front from waist to knees but leaving their backside bare' (Jane C Goodale, *Tiwi Wives: A Study of the Women of Melville Island, North Australia*, University of Washington Press, 1971, p. 233). Spencer, who photographed the image on p. 96, has a description that is closer to Goodale's than to what he photographed. He referred to Tiwi women wearing 'curious bark aprons' (Baldwin Spencer, *Native Tribes of the Northern Territory*

of Australia, Macmillan, 1914, p. 401). If they had to be held up by hand, they could not have been apparel used while working with the hands.

12 John Morton (pers. comm., 18 January 20) points out that skin is itself a kind of clothing. It is often decorated with scarification in Aboriginal traditions, modifications designed to be seen and valued.

13 RMW Dixon, 'Preface'. In JRB Love, *The Grammatical Structure of the Worora Language of North-western Australia* (Lincom Europa, 2000), p. 1.

14 JRB Love, 2000, p. 5.

15 JRB Love (comp. & ed. by David M Welch), *Kimberley People: Stone Age Bushmen of Today* (David M Welch, 2009), p. 67; and see photos on pp. 155–7, 220, 228, 236 and 244.

16 For example, Howitt's photo of a Victorian man wearing a possum skin rug (AW Howitt, *The Native Tribes of South-east Australia*, Macmillan, 1904, p. 40); Berndt and Berndt's cloaked man (Ronald M Berndt & Catherine H Berndt with John Stanton, *A World that Was: The Yaraldi of the Murray River and the Lakes, South Australia*, Melbourne University Press at The Miegunyah Press, 1993, p. 62; actually a drawing); Norman B Tindale, *Aboriginal Tribes of Australia: Their Terrain, Environmental Controls, Distribution, Limits, and Proper Names* (University of California Press, 1974): black-and-white photo plates 5–32, taken 1935); Herbert Basedow (comp. & ed. David M Welch), *Notes on Some Native Tribes of Central Australia* (David M Welch, 2008): plates 3–11, 13–15, 18, 43, 45–7, taken 1903).

17 David Collins, *An Account of the English Colony in New South Wales* (T Cadell Jun. & W Davies, 1798), p. 551.

18 Collins, p. 562.

19 Ursula McConnel, 'Native arts and industries on the Archer, Kendall and Holroyd rivers, Cape York Peninsula, north Queensland', *Records of the South Australian Museum* 11, 1953, p. 15.

20 McConnel, p. 29, Plate XIq.

21 McConnel, pp. 15–18.

Chapter 8: 'Aquaculture' or fishing and trapping?

1 Simone Barlow & Ashlee Horyniak, *Dark Emu in the Classroom: Teacher Resources for High School Geography* (Magabala Books, 2019), p. 16.

2 'Short-finned eel: Life history' (n.d.), in *Wikipedia*, https://en.wikipedia.org/wiki/Short-finned_eel#Life_history (accessed 20 July 2020).

3 Australian Government Department of Agriculture, Water and the Environment, *Aquaculture*, DAWE website, n.d., https://www.agriculture.gov.au/fisheries/aquaculture (accessed 12 January 2021).

4 UNESCO, *Budj Bim Cultural Landscape*, UNESCO website, n.d., https://whc.unesco.org/en/list/1577/ (accessed 5 March 2020).

5 Donald F Thomson, 'A new type of fish trap from Arnhem Land, Northern Territory of Australia', *Man* 38, 1938, p. 195.

6 Thomson, 1938, p. 193.

7 Thomson, 1938, p. 194; Donald F Thomson (comp. Nicolas Peterson), *Donald Thomson in Arnhem Land* (Currey O'Neil, 1983), p. 94.

8 Judith Wiseman, *Thomson Time: Arnhem Land in the 1930s: A Photographic Essay* (Museum of Victoria, 1996), p. 43.

9 Ian Keen, *Aboriginal Economy and Society: Australia at the Threshold of Colonisation* (Oxford University Press, 2004), p. 101.

10 Paul Memmott, *Gunyah, Goondie + Wurley: The Aboriginal Architecture of Australia* (University of Queensland Press, 2007), p. 179.

11 Donald F Thomson, *Economic Structure and the Ceremonial Exchange Cycle in Arnhem Land* (Macmillan, 1949), p. 62.

12 Geoffrey Blainey, *Triumph of the Nomads: A History of Ancient Australia* (Macmillan, 1983), pp. 140–1.

13 Paul Memmott & Shaneen Fantin, 'The study of indigenous ethno-architecture in Australia'. In Bruce Rigsby & Nicolas Peterson (eds), *Donald Thomson, the Man and Scholar* (Academy of the Social Sciences in Australia, 2005), p. 206.

14 Bruce Pascoe, *Young Dark Emu: A Truer History* (Magabala Books, 2019a), p. 43.

15 For example, see the maps in DS Davidson, 'The chronology of Australian watercraft', *Journal of the Polynesian Society* 44, 1935, pp. 21, 28, 136; Donald F Thomson, 'The fishermen and dugong hunters of Princess Charlotte Bay', *Walkabout* 22(11), 1956, p. 83; William Arthur & Frances Morphy (eds), *Macquarie Atlas of Indigenous Australia: Culture and Society through Space and Time* (Macquarie Library, 2005), p. 55 (here the map on p. 3 of the picture section); and Rupert Gerritsen, *Australia and the Origins of Agriculture* (British Archaeological Reports, 2008), p. 10.

Chapter 9: Dwellings

1 James Dawson, *Australian Aborigines: The Languages and Customs of Several Tribes of Aborigines in the Western District of Victoria, Australia* (George Robertson, 1881), pp. 10–11.

2 The biggest encampment Thomas described was of 150 huts. If the whole or most of a 'tribe' was present, the encampment was subdivided into 'small hamlets' of about six huts each—see William Thomas, 'Brief account of the Aborigines of Australia Felix', in TF Bride (ed.), *Letters from Victorian Pioneers: Being a Series of Papers on the Early Occupation of the Colony, the Aborigines, etc.* (Trustees of the Public Library, 1898), p. 93.

3 Thomas, pp. 65, 66.

4 Thomas, p. 66.

5 Pardoe and Hutton refer to middle Murray encampments as 'villages', even though they were only occupied for an estimated five months a year. See Colin Pardoe & Dan Hutton, 'Aboriginal heritage as ecological proxy in south-eastern Australia: A Barapa wetland case study', preprint, *Australasian Journal of Environmental Management*, 2020, https://www.researchgate.net/publication/338688722_Aboriginal_heritage_as_ecological_proxy_in_south-eastern_Australia_A_Barapa_wetland_case_study (accessed 8 July 2020).

6 Peter Beveridge, *The Aborigines of Victoria and Riverina* (ML Hutchinson, 1889), p. 102. 'Rudest' here means 'simplest'.

7 Paul Memmott, *Gunyah, Goondie + Wurley: The Aboriginal Architecture of Australia* (University of Queensland Press, 2007), pp. 199–200.

8 Sue O'Connor, 'The stone house structures of High Cliffy Island, north-west Kimberley, WA', *Australian Archaeology* 25, 1987, p. 34.

9 O'Connor, 1987, p. 33.

10 Sue O'Connor, '30,000 years of Aboriginal occupation: Kimberley, north-west Australia', *Terra Australis* 14 (ANH Publications and Centre for Archaeological Research, Australian National University, 1999), p. 113.

11 O'Connor, 1987, p. 37.

12 O'Connor, 1999, pp. 95–6.

13 Norman B Tindale, *Aboriginal Tribes of Australia: Their Terrain, Environmental Controls, Distribution, Limits, and Proper Names* (University of California Press, 1974), pp. 147, 242.

14 Language group intermarriage varied widely, but as a rule of thumb, the smaller the group, the greater the degree to which its members married members of neighbouring linguistic country groups. For example, see Peter Sutton, 'Comment on Denham's *Beyond Fictions of Closure in Australian Aboriginal Kinship*', *Mathematical Anthropology and Cultural Theory* 5(5), 2013a, pp. 1–5, http://mathematicalanthropology.org/Pdf/Sutton_MACT0513.pdf; Peter Sutton, 'Cross-comment on Denham's *Beyond Fictions of Closure in Australian Aboriginal Kinship*', *Mathematical Anthropology and Cultural Theory* 5(6), 2013b, pp. 1–6, http://mathematicalanthropology.org/Pdf/Sutton2_MACT0513.pdf (Sutton 2013a and 2013b accessed on 20 January 2021); Peter Sutton, 'Small language survival and large language expansion on a hunter-gatherer continent', in Tom Güldemann, Patrick McConvell & Richard A Rhodes (eds), *The Language of Hunter-Gatherers* (Cambridge University Press, 2020), pp. 356–91.

15 R Lauriston Sharp, *The Social Anthropology of a Totemic System in North Queensland, Australia*, PhD dissertation, Harvard University, 1937, pp. 13–27.

16 From my own fieldwork with Wangkangurru claimants in two Simpson Desert land claims in the 1980s–1990s.

17 Rhys Jones, 'Tasmanian tribes'. Appendix in Tindale, p. 333.

18 John Morgan, *The Life and Adventures of William Buckley: Thirty-two Years a Wanderer Amongst the Aborigines of the then Unexplored Country around Port Phillip, now the Province of Victoria* (William Heinemann, 1967).

19 Morgan, p. 35. Yawangcontes means 'native hut lake'.

20 Page references are from Morgan.

21 Peter Manifold in A Kenyon, 'Stone structures of the Australian Aboriginal', *Victorian Naturalist* 47(5), 1930, p. 71.

22 Dawson, p. 11.

23 Kenyon, p. 71.

24 Kenyon, p. 72.

25 Thomas Worsnop, *The Prehistoric Arts, Manufactures, Works, Weapons, etc., of the Aborigines of Australia* (CE Bristow, Government Printer, 1897), p. 77. Worsnop was town clerk of Adelaide from 1886 to 1898.

26 Worsnop, p. 77.

27 Matthew Flinders, *A Voyage to Terra Australis*, vol. 2 (G & W Nicol, 1814), pp. 172–3. These were stonelines built by Macassan trepangers to support the

cauldrons used to boil sea slugs—see CC Macknight, *The Voyage to Marege':*
Macassan Trepangers in Northern Australia (Melbourne University Press, 1976),
pp. 51–2.

28 Memmott, pp. 182–207.

29 Memmott, p. 185.

30 R Brough Smyth, *The Aborigines of Victoria, with Notes Relating to the Habits of*
the Natives of Other Parts of Australia and Tasmania (John Ferres, Government
Printer, 1878), pp. 136–7. This or perhaps another version from the same
source, Assistant Protector of Aborigines in Victoria William Thomas, appears
to be the source of Pascoe's unsourced passages on the 'important philosopher'
'Kuller Kullup' on pp. 91, 129–30; cf. Thomas, p. 98.

31 The term is used in local tourist signage and literature on the Budj Bim (Mount
Eccles) area, for example, Gib Wettenhall with the Gunditjmara People, *The*
People of Budj Bim: Engineers of Aquaculture, Builders of Stone House Settlements
and Warriors Defending Country (em Press Publishing, 2010).

32 A sign near this reconstruction refers to 'stone houses' and has a drawing of
a house with stone walls from floor to roof. It bears no resemblance to the
reconstruction and is an imagined structure only.

33 Memmott, p. 185.

34 Memmott, p. 185.

35 Worsnop, p. 73.

36 Phillip Parker King, *Narrative of a Survey of the Intertropical and Western Coasts of*
Australia Performed between the Years 1818 and 1822, vol. 1 (John Murray, 1827),
pp. 431–2.

37 Paul Memmott pers. comm., 26 May 2020.

38 Page references in this list refer to Memmott, 2007.

39 Specialists in the archaeology of the Sydney area (Val Attenbrow, pers. comm.,
16 June 2020; Paul Irish, pers. comm., 16 July 2020) have not found any evidence of an ongoing presence of Aboriginal people in the northern beaches in
the form of the Warringah sandstone house foundations described in Memmott
(p. 186). No evidence relating to pre-conquest stone house foundations in the
Sydney region appears in Val Attenbrow, *Sydney's Aboriginal Past: Investigating*
the Archaeological and Historical Records, 2nd edn (UNSW Press, 2010); Paul Irish,
'Changing perspectives in Australian archaeology, Part III: Hidden in plain
view: The Sydney Aboriginal Historical Places Project', *Technical Reports of the*
Australian Museum, Online 23(3), 2011, pp. 31–44; Paul Irish, *Hidden in Plain*
View: The Aboriginal People of Coastal Sydney (NewSouth Publishing, 2017); or
Melinda Hinkson, *Aboriginal Sydney: A Guide to Important Places of the Past and*
Present (Aboriginal Studies Press, 2001).

40 Paul Memmott pers. comm., 26 May 2020.

41 Worsnop, p. 80.

42 Worsnop, p. 107.

43 For example, Fred Myers, *Pintupi Country, Pintupi Self: Sentiment, Place, and*
Politics among Western Desert Aborigines (Smithsonian Institution Press, 1986),
maps 3a to 3h 'Maantja's travels'; Robert Layton, *Uluru: An Aboriginal History of*
Ayers Rock (AIAS, 1986), pp. 32–3.

44 Athol Chase & Peter Sutton, 'Hunter-gatherers in a rich environment: Aboriginal coastal exploitation in Cape York Peninsula', in A Keast (ed.), *Ecological Biogeography of Australia* (W Junk, 1981), pp. 1817–52.

45 In the case of north-east Arnhem Land, the seasons were referred to in Donald F Thomson, *Economic Structure and the Ceremonial Exchange Cycle in Arnhem Land* (Macmillan, 1949), p. 16 as the 'six or more phases or seasons which they name from the winds, the weather conditions, or from the food supplies which characterise them'. They were laid out in detail for the Daly River area in WEH Stanner, 'The Daly River tribes: A report on field work in north Australia', Part 1, *Oceania* 3, 1933, p. 385; for Groote Eylandt in Julie Waddy, *Classification of Plants & Animals from a Groote Eylandt Aboriginal Point of View* (ANU North Australia Research Unit, 1988), vol. 1, p. 53; for various regions of Cape York Peninsula in Donald F Thomson, 'The seasonal factor in human culture illustrated from the life of a contemporary nomadic group', *Proceedings of the Prehistoric Society* 5, 1939, pp. 214–15, and in Chase & Sutton, pp. 1831, 1835, 1838; for Wik-Mungkan in Cape York by Philip Clarke in *Where the Ancestors Walked: Australia as an Aboriginal Landscape* (Allen & Unwin, 2003), p. 172; for south-east Cape York in Christopher Anderson, 'Regional variation', in Susan Bambrick (ed.), *The Cambridge Encyclopedia of Australia* (Cambridge University Press, 1994), p. 66; for the Borroloola region (NT) in Richard Baker, 'Traditional Aboriginal land use in the Borroloola region', in Nancy M Williams & Graham Barnes (eds), *Traditional Ecological Knowledge: Wisdom for Sustainable Development* (Centre for Resource and Environmental Studies, 1993), p. 129; for north-east Arnhem Land in Stephen Davis, *Man of All Seasons* (Angus & Robertson, 1989); for western Arnhem Land in Ronald M Berndt & Catherine H Berndt, *Man, Land and Myth in North Australia: The Gunwinggu People* (Ure Smith, 1970), p. 31, and in Bill Neidjie, Stephen Davis & Allan Fox, *Kakadu Man ... Bill Neidjie* (Mybrood, 1985), pp. 18–23, and in Diane Lucas & Ken Searle, *Walking with the Seasons in Kakadu* (Allen & Unwin, 2005); and for different parts of the Kimberley region in Phyllis Kaberry, *Aboriginal Woman, Sacred and Profane* (George Routledge & Sons, 1939), p. 11, and in Hermann Nekes & Ernest A Worms, *Australian Languages* (Micro-Bibliotheca Anthropos, 10, Anthropos Institut, 1953/2006), pp. 78–81.

46 Bureau of Meteorology, Australian Government, *Indigenous Weather Knowledge: Yawuru Calendar*, 2016, BOM website, http://www.bom.gov.au/iwk/calendars/yawuru.shtml (accessed 20 December 2019).

47 Memmott, pp. 156–81.

48 W Lloyd Warner, *A Black Civilization: A Social Study of an Australian Tribe* (Harper & Brothers, 1937), pp. 471–5.

49 Pascoe, 2014, pp. 88–9.

50 'Eastern Trans-Fly languages' (n.d.), in *Wikipedia*, https://en.wikipedia.org/wiki/Eastern_Trans-Fly_languages (accessed 20 December 2019); Jeremy Beckett, *Torres Strait Islanders: Custom and Colonialism* (Cambridge University Press, 1987), p. 114.

51 Memmott, p. 19.

52 Bruce Pascoe, *Dark Emu: Aboriginal Australia and the Birth of Agriculture*, 2nd edn (Magabala Books, 2018), p. 22.

53 Bruce Pascoe, *Young Dark Emu: A Truer History* (Magabala Books, 2019a), pp. 45–6.

54 WEH Stanner, 'Caliban discovered'. In WEH Stanner, *White Man Got No Dreaming: Essays 1938–1973* (ANU Press, 1979 (1962)), p. 162.

55 Walter E Roth, 'North Queensland Ethnography Bulletin no. 16: Huts and shelters', *Records of the Australian Museum* 8(1), 1910, Plate XII, Figure 2.

56 Roth, p. 59.

57 James Davis, 'James Davis 1861: Evidence of Davis to the Select Committee into the Native Police and the Condition of the Aborigines generally', *Queensland Ethnohistorical Transcripts* 1(1), 1982, p. 12.

58 RM Williams, *Song in the Desert* (Angus & Robertson, 1998).

59 From Nicolas Peterson with Jeremy Long, *Australian Territorial Organization: A Band Perspective* (Oceania Monographs, 1986), p. 40.

60 Peterson & Long, pp. 74–141.

61 Peterson & Long, p. 135.

62 Page numbers in Table 7 refer to Morgan, 1967.

63 For example, Peterson & Long, p. 30. Frederick Rose, in his book on the 'traditional mode of production' of the Old People (Frederick GG Rose, *The Traditional Mode of Production of the Australian Aborigines*, Angus & Robertson, 1987, pp. 169ff), used the term 'foraging group' for what we generally refer to here as 'camps' or 'bands'.

64 Harry Lourandos, 'Aboriginal spatial organization and population: South western Victoria reconsidered', *Archaeology and Physical Anthropology in Oceania* 12, 1977, pp. 202–25.

65 Peter Sutton, *Native Title in Australia: An Ethnographic Perspective* (Cambridge University Press, 2003), p. 70.

66 Lourandos, p. 211.

67 Rhys Jones, 'The demography of hunters and farmers in Tasmania'. In DJ Mulvaney & J Golson (eds), *Aboriginal Man and Environment in Australia* (ANU Press, 1971), pp. 277–8.

68 Pascoe, 2019a, p. 51.

69 Pascoe, 2019a, p. 49.

70 For a similar house photographed at Mer in 1928 by Charles Yonge, see 'Old type of house, Meer Island, Queensland, ca. 1928', National Library of Australia Catalogue, https://catalogue.nla.gov.au/Record/4189451 (accessed 13 July 2020).

71 Simone Barlow & Ashlee Horyniak, *Dark Emu in the Classroom: Teacher Resources for High School Geography* (Magabala Books, 2019), p. 27.

72 Barlow & Horyniak, p. 15.

Chapter 10: Mobility

1 John Morgan, *The Life and Adventures of William Buckley: Thirty-two Years a Wanderer Amongst the Aborigines of the then Unexplored Country around Port Phillip, now the Province of Victoria* (William Heinemann, 1967).

2 Page numbers here refer to Norman B Tindale, *Aboriginal Tribes of Australia: Their Terrain, Environmental Controls, Distribution, Limits, and Proper Names* (University of California Press, 1974).

3 Tindale's 'horde' was usually a confusion of a land-owning descent group with a camp, but here he probably means the estate or country of a descent-based land-owning group, not a camp of mixed relatives.

4 Edmund Gregory, *Sketch of the Residence of James Morrill among the Aboriginals of Northern Queensland for Seventeen Years* ('Courier' General Printing Office, 1866), http://handle.slv.vic.gov.au/10381/114510, p. 18.

5 Paul Memmott & Robyn Horsman, *A Changing Culture: The Lardil Aborigines of Mornington Island* (Social Science Press, 1991), p. 68.

6 Memmott & Horsman, p. 121.

7 Petronella Vaarzon-Morel (ed.), *Warlpiri Women's Voices (Warlpiri Karnta Karnta-kurlangu Yimi): Our Lives, Our History* (IAD Press, 1995).

8 RMW Dixon (comp. & ed.), *Words of Our Country: Stories, Place Names and Vocabulary in Yidiny, the Aboriginal Language of the Cairns-Yarrabah Region* (University of Queensland Press, 1991), pp. 56–8.

9 Sylvia Hallam, *Fire and Hearth: A Study of Aboriginal Usage and European Usurpation in South-western Australia* (AIAS, 1979), p. 147; cf. Pascoe, 2014, pp. 21–2.

10 Baldwin Spencer, 'Aborigines'. In AW Jose & HJ Carter (eds), *The Australian Encyclopaedia, Vol. 1: A to LYS* (Angus & Robertson, 1927), p. 16.

11 Charles Barrett, *Blackfellows of Australia* (Lawrence Kay for Pictorial Newspapers, a Sun book, c1936), p. 16.

12 JW Bleakley, *The Aborigines of Australia: Their History, Their Habits, Their Assimilation* (Jacaranda Press, 1961), p. 12.

13 Charles P Mountford, *The Aborigines and Their Country* (Rigby, 1969), p. 71.

14 Earlier he was a blacksmith's striker and tram conductor (Max Lamshed, *'Monty': The Biography of CP Mountford*, Rigby, 1972, pp. 17–21, 41). Norman Tindale was also a self-taught ethnographer, albeit one with a Bachelor of Science degree, but he was far better at it and his interests were vastly wider than Mountford's. Unlike Mountford, Tindale took a special interest in Aboriginal social organisation, languages, territories, economy and food technology, including seed grinding, as I explore later in this chapter.

15 Mountford, p. 7.

16 Charles Chewings, *Back in the Stone Age: The Natives of Central Australia* (Angus & Robertson, 1936), p. viii.

17 AW Reed, *An Illustrated Encyclopedia of Aboriginal Life* (AH & AW Reed, 1969), p. 5.

18 Reed, p. 6.

19 'Alexander Wyclif Reed', (n.d.), in *Wikipedia*, https://en.wikipedia.org/wiki/Alexander_Wyclif_Reed (accessed 1 January 2020).

20 Reed, p. 70.

21 Ronald M Berndt & Catherine H Berndt, *The World of the First Australians: An Introduction to the Traditional Life of the Australian Aborigines*, 1st edn (Ure Smith, 1964), and *The World of the First Australians: Aboriginal Traditional Life, Past and Present*, 4th rev. edn with additions (Aboriginal Studies Press, 1988).

22 Berndt & Berndt, 1964, p. 9.

23 Berndt & Berndt, 1964, p. 24.

24 Berndt & Berndt, 1964, p. 92.

25 Berndt & Berndt, 1964, p. 93.

26 Berndt & Berndt, 1964, p. 93.

27 Berndt & Berndt, 1964, p. 95.

28 Norman B Tindale, 'Ecology of primitive aboriginal man in Australia'. In A Keast, RL Crocker & CS Christian (eds), *Biogeography and Ecology in Australia* (Junk, 1959), pp. 37–51.

29 Berndt & Berndt, 1964, p. 99.

30 Catherine H Berndt & Ronald M Berndt, *Aborigines in Australian Society* (Pitman, 1985), pp. 14–15.

31 Berndt & Berndt, 1985, p. 29.

32 There is no fixed and precise meaning for 'semi-nomadic' or 'semi-sedentary', and the two would be hard to distinguish from each other. Basically the intent is to label a pattern whereby staying in one place for weeks or months alternates with greater mobility and shorter overnight stays at different locations.

33 AP Elkin, *The Australian Aborigines: How to Understand Them* (Angus & Robertson, 1938), p. 15.

34 For example, AP Elkin, *The Australian Aborigines* (Angus & Robertson, 1981).

35 Phyllis Kaberry, *Aboriginal Woman, Sacred and Profane* (George Routledge & Sons, 1939), p. 10.

36 Ursula H McConnel, 'The Wik-Munkan tribe of Cape York Peninsula, Part 1', *Oceania* 1, 1930a, pp. 100–4.

37 WEH Stanner, 'Caliban discovered'. In WEH Stanner, *White Man Got No Dreaming: Essays 1938–1973* (ANU Press, 1979 (1962)), p. 161.

38 David Nash pers. comm., 14 January 2020; *The Australian Encyclopaedia in Ten Volumes: Volume 1: Abbott to Birch* (Grolier Society, 1962).

39 Peter Sutton (ed.), *Dreamings: The Art of Aboriginal Australia* (Asia Society Galleries & George Braziller; Viking/Penguin, 1988).

40 See J Korff, *Alcheringa*, Creative Spirits website, https://www.creativespirits.info/resources/movies/alcheringa (accessed 22 January 2020).

41 Norman B Tindale & HA Lindsay, *Aboriginal Australians* (Jacaranda Press, 1963), p. 5.

42 Tindale & Lindsay, pp. 58–9.

43 Donald F Thomson, 'The Aborigines of Australia'. In *Australian Junior Encyclopaedia*, Vol. 1 (2nd edn, Australian Education Foundation, 1956a), pp. 70–97.

44 Thomson, 1956a, p. 94.

45 Donald F Thomson, 'The fishermen and dugong hunters of Princess Charlotte Bay', *Walkabout* 22(11), 1956b, p. 33.

46 R Lauriston Sharp, 'People without politics'. In Verne F Ray (ed.), *Systems of Political Control and Bureaucracy in Human Societies* (University of Washington Press, 1959), p. 3.

47 R Lauriston Sharp, *The Social Anthropology of a Totemic System in North Queensland, Australia*, PhD dissertation, Harvard University, 1937, pp. 318–19.

48 Sharp, 1937, pp. 320–1.

49 The later revised and expanded edition is John Mulvaney & Johan Kamminga, *Prehistory of Australia* (Allen & Unwin, 1999).

50 As described in Ronald M Berndt & Catherine H Berndt with John Stanton, *A World that Was: The Yaraldi of the Murray River and the Lakes, South Australia* (Melbourne University Press at The Miegunyah Press, 1993), p. 17.

51 DJ Mulvaney, *The Prehistory of Australia* (Thames & Hudson, 1969), p. 67. Much of this passage remained intact in the revised edition thirty years later (Mulvaney & Kamminga, p. 275). Pardoe and Hutton estimate that people returned annually to the Pollack Swamp area, middle Murray River, for 'perhaps five months each year' (Colin Pardoe & Dan Hutton, 'Aboriginal heritage as ecological proxy in south-eastern Australia: A Barapa wetland case study', preprint, *Australasian Journal of Environmental Management*, 2020, p. 12; https://www.researchgate.net/publication/338688722_Aboriginal_heritage_ as_ecological_proxy_in_south-eastern_Australia_A_Barapa_wetland_case_ study, accessed 8 July 2020).

52 Aldo Massola, *Aboriginal Mission Stations in Victoria* (Hawthorn Press, 1970), p. 94.

53 Peter Latz & GF Griffin, 'Changes in Aboriginal land management in relation to fire and to food plants in Central Australia', in BS Hetzel & HJ Frith (eds), *The Nutrition of Aborigines in Relation to the Ecosystem of Central Australia* (CSIRO, 1978), p. 77.

54 Robert Tonkinson, *The Mardu Aborigines: Living the Dream in Australia's Desert* (Holt, Rinehart & Winston, 1991), p. 40.

55 WH Edwards, *An Introduction to Aboriginal Societies* (Social Science Press, 1988), p. 43.

56 Catherine H Berndt & Ronald M Berndt, *Pioneers and Settlers: The Aboriginal Australians* (Pitman, 1978), p. 14.

57 Colin Bourke, Eleanor Bourke & Bill Edwards (eds), *Aboriginal Australia: An Introductory Reader in Aboriginal Studies* (University of Queensland Press, 1994), pp. 179–80. This book also had sections on Lake Condah, the Brewarrina fish traps, firestick farming and land degradation by stock, four topics revisited by Pascoe; see Olga Gostin & Alwin Chong, 'Living wisdom: Aborigines and the environment', pp. 134–6; Colin Bourke, 'Economics: Independence or welfare', pp. 180–1.

58 Donald F Thomson, 'The seasonal factor in human culture illustrated from the life of a contemporary nomadic group', *Proceedings of the Prehistoric Society* 5, 1939, p. 209.

59 Donald F Thomson, *Kinship and Behaviour in North Queensland: A Preliminary Account of Kinship and Social Organisation on Cape York Peninsula* (AIAS, 1972), p. 1.

60 Judith Wiseman, *Thomson Time: Arnhem Land in the 1930s: A Photographic Essay* (Museum of Victoria, 1996), p. x.

61 Donald F Thomson, *Economic Structure and the Ceremonial Exchange Cycle in Arnhem Land* (Macmillan, 1949), p. 8.

62 Thomson, 1949, p. 16.

63 Marcia Langton, 'Prologue'. In Rachel Perkins & Marcia Langton (eds), *First Australians: An Illustrated History* (Melbourne University Press at The Miegunyah Press, 2008), p. xxiv.

64 Langton, p. xxiv.

65 Patrick Wolfe, 'Robert Manne, the apology, and genocide', *The Monthly* 94, 2008, p. 31.

66 Marji Hill & Alex Barlow, *Black Australia: An Annotated Bibliography and Teacher's Guide to Resources on Aborigines and Torres Strait Islanders* (AIAS, 1978).

67 David Horton (ed.), *The Encyclopaedia of Aboriginal Australia: Aboriginal and Torres Strait Islander History, Society and Culture*, 2 vols (Aboriginal Studies Press, 1994). That work and Sylvia Kleinert & Margo Neale (eds), *The Oxford Companion to Aboriginal Art and Culture* (Oxford University Press, 2000), which is very comprehensive and contains over 400 images, have long been major standard reference volumes.

68 Horton (ed.), p. xxi.

69 Horton (ed.), pp. 374–86.

70 Cribb in Horton (ed.), pp. 382–3.

71 Ian Bryson provides a history of the unit in his *Bringing to Light: A History of Ethnographic Filmmaking at the Australian Institute of Aboriginal and Torres Strait Islander Studies* (Aboriginal Studies Press, 2002).

72 Scott Cane, *First Footprints: The Epic Story of the First Australians* (Allen & Unwin, 2013).

73 Ronald M Berndt, 'The Walmadjeri and Gugadja'. In MG Bicchieri (ed.), *Hunters and Gatherers Today: A Socioeconomic Study of Eleven Such Cultures in the Twentieth Century* (Holt, Rinehart & Winston, 1972), p. 183.

74 Fred Myers, *Pintupi Country, Pintupi Self: Sentiment, Place, and Politics among Western Desert Aborigines* (Smithsonian Institution Press, 1986), p. 77.

75 Lamshed (in Max Lamshed, 'Native's odyssey: Remarkable record of year's travel: 400 places named', *The Advertiser* (Adelaide), 26 August 1932, p. 19) gives the figure of '400 places named' but it seems to have actually been 332 (Paul Monaghan, *Laying Down the Country: Norman B Tindale and the Linguistic Construction of the North-west of South Australia*, PhD thesis, University of Adelaide, 2003, p. 58). Identification of youth from South Australian Museum Anthropology Archives AA346 Mount Liebig data.

76 Lamshed.

77 Bill Gammage, *The Biggest Estate on Earth: How Aborigines Made Australia* (Allen & Unwin, 2011), p. 300.

78 Diane E Barwick, 'Changes in the Aboriginal population of Victoria, 1863–1966'. In DJ Mulvaney & J Golson (eds), *Aboriginal Man and Environment in Australia* (ANU Press, 1971), p. 288.

79 Harry Lourandos, 'Aboriginal spatial organization and population: South western Victoria reconsidered', *Archaeology and Physical Anthropology in Oceania* 12, 1977, pp. 218–19; see also Chapter 13 of this book.

80 Josephine Flood, *Archaeology of the Dreamtime: The Story of Prehistoric Australia and Its People* (JB Publishing, 2006), p. 198.

81 William Arthur & Frances Morphy (eds), *Macquarie Atlas of Indigenous Australia: Culture and Society through Space and Time* (Macquarie Library, 2005), p. 69.

82 Flood, p. 299. Not all scholars are averse to using the term 'village' for large encampments. Peterson and Long used the term once or twice (Nicolas Peterson with Jeremy Long, *Australian Territorial Organization: A Band Perspective*, Oceania Monographs, 1986, p. 31). See also Pardoe & Hutton.

83 Old-fashioned now, in earlier English 'fancy' meant 'preference' (as well as imagination), as in Aboriginal English 'fancy-man' (*bandjiman*, often shortened to *bandji*), meaning 'boyfriend', 'girlfriend' or cross-cousin. So Buckley here is probably not referring to a fantasy but a choice.

84 Buckley in Morgan, p. 58.

Chapter 11: The explorers' records

1 Frederick GG Rose, *The Traditional Mode of Production of the Australian Aborigines* (Angus & Robertson, 1987).

2 Thomas L Mitchell, *Three Expeditions into the Interior of Eastern Australia; with Descriptions of the Recently Explored Region of Australia Felix, and of the Present Colony of New South Wales* (T & W Boone, 1839), vol. 1, pp. 237–8.

3 Mitchell, 1839, vol. 2, p. 194.

4 Mitchell, 1839, vol. 2, p. 194.

5 Alan EJ Andrews (ed.), *Stapylton: With Major Mitchell's Australia Felix Expedition, 1836, Largely from the Journal of Granville William Chetwynd Stapylton* (Blubber Head Press, 1986), p. 146.

6 George Grey, *Journals of Two Expeditions of Discovery in North-west and Western Australia During the Years 1837, 38 and 39* (T & W Boone, 1841), vol, 2, pp. 2, 11, 12, 19.

7 Rupert Gerritsen, *Australia and the Origins of Agriculture* (British Archaeological Reports, 2008), p. 33.

8 Grey, vol. 2, p. 19.

9 Common name yam daisy, although it is not a yam but a tuber: *Microseris lanceolata*.

10 For example, Lesley Head, *Second Nature: The History and Implications of Australia as Aboriginal Landscape* (Syracuse University Press, 2000), pp. 41, 59; Bruce Pascoe, *Dark Emu: Aboriginal Australia and the Birth of Agriculture*, 2nd edn (Magabala Books, 2018), pp. 18–23; Tim Denham, 'Traditional forms of plant exploitation in Australia and New Guinea: The search for common ground', *Vegetation History and Archaeobotany* 17, 2008, p. 246; Gerritsen, pp. 33–5, 112; Bill Gammage, *The Biggest Estate on Earth: How Aborigines Made Australia* (Allen & Unwin, 2011), pp. 289–90; Peter White, 'Revisiting the "Neolithic problem" in Australia', *Records of the Western Australian Museum* 79, 2011, p. 88. The yam daisy example is also used in Simone Barlow & Ashlee Horyniak, *Dark Emu in the Classroom: Teacher Resources for High School Geography* (Magabala Books, 2019), pp. 33–4, minus Grey on the *warran*.

11 Denham, p. 246; see also Harriet V Hunt, Hannah M Moots & Peter J Matthews, 'Genetic data confirms field evidence for natural breeding in a wild taro population (*Colocasia esculenta*) in northern Queensland, Australia', *Genetic Resources and Crop Evolution* 60, 2013.

12 John Hunter, *An Historical Journal of the Transactions at Port Jackson and Norfolk Island* (John Stockdale, 1793), p. 150.

13 Batey's birth date from National Library of Australia, 'Isaac Batey: Reminiscences of settlement of Melbourne and the Sunbury district (1840–70)', *Trove*, https://trove.nla.gov.au/work/227765754?q&versionId=249938056 (accessed 9 January 2020).

14 Thomas L Mitchell, *Journal of an Expedition into the Interior of Tropical Australia in Search of a Route from Sydney to the Gulf of Carpentaria* (Longman, Brown, Green, & Longmans, 1848), p. 274.

15 Mitchell, 1848, p. 65. This is a reference to the banishment of Eve and Adam from the Garden of Eden after they fell from grace and committed original sin. Among their punishments were that Adam was condemned to henceforth engage in agriculture (presumably Adam and Eve were initially hunter-gatherers): 'Therefore the Lord God sent him forth from the garden of Eden, to till the ground from whence he was taken' (Genesis 3:23). Peter Hiscock, in 'Creators or destroyers? The burning questions of human impact in ancient Aboriginal Australia', *Humanities Australia* 5, 2014, links this fall-from-grace mythology to the work of Gammage.

16 There is a large literature on Aboriginal sharing: a good starting point is Nicolas Peterson, 'Demand sharing: Reciprocity and the pressure for generosity among foragers', *American Anthropologist* 95, 1993, pp. 860–74. On 'the sustaining ideals of Aboriginal societies' see TGH Strehlow, *The Sustaining Ideals of Aboriginal Societies* (Aborigines Advancement League Inc. of South Australia, 1956). Strehlow summarised his defence of Aboriginal society in this way: '... we may say that among the strongest ideals which sustained the aboriginal Australian societies were the principles of co-operation, not subordination; of differentiation without inequality; of tolerance for the customs of other peoples in their own country; and of respect for the hunting grounds of other tribes' (p. 11). The technological 'progress' that had created the threat of nuclear annihilation was part of the shadow of concern that lay over Strehlow at that time.

17 Geoffrey Bagshaw pers. comm., 19 January 2020.

18 Peter Sutton, *Wik: Aboriginal Society, Territory and Language at Cape Keerweer, Cape York Peninsula, Australia*, PhD thesis, University of Queensland, 1978, pp. 70–2.

19 Mitchell, 1839, vol. 2, p. 65.

20 John McKinlay, *McKinlay's Journal of Exploration in the Interior of Australia (Burke Relief Expedition)* (FF Bailliere, 1861), p. 50.

21 McKinlay's location provided by Tom Gara pers. comm., 20 February 2020.

22 Robert Etheridge (Jnr), 'On an Aboriginal implement, believed to be undescribed, and supposed to be a hoe', *Journal of the Linnean Society of New South Wales* 9, 1894, pp. 109–12.

23 Etheridge (Jnr), pp. 111–12.

24 Etheridge (Jnr), p. 110.

25 Augustus Charles Gregory, 'Appendix II: Memoranda on the Aborigines of Australia'. In H Ling Roth, 'On the origin of agriculture', *Journal of the Anthropological Institute of Great Britain and Ireland* 16, 1887, p. 131.

26 Gregory, p. 131. Pascoe refers to Augustus Gregory twice but does not use this source. Gammage (p. 298) does cite this source, but only to put it into the

category of 'wrong' statements. He thus claims to know more than Gregory about what people were doing on the west coast of Western Australia prior to 1882, the date when Gregory was interviewed for the 1887 paper by Ling Roth.

27 Charles Sturt, *Narrative of an Expedition into Central Australia* (T & W Boone, 1849), vol. 1, p. 387.

28 See Leonn D Satterthwait, 'Aboriginal Australian net hunting', *Mankind* 16, 1986, pp. 31–48.

29 Peter Beveridge, *The Aborigines of Victoria and Riverina* (ML Hutchinson, 1889), p. 10.

Chapter 12: 'Agricultural' implements and antiquity

1 Robert Etheridge (Jnr), 'On an Aboriginal implement believed to be undescribed, and supposed to be a hoe', *Journal of the Linnean Society of New South Wales* 9, 1894, pp. 109–12.

2 Walter Harper, 'A description of certain objects of unknown significance, formerly used by some New South Wales tribes', *Proceedings of the Linnean Society* 23, 1898, pp. 420–36; Robert Etheridge (Jnr), 'The cylindro-conical and cornute stone implements of Western New South Wales and their significance', *Memoirs of the Geological Survey of New South Wales, Ethnological Series* 2, 1916, pp. 1–42; WW Thorpe, 'Ethnological notes, no. 1', *Records of the Australian Museum* 16(5), 1928, pp. 241–53 and 'Ethnological notes, no. 4', *Records of the Australian Museum* 18(6), 1932, pp. 302–11; Lindsay Black, *Cylcons: The Mystery Stones of the Darling River Valley* (The author, 1942); George Horne, 'Aboriginal stone implements of south-eastern Victoria', paper, Australasian Association for the Advancement of Science, 1921; Frederick D McCarthy, 'The grooved-conical stones of New South Wales', *Memoirs of the Australian Museum (Mankind)* II, 1939, pp. 161–9; Frederick D McCarthy, 'Some unusual cylindro-conical stones from New South Wales and Java', *Records of the Australian Museum* 21(5), 1944, pp. 257–60; Frederick D McCarthy, *Australian Aboriginal Stone Implements*, 2nd edn (Australian Museum Trust, 1976); Frederick D McCarthy, Elsie Bramwell & HVV Noone, 'The stone implements of Australia', *Australian Museum Memoir* 9, 1946, pp. 1–94.

3 Harper; Etheridge (Jnr), 1916; Black.

4 Thorpe, 1928; McCarthy, 1939 and 1976; McCarthy, Bramwell & Noone.

5 Nici Cumpston & Jonathon Jones, *Riverland: Yvonne Koolmatrie: A Retrospective of Ngarrindjeri Weaver Yvonne Koolmatrie* (Art Gallery of South Australia, 2015).

6 Bruce Pascoe, *Dark Emu: Aboriginal Australia and the Birth of Agriculture*, 2nd edn (Magabala Books, 2018). The image is poorly produced and simply labelled 'stone picks'. It is attributed to J Jones.

7 Harper, p. 436.

8 McCarthy, 1944.

9 Etheridge (Jnr), 1916.

10 Harper; Etheridge (Jnr), 1916; Black.

11 Harper, p. 435.

12 Harper, p. 425.

13 Harper, p. 425.
14 Harper, p. 426.
15 Etheridge (Jnr), 1916, p. 4.
16 Etheridge (Jnr), 1916, p. 40.
17 Etheridge (Jnr), 1916, p. 41.
18 Etheridge (Jnr), 1916, p. 15.
19 Etheridge (Jnr), 1916, p. 17.
20 Mathews cited in Etheridge (Jnr), 1916, p. 40.
21 Etheridge (Jnr), 1916, p. 19.
22 Etheridge (Jnr), 1916, p. 40.
23 Black, p. 24.
24 Etheridge (Jnr), 1916; Black; McCarthy, 1944.
25 McCarthy, 1944.
26 Nici Cumpston, Jonathon Jones & Lorena Allam, *Bunha-Bunhanga: Aboriginal Agriculture in the South-East* (Board of the Botanic Gardens and State Herbarium, 2019), paragraph 5, lines 26–9.
27 Cumpston, Jones & Allam, paragraph 11, lines 1–3.
28 Horne; McCarthy, 1976.
29 See NMA Object Summary with Images, https://static1.squarespace. com/static/5cf30ff26df8f90001ae648d/t/5d397c8aa48d2b0001f3f8bb/ 1564048526233/atsip_objectlistmultiplenewlogo.pdf (accessed 12 July 2020).
30 Harper; Etheridge (Jnr), 1916; McCarthy, 1944.
31 Etheridge (Jnr), 1916; Thorpe, 1928; McCarthy, 1939 and 1944.
32 McCarthy, Bramwell & Noone; later published as Frederick D McCarthy, 1967, (1st edn) and McCarthy, *Australian Aboriginal Stone Implements* (Australian Museum) 1976, (2nd edn, revised).
33 McCarthy, 1944.
34 McCarthy, Bramwell & Noone, p. 2.
35 Tom McCourt, *Aboriginal Artefacts* (Rigby, 1975); Simon Holdaway & Nicola Stern, *A Record in Stone: The Study of Australia's Flaked Stone Artefacts* (Melbourne & Canberra: Museum Victoria & AIATSIS, 2004).
36 McCarthy, Bramwell & Noone, p. 9.
37 McCarthy, Bramwell & Noone; McCarthy, 1976.
38 McCarthy, Bramwell & Noone, p. 259.
39 McCarthy, 1939, pp. 166–7.
40 Thorpe, 1928; McCarthy, 1939.
41 Holdaway & Stern, p. 236.
42 Horne, p. 12.
43 Stan Grant (Snr) & John Rudder, *A New Wiradjuri Dictionary* (Restoration House, 2010) p. 318.
44 Lorena Allam in Cumpston, Jones & Allam, paragraph 9, lines 1, 3.
45 Thomas L Mitchell, *Three Expeditions into the Interior of Eastern Australia; with Descriptions of the Recently Explored Region of Australia Felix, and of the Present Colony of New South Wales* (T & W Boone, 1839), vol. 1, p. 336.
46 Mitchell, vol. 1, p. 336.
47 McCarthy, 1976, p. 36.

48 McCarthy, 1976, p. 36; James Knight, 'A broken juin knife from Yandan Creek: Some implications', *Archaeology in Oceania* 25(2), 1990, pp. 68–74; Holdaway & Stern, p. 264.

49 Knight.

50 Holdaway & Stern, p. 264.

51 Norman B Tindale, 'Culture succession in south eastern Australia from late Pleistocene to the present', *Records of the South Australian Museum* 13(1), 1957, p. 29.

52 Knight, pp. 70–1.

53 Knight, p. 72.

54 DA Casey, IM Crawford & RVS Wright, 'The recognition, description, classification and nomenclature of Australian stone implements: The report of the Stone Implement Committee, 1967', Australian National University, 1967, http://rubens.anu.edu.au/raid1/student_projects/tools/casey.html (accessed 8 February 2020).

55 Suzanne Nugent, *Sticks and Stones: A Functional Analysis of Aboriginal Spears from Northern Australia*, PhD thesis, University of Queensland, 2015.

56 Augustus Charles Gregory, 'Appendix II: Memoranda on the Aborigines of Australia'. In H Ling Roth, 'On the origin of agriculture', *Journal of the Anthropological Institute of Great Britain and Ireland* 16, 1887, p. 132.

57 Rupert Gerritsen, *Australia and the Origins of Agriculture* (British Archaeological Reports, 2008), p. 78.

58 Johan Kamminga, 'Over the edge: Functional analysis of Australian stone tools', *Occasional Papers in Anthropology* (Anthropology Museum, University of Queensland), 12, 1982; Peter Hiscock & Tim Maloney, 'Australian lithic technology: Evolution, dispersion and connectivity', in T Hodos (ed.), *The Routledge Handbook of Archaeology and Globalization* (Routledge, 2017), pp. 301–80.

59 R Tobler et al., 'Aboriginal mitogenomes reveal 50,000 years of regionalism in Australia', *Nature* 544, 2017, pp. 180–4; James F O'Connor et al., 'When did *Homo sapiens* first reach Southeast Asia and Sahul?' *Proceedings of the National Academy of Sciences of the United States of America*, 115(34), 2018, pp. 8482–90; R Wood et al., 'Towards an accurate and precise chronology for the colonization of Australia: The example of Riwi, Kimberley, Western Australia', *PLOS One* 11(9), 2016.

60 Aboriginal Victoria, Victorian Government, *Fact Sheet: Aboriginal Coastal Shell Middens*, 2019, Aboriginal Victoria website, https://www.aboriginalvictoria.vic.gov.au/fact-sheet-aboriginal-coastal-shell-middens (accessed 15 February 2020).

61 BD Koppel, *Disentangling Shell Middens: Exploring the Complexities of Deposit Formation and Transformation Using Amino Acid Racemisation*, PhD thesis, University of Wollongong, 2017, pp. 2–5.

62 Koppel, p. 24.

63 JR Prescott & JE Sherwood, 'Thermoluminescence ages for an unusual shell deposit at Point Ritchie, Warrnambool, Australia'. In JR Prescott (ed.), *Archaeometry: Australasian Studies* (Department of Physics and Mathematical Physics, University of Adelaide, 1988), pp. 61–9.

64 Ian J McNiven et al., 'The Moyjil site, south-west Victoria, Australia: Excavation of a last interglacial charcoal and burnt stone feature: Is it a hearth?' *Royal Society of Victoria* 130, 2018, pp. 94–116.

65 JE Sherwood, 'The Moyjil site, south-west Victoria, Australia: Prologue: Of people, birds, shell and fire', *Royal Society of Victoria* 130, 2018, p. 11.

66 Jim M Bowler at al., 'The Moyjil site, south-west Victoria, Australia: Fire and environment in a 120,000-year coastal midden: Nature or people?' *Royal Society of Victoria* 130, 2018, pp. 71–93.

67 McNiven et al., p. 111.

68 Stephen P Carey et al., 'The Moyjil site, south-west Victoria, Australia: Stratigraphic and geomorphic context', *Royal Society of Victoria* 130, 2018, p. 16.

69 Wood et al.

70 Tobler et al.; James F O'Connell et al., 'When did *Homo sapiens* first reach Southeast Asia and Sahul?' *Proceedings of the National Academy of Sciences of the United States of America*, 115(34), 2018, pp. 8482–90; A Cooper, A Williams & N Spooner, 'When did Aboriginal people first arrive in Australia?' *The Conversation*, 7 August 2018. By using the human fossil record and genetic signals, these researchers cannot find strong evidence for an exodus from Africa earlier than 50,000–55,000 years ago. They suggest that processes operating on some archaeological deposits have left deposits younger than 50,000 years old, with older age outcomes. See also Appendix 1 of this book.

71 Sue O'Connor, '30,000 years of Aboriginal occupation: Kimberley, north-west Australia', *Terra Australis* 14 (ANH Publications and Centre for Archaeological Research, Australian National University, 1999).

72 Carey et al.; Bowler et al.; McNiven et al.; Sherwood, 2018; JE Sherwood et al., 'The Moyjil site, south-west Victoria, Australia: Chronology', *Royal Society of Victoria* 130, 2018, pp. 32–49; JE Sherwood, IJ McNiven & Laurie Laurenson, 'The Moyjil site, south-west Victoria, Australia: Shells as evidence of the deposit's origin', *Royal Society of Victoria* 130, 2018, pp. 50–70.

73 Bruce Pascoe, *Salt: Selected Essays and Stories* (Black Inc., 2019b), p. 102.

74 CE Dortch & PA Hesp, 'Rottnest Island artifacts and palaeosols in the context of Greater Swan Region prehistory', *Journal of the Royal Society of Western Australia* 77, 1994, pp. 23–2; P Hesp, CV Murray-Wallace & CE Dortch, 'Aboriginal occupation on Rottnest Island, Western Australia, provisionally dated by aspartic acid racemisation assay of land snails to greater than 50 ka', *Australian Archaeology* 49, 1999, pp. 7–12.

75 Dortch & Hesp.

76 Hesp, Murray-Wallace & Dortch, p. 11. The Pleistocene is a geological epoch commencing, in Australia, around 1.5 million years ago and ending about 11,000 years ago. On other continents, the Pleistocene era commences around 2.6 million years ago.

77 AN Williams et al., 'Sea-level change and demography during the last glacial termination and early Holocene across the Australian continent', *Quaternary Science Reviews* 182, 2018, pp. 144–54.

78 Rebe Taylor, *Unearthed: The Aboriginal Tasmanians of Kangaroo Island* (Wakefield Press, 2000); Keryn Walshe, 'Investigator Isles Expedition 2006: Two stone

implements from Flinders Island, South Australia', *Transactions of the Royal Society of South Australia* 132(2), 2008, pp. 45–50; Keryn Walshe, 'Archaeological evidence for a sealer's and wallaby hunter's skinning site on Kangaroo Island, South Australia', *Journal of Island and Coastal Archaeology* 9(1), 2014, pp. 130–43.

79 Taylor; Walshe, 2008; Walshe, 2014; Keryn Walshe, 'Echidna to wolf's head: A nineteenth-century sealer's ornament from Kangaroo Island, South Australia', *The Artefact* 39, 2018, pp. 5–8.

80 Walshe, 2014.

81 David Horton, *The Pure State of Nature: Sacred Cows, Destructive Myths and the Environment* (Allen & Unwin, 2000), p. 67.

82 Horton, p. 61.

83 Horton, p. 67.

84 Horton, p. 65.

85 Horton, p. 69.

Chapter 13: Stone circles and 'smoking' trees

1 See Francis Dahlberg (ed.), *Woman the Gatherer* (Yale University Press, 1981).

2 Richard B Lee & Irven DeVore, *Man the Hunter* (Aldine, 1968); Marshall Sahlins, *Stone Age Economics* (Aldine, Atherton Inc., 1972).

3 Bryony Orme, 'The advantages of agriculture'. In JVS Megaw (ed.), *Hunters, Gatherers and First Farmers beyond Europe: An Archaeological Survey* (Leicester University Press, 1977), p. 41.

4 Aldo Massola, 'A history of Lake Condah Reserve: An address to the Society on Tuesday evening, 19th June, 1962', *Victorian Historical Magazine* 34(1), 1963, p. 29.

5 Sian Johnson, 'Volcanoes in Victoria reveal fresh evidence of eruptions 37,000 years ago', *ABC News*, 26 February 2020.

6 L Head, D D'Costa & P Edney, 'Pleistocene dates for volcanic activity in western Victoria and implications for Aboriginal occupation'. In MAJ Williams, P de Deckker & AP Kershaw (eds), *The Cainozoic in Australia: A Reappraisal of the Evidence* (Geological Society of Australia, 1991), pp. 302–8.

7 See Neville Rosengren, 'Lake Condah area: Lava surface features', in Anne Clarke, *Lake Condah Project Aboriginal Archaeology* (Occasional Report No. 36, Victoria Archaeological Survey, 1991), pp. 90–103; Heather Builth, 'Mt Eccles lava flow and the Gunditjmara connection: A landform for all seasons', *Proceedings of the Royal Society of Victoria* 116(1), 2004, pp. 165–84; J Tibby et al., 'Environmental change and variability in southwestern Victoria: Changing constraints and opportunities for occupation and land use', in Bruno David, Bryce Barker & Ian J McNiven (eds), *The Social Archaeology of Australian Indigenous Societies* (Aboriginal Studies Press, 2006), pp. 254–69; Heather Builth et al., 'Environmental and cultural change on the Mt Eccles lava-flow landscapes of south-western Victoria, Australia', *The Holocene* 18(3), 2008, pp. 413–24.

8 Rosengren; Context Pty Ltd, *Lake Condah Heritage Management Plan* (report prepared for Victoria Archaeological Survey, 1993).

9 Builth, 2004.

10 Galaxia is anadramous while the short-finned eel is catadramous, which means that galaxia are spawned in fresh water and migrate to sea water to mature, returning to fresh water to spawn their own offspring, whereas the eel is spawned in sea water and migrates to fresh water to mature, leaving for sea water when it is ready to spawn.

11 Massola, 1963, p. 29.

12 Ian J McNiven et al., 'Phased redevelopment of an ancient Gunditjmara fish trap over the past 800 years: Muldoons trap complex, Lake Condah, southwestern Victoria', *Australian Archaeology* 81, 2015, pp. 44–58; Ian J McNiven et al., 'Kurtonitj stone house: Excavation of a mid-nineteenth century Aboriginal frontier site from Gunditjmara country, south east Victoria', *Archaeology in Oceania* 52, 2017, pp. 171–97.

13 See Aldo Massola, 'The native fish traps at Toolondo, in the Wimmera', *Victorian Naturalist* 79, 1962, pp. 162–6; Massola, *Journey to Aboriginal Victoria* (Rigby, 1969); Massola, *The Aborigines of South East Australia as They Were* (Heinemann, 1971); Harry Lourandos, 'Aboriginal settlement and land use in south-western Victoria: A report on current field work', *Artefact* 1, 1976, pp. 174–93; Lourandos, *Continent of Hunter-Gatherers: New Perspectives in Australian Prehistory* (Cambridge University Press, 1997); Peter JF Coutts, RK Frank & P Hughes, 'Aboriginal engineers of the Western District, Victoria', *Records of the Victorian Archaeological Survey* 7, 1978; Jill Wesson, *Excavations of Stone Structures in the Condah Area, Western Victoria*, Masters preliminary thesis, La Trobe University, Melbourne, 1981; Steven Hemming, 'An Aboriginal fish trap from Lake Condah, Victoria', *Journal of the Anthropological Society of South Australia* 23(4), 1985, pp. 2–6; Katrina Geering, *Management Recommendations for Aboriginal Stone Houses at Allambie, near Macarthur, South West Victoria: Report of the Victoria Archaeological Survey* (Ministry of Planning and Environment, 1985); Elizabeth Williams, *Wet Underfoot? Earth Mound Sites and the Recent Prehistory of South West Victoria*, PhD thesis, Australian National University, 1985; Williams, 'Complex hunter-gatherers: A view from Australia', *Antiquity* 61(232), 1987, pp. 310–21; Williams, *Complex Hunter-Gatherers: A Late Holocene Example from Temperate Australia* (British Archaeological Reports, 1988); Context Pty Ltd; Anne Clarke, 'Romancing the stones: The cultural construction of an archaeological landscape in the Western District of Victoria', *Archaeology in Oceania* 29, 1994, pp. 1–15; Heather Builth, *Lake Condah Revisited: Archaeological Constructions of a Cultural Landscape*, Honours thesis, Faculty of Aboriginal and Torres Strait Islander Studies, University of South Australia, Adelaide, 1996; Builth, 'Analysing Gunditjmara settlement: The use of an appropriate methodology', in G Carver & K Stankowski (eds), *Proceedings of the Third National Archaeology Students' Conference* (Southern Archaeology, 2002a), pp. 15–32; Builth, *The Archaeology and Socioeconomy of the Gunditjmara: A Landscape Analysis from Southwest Victoria, Australia*, PhD thesis, Department of Archaeology, Flinders University of South Australia, 2002b; Builth, 2004; Thomas Richards, 'A late nineteenth-century map of an Australian Aboriginal fishery at Lake Condah', *Australian Aboriginal Studies* 2, 2011, pp. 64–87; Ian McNiven, & IJ Bell, 'Fishers and farmers: Historicising the Gunditjmara

freshwater fishery, western Victoria'. *La Trobe Journal* 85, 2010, pp. 83–105; McNiven et al., 'Dating Aboriginal stone-walled fishtraps at Lake Condah, southeast Australia', *Journal of Archaeological Science* 39, 2012, pp. 268–86.

14 Massola, 1963.

15 Lourandos, 1976.

16 Peter Coutts et al., 'The mound people of western Victoria: A preliminary statement', *Records of the Victorian Archaeological Survey* (Ministry for Conservation) 1, 1976; Peter JF Coutts, P Henderson & R Fullagar, 'Preliminary investigation of Aboriginal mounds in north-western Victoria', *Records of the Victorian Archaeological Survey* (Ministry for Conservation) 9, 1979.

17 Coutts, Frank & Hughes, p. 24.

18 The page numbers in the main text of this chapter are from the second edition of *Dark Emu*, published by Magabala Books in 2018.

19 Context Pty Ltd.

20 Context Pty Ltd.

21 Coutts, Frank & Hughes; Clarke, 1994.

22 Coutts, Frank & Hughes, p. 16.

23 Coutts, Frank & Hughes, p. 42.

24 *The Age*, 21 January 1981, cited in Clarke, 1994, p. 13.

25 Lourandos, 1976.

26 Lourandos, 1997, p. 112.

27 Approximately 220 stone circles had been recorded by 1990 (Context Pty Ltd).

28 Context Pty Ltd, p. 69.

29 Clarke, 1991 and 1994.

30 Cited in Clarke, 1994, p. 12.

31 Clarke, 1994, p. 13.

32 Context Pty Ltd.

33 Pascoe, 2018, p. 85.

34 Clarke, 1991 and 1994.

35 Pahoehoe lava flows are gently undulating and smooth, sometimes hummocky. See 'Pahoehoe: Lava flow', Encyclopedia Britannica website, n.d., https://www.britannica.com/science/pahoehoe (accessed 20 July 2020).

36 Rosengren, p. 92.

37 Rosengren, p. 93.

38 Rosengren, p. 94.

39 Context Pty Ltd, p. 69.

40 Clarke, 1994, p. 6.

41 Clarke, 1994, p. 5.

42 Context Pty Ltd, p. 69.

43 Context Pty Ltd, p. 71.

44 Wesson.

45 McNiven et al., 2017.

46 Builth, 2002b, p. 316.

47 Builth, 2002b, p. 317.

48 Builth, 2002b, p. 68.

49 Pascoe, 2018, p. 84.

50 Builth, 2002b, p. 117.

51 Rosengren, p. 91.

52 Rosengren, p. 90.

53 Builth, 2002a and 2002b.

54 Builth, 2002b, pp. 150–1.

55 Coutts, Frank & Hughes; Clarke, 1991 and 1994.

56 Builth, 2002b, p. 134.

57 Massola, 1963, p. 38; Aldo Massola, *Aboriginal Mission Stations in Victoria* (Hawthorn Press, 1970), p. 99.

58 *Portland Guardian*, 23 February 1891, p. 4.

59 See Charlotte Beck & George Jones, 'Bias and archaeological classification', *American Antiquity* 54(2), 1989, pp. 244–62.

60 Clarke, 1991, p. 19.

61 Builth, 2002b, p. 163.

62 Builth, 2002b, p. 209.

63 James Dawson, *Australian Aborigines: The Languages and Customs of Several Tribes of Aborigines in the Western District of Victoria, Australia* (George Robertson, 1881), pp. 94–5.

64 Daisy M Bates (ed. Isobel White), *The Native Tribes of Western Australia* (National Library of Australia, 1985); Ronald M Berndt & Catherine H Berndt, *The World of the First Australians: An Introduction to the Traditional Life of the Australian Aborigines*, 1st edn (Ure Smith, 1964), pp. 110–12.

65 Dawson, p. 95.

66 Builth, 2002b, p. 314.

67 Builth, 2002b, p. 173.

68 Robert Edwards, *Aboriginal Bark Canoes of the Murray Valley* (Rigby, 1972).

69 Edwards; Rhys Roberts, *The Peramangk and Culturally Modified Trees: Significant Heritage Sites*, Honours thesis, Department of Archaeology, Flinders University of South Australia, 2000; Greg Carver, *An Examination of Indigenous Australian Culturally Modified Trees in South Australia*, Honours thesis, Department of Archaeology, Flinders University of South Australia, 2002; Andrew Long, *Aboriginal Scarred Trees in New South Wales: A Field Manual* (NSW Department of Conservation, 2005).

70 Long.

71 Builth, 2002b, p. 137.

72 An example is shown on p. 163 of Builth, 2002b.

73 Builth, 2002b, p. 177.

74 National Center for Biotechnology Information. *Pubchem Compound Summary For CID 444899, Arachidonic Acid*, n.d., https://pubchem.ncbi.nlm.nih.gov/compound/Eicosapentaenoic-acid and *Pubchem Compound Summary For CID 446284, Eicosapentaenoic Acid*, n.d., https://pubchem.ncbi.nlm.nih.gov/compound/Eicosapentaenoic-acid (accessed 22 January 2020).

75 Coutts, Frank & Hughes, p. 13.

76 Ian Keen, 'Constraints on the development of enduring inequalities in late Holocene Australia', *Current Anthropology* 47, 2006, p. 27.

77 *The Leader* (Melbourne), 7 September 1867, p. 20 (3).

78 WB Emison et al., 'Survey of the vertebrate fauna in the Grampians-Edenhope area of southwestern Victoria', *Memoirs of the Victoria Museum* 39, 1978, pp. 281–365.

79 Builth, 2002b.

80 Ronald Strahan (ed.), *Mammals of Australia* (Smithsonian Institution Press, 1995) and references therein.

81 Interestingly, dingoes lack the enzyme necessary for digesting starch, which is a marker of dogs closely associated with agricultural communities; see Alex Cagan & Torsten Blass, 'Identification of genomic variants putatively targeted by selection during dog domestication', *BMC Evolutionary Biology* 16 (10), 2016, pp. 1–13.

82 Builth, 2004, p. 179, Figure 9.

83 Gib Wettenhall with the Gunditjmara People, *The People of Budj Bim: Engineers of Aquaculture, Builders of Stone House Settlements and Warriors Defending Country*, Heywood, Vic.: em PRESS Publishing, 2010.

84 Builth, 2002b, p. 163.

85 For example, see Michal Rybka, 'Smoked eel: A delicacy made in your back yard', Tasfish website, 2014, https://www.tasfish.com/196-other/eel/2533-smoked-eel-a-delicacy-made-in-your-back-yard-michal-rybka (accessed 24 January 2020).

86 For example, Berndt & Berndt, 1964, p. 110.

87 Builth, 2002b, p. 208.

88 Keen, p. 27, citing Blandowski.

89 Dawson, p. 94.

90 Wesson; McNiven et al., 2017.

91 LR Smyth, *The Aboriginal Population of Australia* (Aborigines in Australian Society no. 14, Canberra: ANU Press, 1980), p. 111.

92 Aboriginal Heritage Office, A Brief Aboriginal History, Aboriginal Heritage Office website, 2014, https://www.aboriginalheritage.org/history/history/ (accessed 15 January 2020).

93 Context Pty Ltd; Aboriginal Affairs Victoria, *Lake Condah Heritage Management Strategy and Plan: Report by AAV in Conjunction with the Kerrup Jmara Elders Aboriginal Corporation* (Aboriginal Affairs Victoria, 1993).

94 Department of Agriculture, Water and the Environment, Australian Government, World Heritage Places: Budj Bim Cultural Landscape, DAWE website, n.d., http://environment.gov.au/heritage/places/world/budj-bim (accessed 15 January 2020).

Conclusion

1 Peter Sutton & Ken Hale, *Linguistic Organisation and Native Title: The Wik Case, Australia* (Asia-Pacific Linguistics, 2021; in press).

2 For a lay reader's introduction to the rich ethnographic fields of Aboriginal land tenure, see Peter Sutton, *Native Title in Australia: An Ethnographic Perspective* (Cambridge University Press, 2003).

Appendix 1: When did Indigenous people arrive in Australia?

1 R Wood et al., 'Towards an accurate and precise chronology for the colonization of Australia: The example of Riwi, Kimberley, Western Australia', *PLOS
   One* 11(9), 2016.

2 C Clarkson, Z Jacobs, B Marwick, R Fullagar, L Wallis, M Smith, C Pardoe,
   'Human Occupation of northern Australia by 65,000 years ago', *Nature* 547,
   2017, pp. 306–10.

3 M A Smith, I Ward, I Moffat, 'How do we distinguish termite stone lines
   from artefact horizons? A challenge for geoarchaeology in tropical Australia',
   Geoarchaeology, 35(2), 2020, pp. 232–42.

4 M A J Williams, N A Spooner, K McDonnell, J F O'Connell, 'Identifying disturbance in archaeological sites in tropical northern Australia: Implications for
   previously proposed 65,000-year continental occupation date', *Geoarchaeology*,
   36, 2021, pp. 92–108.

5 Q Fu et al, 'The genome sequence of a 45,000-year-old modern human from
   western Siberia', *Nature*, 514(7523), 2014, pp. 445–9.

6 Tobler et al, 2017; James F O'Connell et al., 'When did *Homo sapiens* first reach
   Southeast Asia and Sahul?' *Proceedings of the National Academy of Sciences of the
   United States of America*, 115(34), 2018, pp. 8482–90.

7 J-J Hublin, 'How old are the oldest *Homo sapiens* in Far East Asia?', *PNAS*
   118(10), 2021.

8 O'Connell et al; Williams et al.

Appendix 2: Band movements recorded by William Buckley

1 Ian D Clark, *Aboriginal Languages and Clans: An Historical Atlas of Western and
   Central Victoria, 1800–1900* (Monash University, 1990), p. 317.

2 Buckley gave a reason for leaving: '… we started again for a new locality, our
   supplies of game beginning to fall short in consequence of our continued
   hunting' (Morgan, p. 31).

References

Abbott, Ian. 'The importation, release, establishment, spread, and early impact on prey animals of the red fox *Vulpes vulpes* in Victoria and adjoining parts of south-eastern Australia'. *Zoologist* 35(3), 2011, pp. 463–533.

Aboriginal Affairs Victoria. *Lake Condah Heritage Management Strategy and Plan: Report by AAV in Conjunction with the Kerrup Jmara Elders Aboriginal Corporation.* Melbourne: Aboriginal Affairs Victoria, 1993.

Akerman, Kim. *From the Bukarikara: The Lore of the Southwest Kimberley through the Art of Butcher Joe Nangan.* Perth: UWA Publishing, 2020.

Allam, Lorena. *Bunha-Bunhanga: Aboriginal Agriculture in the South-East.* Adelaide: Art Gallery of South Australia, 2020.

Allen, Harry. 'The Bagundji of the Darling Basin: Cereal gatherers in an uncertain environment'. *World Archaeology* 5, 1974, pp. 309–22.

——'Aborigines of the western plains of New South Wales'. In Christine Haigh & Wendy Goldstein (eds), *The Aborigines of New South Wales*, Sydney: NSW National Parks & Wildlife Service, 1980, pp. 33–43.

Allen, Harry (ed.). *Australia: William Blandowski's Illustrated Encyclopedia of Aboriginal Australia.* Canberra: Aboriginal Studies Press, 2010.

Allen, Jim. 'The hunting Neolithic: Adaptations to the food quest in prehistoric Papua New Guinea'. In JVS Megaw (ed.), *Hunters, Gatherers and First Farmers beyond Europe: An Archaeological Survey*, Leicester: Leicester University Press, 1977, pp. 167–88.

Altman, Jon C. *Hunter-Gatherers Today: An Aboriginal Economy in North Australia.* Canberra: AIAS [AIATSIS], 1987.

Anderson, Christopher. *The Political and Economic Basis of Kuku-Yalanji Social History.* PhD thesis, University of Queensland, 1984.

——'Regional variation'. In Susan Bambrick (ed.), *The Cambridge Encyclopedia of Australia*, Cambridge: Cambridge University Press, 1994, pp. 65–8.

Anderson, Stephanie. *Pelletier: The Forgotten Castaway of Cape York.* Melbourne: Melbourne Books, 2009.

Andrews, Alan EJ (ed.). *Stapylton: With Major Mitchell's Australia Felix Expedition, 1836, Largely from the Journal of Granville William Chetwynd Stapylton.* Hobart: Blubber Head Press, 1986.

Arthur, William & Morphy, Frances (eds). *Macquarie Atlas of Indigenous Australia: Culture and Society through Space and Time.* North Ryde, NSW: Macquarie Library, 2005.

Attenbrow, Val. *Sydney's Aboriginal Past: Investigating the Archaeological and Historical Records*. 2nd edn. Sydney: UNSW Press, 2010.

Austin, Peter. *A Grammar of Diyari, South Australia*. Cambridge: Cambridge University Press, 1981.

——'Diyari language postcards and Diyari literacy'. *Aboriginal History* 10(2), 1986, pp. 175–92.

Baker, Richard. 'Traditional Aboriginal land use in the Borroloola region'. In Nancy M Williams & Graham Barnes (eds), *Traditional Ecological Knowledge: Wisdom for Sustainable Development*, Canberra: Centre for Resource and Environmental Studies, 1993, pp. 126–43.

Balme, Jane & Beck, Wendy. 'Earth mounds in south eastern Australia'. *Australian Archaeology* 42, 1996, pp. 39–51.

Bar-Yosef, Ofer & Kislev, Mordechai E. 'Early farming communities in the Jordan Valley'. In DR Harris & GC Hillman (eds), *Foraging and Farming: The Evolution of Plant Exploitation*, London: Unwin Hyman, 1989, pp. 632–42.

Barfield, Thomas (ed.). *The Dictionary of Anthropology*. Oxford: Blackwell Publishing, 1997.

Barlow, Simone & Horyniak, Ashlee. *Dark Emu in the Classroom: Teacher Resources for High School Geography*. Broome: Magabala Books, 2019.

Barrett, Charles. *Blackfellows of Australia*. Melbourne: Lawrence Kay for Pictorial Newspapers, a Sun book, c1936.

Barwick, Diane E. 'Changes in the Aboriginal population of Victoria, 1863–1966'. In DJ Mulvaney & J Golson (eds), *Aboriginal Man and Environment in Australia*. Canberra: ANU Press, 1971, pp. 288–315.

Basedow, Herbert. *The Australian Aboriginal*. Adelaide: FW Preece & Sons, 1925.

Basedow, Herbert (comp. & ed. David M Welch). *Notes on Some Native Tribes of Central Australia*. Virginia, NT: David M Welch, 2008.

Bates, Daisy M. *Aboriginal Perth and Bibbulmun Biographies and Legends*. Perth: Hesperian Press, 1992.

Bates, Daisy M (ed. Isobel White). *The Native Tribes of Western Australia*. Canberra: National Library of Australia, 1985.

Beattie, Susie (ed.). *Collins German Dictionary and Grammar*. Glasgow: HarperCollins, 2014.

Beck, Charlotte & Jones, George. 'Bias and archaeological classification'. *American Antiquity* 54(2), 1989, pp. 244–62.

Beckett, Jeremy. *Torres Strait Islanders: Custom and Colonialism*. Cambridge: Cambridge University Press, 1987.

Bellwood, Peter. *First Farmers: The Origins of Agricultural Societies*. Oxford: Blackwell, 2005.

Berndt, Catherine H & Berndt, Ronald M. *Pioneers and Settlers: The Aboriginal Australians*. Carlton, Vic.: Pitman, 1978.

——*Aborigines in Australian Society*. Carlton, Vic.: Pitman, 1985.

Berndt, Ronald M. 'The Walmadjeri and Gugadja'. In MG Bicchieri (ed.), *Hunters and Gatherers Today: A Socioeconomic Study of Eleven Such Cultures in the Twentieth Century*. New York: Holt, Rinehart & Winston, 1972, pp. 177–216.

——*Australian Aboriginal Religion* (the four fascicles in one). Leiden: EJ Brill, 1974.

Berndt, Ronald M & Berndt, Catherine H. *The World of the First Australians: An Introduction to the Traditional Life of the Australian Aborigines.* 1st edn. Sydney: Ure Smith, 1964.

——*Man, Land and Myth in North Australia: The Gunwinggu People.* Sydney: Ure Smith, 1970.

——*The World of the First Australians: Aboriginal Traditional Life, Past and Present.* 4th rev. edn with additions. Canberra: Aboriginal Studies Press, 1988.

Berndt, Ronald M & Berndt, Catherine H with John Stanton. *A World that Was: The Yaraldi of the Murray River and the Lakes, South Australia.* Melbourne: Melbourne University Press at The Miegunyah Press, 1993.

Beveridge, Peter. *The Aborigines of Victoria and Riverina.* Melbourne: ML Hutchinson, 1889.

——*The Aborigines of Victoria and Riverina.* Illustrated edn. Donvale, Vic.: Lowden, 2008.

Blainey, Geoffrey. *Triumph of the Nomads: A History of Ancient Australia.* 1st edn, 1975. Melbourne: Macmillan, 1983.

Black, Lindsay. *Cylcons: The Mystery Stones of the Darling River Valley.* Leeton, NSW: The author, 1942.

Blake, Barry J, Clark, Ian & Krishna-Pillay, Sharnthi H. 'Wathawurrung: The language of the Geelong-Ballarat area'. In BJ Blake (ed.), *Wathawurrung and the Colac Language of Southern Victoria,* Canberra: Pacific Linguistics, 1998, pp. 59–154.

Bleakley, JW. *The Aborigines of Australia: Their History, Their Habits, Their Assimilation.* Brisbane: Jacaranda Press, 1961.

'Boomerangs are booming'. *Australasian Post* 16, July 1964, pp. 16–17.

Bourke, Colin. 'Economics: Independence or welfare'. In C Bourke, E Bourke & B Edwards (eds), *Aboriginal Australia: An Introductory Reader in Aboriginal Studies,* Brisbane: University of Queensland Press, 1994, pp. 179–98.

Bourke, Colin, Bourke, Eleanor & Edwards, Bill (eds). *Aboriginal Australia: An Introductory Reader in Aboriginal Studies.* Brisbane: University of Queensland Press, 1994.

Bowler, Jim M, Price, David M, Sherwood, John E & Carey, Stephen P. 'The Moyjil site, south-west Victoria, Australia: Fire and environment in a 120,000-year coastal midden: Nature or people?' *Royal Society of Victoria* 130, 2018, pp. 71–93.

Bradley, John. 'The social, economic and historical construction of cycad palms among the Yanyuwa'. In B David, B Barker & IJ McNiven (eds), *The Social Archaeology of Australian Indigenous Societies,* Canberra: Aboriginal Studies Press, 2006, pp. 161–81.

Brazier, Rev. Amos. 'Report on Lake Condah Mission'. In *Aboriginal Mission Stations in Victoria,* Melbourne: Hawthorn Press, 1875. Quoted in Massola, 1970, p. 100.

Bryson, Ian. *Bringing to Light: A History of Ethnographic Filmmaking at the Australian Institute of Aboriginal and Torres Strait Islander Studies.* Canberra: Aboriginal Studies Press, 2002.

Builth, Heather. *Lake Condah Revisited: Archaeological Constructions of a Cultural Landscape*. Honours thesis, Faculty of Aboriginal and Torres Strait Islander Studies, University of South Australia, Adelaide, 1996. (Thesis abstract in *Australian Archaeology* 47, 1996, p. 68.)

——'Analysing Gunditjmara settlement: The use of an appropriate methodology'. In G Carver & K Stankowski (eds), *Proceedings of the Third National Archaeology Students' Conference*, Blackwood, SA: Southern Archaeology, 2002a, pp. 15–32.

——*The Archaeology and Socioeconomy of the Gunditjmara: A Landscape Analysis from Southwest Victoria, Australia*. PhD thesis, Department of Archaeology, Flinders University of South Australia, 2002b.

——'Mt Eccles lava flow and the Gunditjmara connection: A landform for all seasons'. *Proceedings of the Royal Society of Victoria* 116(1), 2004, pp. 165–84.

——*Ancient Aboriginal Aquaculture Rediscovered*. Saabrücken, Germany: Lambert Academic Publishing, 2014.

Builth, Heather et al. 'Environmental and cultural change on the Mt Eccles lava-flow landscapes of south-western Victoria, Australia'. *The Holocene* 18(3), 2008, pp. 413–24.

Cagan, Alex & Blass, Torsten. 'Identification of genomic variants putatively targeted by selection during dog domestication'. *BMC Evolutionary Biology* 16(10), 2016, pp. 1–13.

Cahir, Fred, Clark, Ian D & Clarke, Philip A. *Aboriginal Biocultural Knowledge in South-Eastern Australia: Perspectives of Early Colonists*. Clayton South, Vic.: CSIRO Publishing, 2018.

Campbell, Alastair H. 'Elementary food production by the Australian Aborigines'. *Mankind* 6, 1965, pp. 206–88.

Cane, Scott. *First Footprints: The Epic Story of the First Australians*. Sydney: Allen & Unwin, 2013.

Carey, Stephen P et al. 'The Moyjil site, south-west Victoria, Australia: Stratigraphic and geomorphic context'. *Royal Society of Victoria* 130, 2018, pp. 14–31.

Carver, Greg. *An Examination of Indigenous Australian Culturally Modified Trees in South Australia*. Honours thesis, Department of Archaeology, Flinders University of South Australia, 2002.

Casey, DA, Crawford, IM & Wright, RVS. 'The recognition, description, classification and nomenclature of Australian stone implements: The report of the Stone Implement Committee, 1967'. Australian National University, 1967. http://rubens.anu.edu.au/raid1/student_projects/tools/casey.html (accessed 8 February 2020).

Chase, Athol. 'Belonging to country: Territory, identity and environment in Cape York Peninsula, northern Australia'. In LR Hiatt (ed.), *Aboriginal Landowners*, Sydney: Oceania, 1984, pp. 104–28.

——'Domestication and domiculture in northern Australia: A social perspective'. In DR Harris & GC Hillman (eds), *Foraging and Farming: The Evolution of Plant Exploitation*, London: Unwin Hyman, 1989, pp. 42–78.

Chase, Athol & Sutton, Peter. 'Hunter-gatherers in a rich environment: Aboriginal coastal exploitation in Cape York Peninsula'. In A Keast (ed.), *Ecological Biogeography of Australia*, The Hague: W Junk, 1981, pp. 1817–52.

Chaseling, Wilbur S. *Yulengor: Nomads of Arnhem Land*. London: Epworth Press, 1957.

Chewings, Charles. *Back in the Stone Age: The Natives of Central Australia*. Sydney: Angus & Robertson, 1936.

Chivers, IH & Raulings, KA. *Australian Native Grasses: Key Species and Their Uses*. 4th edn. Cheltenham, Vic.: Native Seeds, 2009.

Christie, MF. *Aborigines in Colonial Victoria, 1835–86*. Sydney: Sydney University Press, 1979.

Clark, Ian D. *Aboriginal Languages and Clans: An Historical Atlas of Western and Central Victoria, 1800–1900*. Melbourne: Monash University, 1990.

Clarke, Anne. *Lake Condah Project, Aboriginal Archaeology*. Occasional Report No. 36. Victoria Archaeological Survey, 1991.

——'Romancing the stones: The cultural construction of an archaeological landscape in the Western District of Victoria'. *Archaeology in Oceania* 29, 1994, pp. 1–15.

Clarke, Philip. *Where the Ancestors Walked: Australia as an Aboriginal Landscape*. Sydney: Allen & Unwin, 2003.

——*Aboriginal People and Their Plants*. Dural, NSW: Rosenberg, 2007.

——*Discovering Aboriginal Plant Use: Journeys of an Australian Anthropologist*. Dural, NSW: Rosenberg, 2014.

Clarkson, C, Jacobs, Z, Marwick, B, Fullagar, R, Wallis, L, Smith, M, Pardoe, C. 'Human Occupation of northern Australia by 65,000 years ago'. *Nature* 547, 2017, pp. 306–10.

Clemens, Helen. 'The Aborigines: Hunter-gatherers: Why not agriculturists?' In Christine Haigh & Wendy Goldstein (eds), *The Aborigines of New South Wales*, Sydney: NSW National Parks & Wildlife Service, 1980, pp. 52–3.

Collins, David. *An Account of the English Colony in New South Wales: With Remarks on the Dispositions, Customs, Manners &c. of the Native Inhabitants of that Country: To which are Added, some Particulars of New Zealand; compiled, by permission, from the Mss. of Lieutenant-Governor King*. London: T Cadell Jun. & W Davies, 1798.

Context Pty Ltd. *Lake Condah Heritage Management Plan*. Report prepared for Victoria Archaeological Survey, 1993.

Cooper, A, Williams, A & Spooner, N. 'When did Aboriginal people first arrive in Australia?' *The Conversation*, 7 August 2018.

Cornish, Brian, Solomon, Lucien B & Walshe, Keryn. 'Surviving multi-trauma in the past'. *Australian and New Zealand Journal of Surgery* 80, 2010, pp. 912–16.

Coutts, Peter JF, Frank, RK & Hughes, P. 'Aboriginal engineers of the Western District, Victoria'. *Records of the Victorian Archaeological Survey* (Melbourne: Ministry for Conservation) 7, 1978.

Coutts, Peter JF, Henderson, P & Fullagar, R. 'Preliminary investigation of Aboriginal mounds in north-western Victoria'. *Records of the Victorian Archaeological Survey* (Melbourne: Ministry for Conservation) 9, 1979.

Coutts, Peter JF, Witter, D, McIlwraith, M & Frank, R. 'The mound people of western Victoria: A preliminary statement'. *Records of the Victorian Archaeological Survey* (Melbourne: Ministry for Conservation) 1, 1976.

Cribb, Roger, Walmbeng, Rex, Wolmby, Raymond & Taisman, Charles. 'Landscape as cultural artefact: Shell mounds and plants in Aurukun, Cape York Peninsula'. *Australian Aboriginal Studies* 2, 1988, pp. 60–73.

Cumpston, Nici & Jones, Jonathon. *Riverland: Yvonne Koolmatrie: A Retrospective of Ngarrindjeri Weaver Yvonne Koolmatrie.* Adelaide: Art Gallery of South Australia, 2015.

Cumpston, Nici, Jones, Jonathon & Allam, Lorena. *Bunha-Bunhanga: Aboriginal Agriculture in the South-East.* Santos Museum of Economic Botany, 13 September 2019 – 27 January 2020. Adelaide: Board of the Botanic Gardens and State Herbarium, 2019.

Dahlberg, Francis (ed.). *Woman the Gatherer.* New Haven: Yale University Press, 1981.

Davidson, DS. 'The chronology of Australian watercraft'. *Journal of the Polynesian Society* 44, 1935, pp. 1–63.

——'Footwear of the Australian Aborigines: Environmental vs cultural determination'. *Southwest Journal of Anthropology* 3, 1947, pp. 114–23.

Davidson, DS & McCarthy, FD. 'The distribution of stone implements in Western Australia'. *Anthropos* 52, 1957, pp. 390–458.

Davis, James. 'James Davis 1861: Evidence of Davis to the Select Committee into the Native Police and the Condition of the Aborigines generally'. *Queensland Ethnohistorical Transcripts* 1(1), 1982, pp. 11–19.

Davis, Stephen. *Man of All Seasons.* Sydney: Angus & Robertson, 1989.

Dawson, James. *Australian Aborigines: The Languages and Customs of Several Tribes of Aborigines in the Western District of Victoria, Australia.* Melbourne: George Robertson, 1881.

de Leaniz, Carlos G, Gajardo, G & Consuegra, S. 'From best to pest: Changing perspectives on the impact of exotic salmonids in the southern hemisphere'. *Systematics and Biodiversity* 8, 2010, pp. 447–59.

Denham, Tim. 'Traditional forms of plant exploitation in Australia and New Guinea: The search for common ground'. *Vegetation History and Archaeobotany* 17, 2008, pp. 245–8.

Denham, Tim, Donohue, Mark & Booth, Sara. 'Horticultural experimentation on northern Australia reconsidered'. *Antiquity* 83, 2009, pp. 634–48.

Dix, Warwick & Lofgren, Mance E. 'Kurumi: Possible Aboriginal incipient agriculture associated with a stone arrangement'. *Records of the Western Australian Museum* 3, 1974, pp. 73–7.

Dixon, RMW. 'Preface'. In JRB Love, *The Grammatical Structure of the Worora Language of North-western Australia,* Munich: Lincom Europa, 2000, p. 1.

——*Australian Languages: Their Nature and Development.* Cambridge: Cambridge University Press, 2002.

Dixon, RMW (comp. & ed.). *Words of Our Country: Stories, Place Names and Vocabulary in Yidiny, the Aboriginal Language of the Cairns-Yarrabah Region.* St Lucia, Qld: University of Queensland Press, 1991.

Dortch, CE & Hesp, PA. 'Rottnest Island artifacts and palaeosols in the context of Greater Swan Region prehistory'. *Journal of the Royal Society of Western Australia* 77, 1994, pp. 23–32.

Duncan-Kemp, Alice Monckton. *Our Sandhill Country: Nature and Man in South-western Queensland*. Sydney: Angus & Robertson, 1934.

Edwards, Robert. *Aboriginal Bark Canoes of the Murray Valley*. Adelaide: Rigby, 1972.

Edwards, WH. *An Introduction to Aboriginal Societies*. Tuggerah, NSW: Social Science Press, 1988.

Elkin, AP. 'Totemism in north-western Australia (the Kimberley division)'. *Oceania* 3, 1933, pp. 257–96.

——'Cult-totemism and mythology in northern South Australia'. *Oceania* 5, 1934, pp. 171–92.

——*The Australian Aborigines: How to Understand Them*. Sydney: Angus & Robertson, 1938.

——*The Australian Aborigines*. Sydney: Angus & Robertson, 1981.

Ellis, Bob. 'Iga: The tree that walked'. *South Australian Geographical Journal* 112, 2013, pp. 5–18.

Emison, WB, Porter, JW, Norris KC & Apps, GJ. 'Survey of the vertebrate fauna in the Grampians-Edenhope area of southwestern Victoria'. *Memoirs of the Victoria Museum* 39, 1978, pp. 281–365.

Etheridge, Robert (Jnr). 'On an Aboriginal implement believed to be undescribed, and supposed to be a hoe'. *Journal of the Linnean Society of New South Wales* 9, 1894, pp. 109–12.

——'The cylindro-conical and cornute stone implements of Western New South Wales and their significance'. *Memoirs of the Geological Survey of New South Wales, Ethnological Series* 2, 1916, pp. 1–42.

Flinders, Matthew. *A Voyage to Terra Australis*. Vol. 2. London: G & W Nicol, 1814.

Flood, Josephine. *Archaeology of the Dreamtime*. Sydney: Collins, 1983.

——*Archaeology of the Dreamtime: The Story of Prehistoric Australia and Its People*. Marleston, SA: JB Publishing, 2006.

Fu, Q et al. 'The genome sequence of a 45,000-year-old modern human from western Siberia'. *Nature*, 514(7523), 2014, pp. 445–9.

Gammage, Bill. *The Biggest Estate on Earth: How Aborigines Made Australia*. Sydney: Allen & Unwin, 2011.

Geering, Katrina. *Management Recommendations for Aboriginal Stone Houses at Allambie, near Macarthur, South West Victoria*. Report of the Victoria Archaeological Survey. Melbourne: Ministry of Planning and Environment, 1985.

Gerritsen, Rupert. *Australia and the Origins of Agriculture*. Oxford: British Archaeological Reports, 2008.

Geytenbeek, Brian & Geytenbeek, Helen. *Gidabal Grammar and Dictionary*. Canberra: AIAS, 1971.

Gilmore, Mary. *Old Days, Old Ways: A Book of Recollections*. Illustrated edn. Sydney: Angus & Robertson, 1986.

Glasgow, Kathleen. *Burarra–Gun-nartpa Dictionary with English Finder List*. Darwin: Summer Institute of Linguistics, 1994.

Glass, Amee Dorothy. *Cohesion in Ngaanyatjarra Discourse*. Darwin: Summer Institute of Linguistics, 1997.

Goddard, Cliff & Kalotas, Arpad (comps & eds). *Punu: Yankunytjatjara Plant Use: Traditional Methods of Preparing Foods, Medicines, Utensils and Weapons from Native Plants*. Sydney: Angus & Robertson, 1985.

Goodale, Jane C. *Tiwi Wives: A Study of the Women of Melville Island, North Australia*. Seattle: University of Washington Press, 1971.

Gostin, Olga & Chong, Alwin. 'Living wisdom: Aborigines and the environment'. In C Bourke, E Bourke & B Edwards (eds), *Aboriginal Australia: An Introductory Reader in Aboriginal Studies*, Brisbane: University of Queensland Press, 1994, pp. 123–39.

Gott, Beth. 'Murnong—*Microseris scapigera*: A study of a staple food of Victorian Aborigines'. *Australian Aboriginal Studies* 2, 1983, pp. 2–18.

Grant (Snr), Stan & Rudder, John. *A New Wiradjuri Dictionary*. Wagga Wagga, NSW: Restoration House, 2010.

Green, Jenny. *Central & Eastern Anmatyerr to English Dictionary*. Alice Springs: IAD Press, 2010.

Gregory, Augustus Charles. *Journals of Australian Explorations*, 1884. Project Gutenberg Australia website. http://gutenberg.net.au/ebooks14/1402621h.html (accessed 24 January 2020).

——'Appendix II: Memoranda on the Aborigines of Australia'. In H Ling Roth, 'On the origin of agriculture', *Journal of the Anthropological Institute of Great Britain and Ireland* 16, 1887, pp. 102–36 (pp. 131–3).

Gregory, Edmund. *Sketch of the Residence of James Morrill among the Aboriginals of Northern Queensland for Seventeen Years*. Brisbane: 'Courier' General Printing Office, 1866. http://handle.slv.vic.gov.au/10381/114510 (accessed 22 December 2019).

Grey, George. *Journals of Two Expeditions of Discovery in North-west and Western Australia during the Years 1837, 38 and 39*. 2 vols. London: T & W Boone, 1841.

Griffiths, Tom. 'Reading Bruce Pascoe', *Inside Story*, 26 November 2019. https://insidestory.org.au/reading-bruce-pascoe/ (accessed 20 January 2020).

Gsell, Francis Xavier. *"The Bishop with 150 Wives": Fifty Years as a Missionary*. Sydney: Angus & Robertson, 1955.

Hall, Jim & McNiven, Ian (eds). *Australian Coastal Archaeology*. Canberra: ANH Publications, Australian National University, 1999.

Hallam, Sylvia. *Fire and Hearth: A Study of Aboriginal Usage and European Usurpation in South-western Australia*. Canberra: AIAS, 1979.

——'Plant usage and management in southwest Australian Aboriginal societies'. In DR Harris & GC Hillman (eds), *Foraging and Farming: The Evolution of Plant Exploitation*, London: Unwin Hyman, 1989, pp. 136–51.

Hamby, Louise (ed.). *Twined Together = kunmadj njalehnjaleken*. Gunbalanya, NT: Injalak Arts & Crafts, 2005.

Hammerton, John A. *For King and Empire: Pictorial Souvenir of the Coronation*. London: Amalgamated Press, 1937.

Hardwick, Jeff. *Wadeye Kardu Murntak Warra: Old People Before: Plant Food Collecting and Processing*. Book 3 of *Traditional Knowledge, Language and Skills of the Aboriginal People from the Wadeye Region, NT, Australia*. Batchelor, NT: The author, 2019.

Harper, Walter. 'A description of certain objects of unknown significance, formerly used by some New South Wales tribes'. *Proceedings of the Linnean Society* 23, 1898, pp. 420–36.

Harris, David R. 'Subsistence strategies across Torres Strait'. In J Allen, J Golson & R Jones (eds), *Sunda and Sahul: Prehistoric Studies in Southeast Asia, Melanesia and Australia*, London: Academic Press, 1977, pp. 421–63.

Harris, David R & Hillman, Gordon C (eds). *Foraging and Farming: The Evolution of Plant Exploitation*. London: Unwin Hyman, 1989.

Head, Lesley. *Second Nature: The History and Implications of Australia as Aboriginal Landscape*. Syracuse, NY: Syracuse University Press, 2000.

Head, L, D'Costa, D & Edney, P. 'Pleistocene dates for volcanic activity in Western Victoria and implications for Aboriginal occupation'. In MAJ Williams, P de Deckker & AP Kershaw (eds), *The Cainozoic in Australia: A Reappraisal of the Evidence*. Special publication no. 18. Melbourne: Geological Society of Australia, 1991, pp. 302–8.

Heath, Jeffrey. *Nunggubuyu Myths and Ethnographic Texts*. Canberra: AIAS, 1980.

——*Nunggubuyu Dictionary*. Canberra: AIAS, 1982.

Hemming, Steven. 'An Aboriginal fish trap from Lake Condah, Victoria'. *Journal of the Anthropological Society of South Australia* 23(4), 1985, pp. 2–6.

Hercus, Luise & Clarke, Peter. 'Nine Simpson Desert wells'. *Archaeology in Oceania* 21, 1986, pp. 51–62.

Hesp, P, Murray-Wallace, CV & Dortch, CE. 'Aboriginal occupation on Rottnest Island, Western Australia, provisionally dated by aspartic acid racemisation assay of land snails to greater than 50 ka'. *Australian Archaeology* 49, 1999, pp. 7–12.

Hill, Marji & Barlow, Alex. *Black Australia: An Annotated Bibliography and Teacher's Guide to Resources on Aborigines and Torres Strait Islanders*. Canberra: AIAS, 1978.

Hinkson, Melinda. *Aboriginal Sydney: A Guide to Important Places of the Past and Present*. Canberra: Aboriginal Studies Press, 2001.

Hiscock, Peter. 'Revitalising artefact analysis'. In Tim Murray (ed.), *Archaeology of Aboriginal Australia: A Reader*, Sydney: Allen & Unwin, 1998, pp. 257–65.

——'Creators or destroyers? The burning questions of human impact in ancient Aboriginal Australia'. *Humanities Australia* 5, 2014, pp. 40–52.

Hiscock, Peter & Maloney, Tim. 'Australian lithic technology: Evolution, dispersion and connectivity'. In T Hodos (ed.), *The Routledge Handbook of Archaeology and Globalization,* Abingdon, UK: Routledge, 2017, pp. 301–80.

Holdaway, Simon & Stern, Nicola. *A Record in Stone: The Study of Australia's Flaked Stone Artefacts*. Melbourne & Canberra: Museum Victoria & AIATSIS, 2004.

Hope, Jeannette & Vines, Gary. *Brewarrina Aboriginal Fisheries Conservation Plan*. Unpublished report for NSW Department of Planning, Industry and Environment, 1994.

Horne, George. 'Aboriginal stone implements of south-eastern Victoria'. Paper, Australasian Association for the Advancement of Science, 1921.

Horne, G & Aiston, G. *Savage Life in Central Australia*. London: Macmillan, 1924.

Horton, David. *The Pure State of Nature: Sacred Cows, Destructive Myths and the Environment*. Sydney: Allen & Unwin, 2000.

Horton, David (ed.). *The Encyclopaedia of Aboriginal Australia: Aboriginal and Torres Strait Islander History, Society and Culture*. 2 vols. Canberra: Aboriginal Studies Press, 1994.

Howitt, AW. *The Native Tribes of South-east Australia*. London: Macmillan, 1904.

Hublin, J-J. 'How old are the oldest *Homo sapiens* in Far East Asia?'. *PNAS* 118(10), 2021.

Hunt, Harriet V, Moots, Hannah M & Matthews, Peter J. 'Genetic data confirms field evidence for natural breeding in a wild taro population (*Colocasia esculenta*) in northern Queensland, Australia'. *Genetic Resources and Crop Evolution* 60, 2013, pp. 1695–707.

Hunter, John. *An Historical Journal of the Transactions at Port Jackson and Norfolk Island*. London: John Stockdale, 1793.

Hynes, Ross & Chase, Athol. 'Plants, sites and domiculture: Aboriginal influence upon plant communities in Cape York Peninsula'. *Archaeology in Oceania* 17, 1982, pp. 38–50.

Irish, Paul. 'Changing perspectives in Australian archaeology, Part III: Hidden in plain view: The Sydney Aboriginal Historical Places Project'. *Technical Reports of the Australian Museum, Online* 23(3), 2011, pp. 31–44.

——*Hidden in Plain View: The Aboriginal People of Coastal Sydney*. Sydney: NewSouth Publishing, 2017.

Irvine, FR. 'Evidence of change in the vegetable diet of Australian Aborigines'. In AR Pilling & RA Waterman (eds), *Diprotodon to Detribalization: Studies of Change among Australian Aborigines*, East Lansing: Michigan State University Press, 1970, pp. 278–84.

Jones, Rhys. 'Fire-stick farming'. *Australian Natural History* 16(7), 1969, pp. 224–8.

——'The demography of hunters and farmers in Tasmania'. In DJ Mulvaney & J Golson (eds), *Aboriginal Man and Environment in Australia*. Canberra: ANU Press, 1971, pp. 271–87.

——'Tasmanian tribes'. Appendix in N Tindale, *Aboriginal Tribes of Australia: Their Terrain, Environmental Controls, Distribution, Limits, and Proper Names*, Berkeley: University of California Press, 1974, pp. 319–54.

——'The Neolithic, Palaeolithic and the hunting gardeners: Man and land in the antipodes'. In RP Suggate & MM Creswell (eds), *Quaternary Studies*, Wellington: Royal Society of New Zealand, 1975, pp. 21–34.

——'Ordering the landscape'. In I Donaldson & T Donaldson (eds), *Seeing the First Australians*, Sydney: George Allen & Unwin, 1985, pp. 181–209.

——'Mindjongork: Legacy of the firestick'. In DB Rose (ed.), *Country in Flames: Proceedings of the 1994 Symposium on Biodiversity and Fire in North Australia*, Canberra & Darwin: Department of the Environment, Sport and Territories / North Australia Research Unit, Australian National University, 1995, pp. 11–17.

Jones, Rhys & Meehan, Betty. 'Plant foods of the Gidjingali: Ethnographic and archaeological perspectives from northern Australia on tuber and seed exploitation'. In DR Harris & GC Hillman (eds), *Foraging and Farming: The Evolution of Plant Exploitation*, London: Unwin Hyman, 1989, pp. 120–35.

Kaberry, Phyllis. *Aboriginal Woman, Sacred and Profane*. London: George Routledge & Sons, 1939.

Kamminga, Johan. 'Over the edge: Functional analysis of Australian stone tools'. *Occasional Papers in Anthropology* (Anthropology Museum, University of Queensland), 12, 1982.

Keen, Ian. *Knowledge and Secrecy in an Aboriginal Religion*. Oxford: Clarendon Press, 1994.

——*Aboriginal Economy and Society: Australia at the Threshold of Colonisation*. Melbourne: Oxford University Press, 2004.

——'Constraints on the development of enduring inequalities in late Holocene Australia'. *Current Anthropology* 47, 2006, pp. 7–38.

——'Foragers or farmers: *Dark Emu* and the debate over Aboriginal agriculture'. *Anthropological Forum*, 2021, DOI: 10.1080/00664677.2020.1861538.

Kelly, Caroline Tennant. 'Tribes on Cherburg [*sic*] settlement, Queensland'. *Oceania* 5, 1935, pp. 461–73.

Kenyon, A. 'Stone structures of the Australian Aboriginal'. *Victorian Naturalist* 47(5), 1930, pp. 71–5.

Kimber, RG. 'Resource use and management in Central Australia'. *Australian Aboriginal Studies* 2, 1984, pp. 12–23.

King, Phillip Parker. *Narrative of a Survey of the Intertropical and Western Coasts of Australia Performed between the Years 1818 and 1822*. Vol. 1. London: John Murray, 1827.

Kleinert, Sylvia & Neale, Margo (eds). *The Oxford Companion to Aboriginal Art and Culture*. Melbourne: Oxford University Press, 2000.

Knight, James. 'A broken juin knife from Yandan Creek: Some implications'. *Archaeology in Oceania* 25(2), 1990, pp. 68–74.

Koppel, BD. *Disentangling Shell Middens: Exploring the Complexities of Deposit Formation and Transformation Using Amino Acid Racemisation*. PhD thesis, University of Wollongong, 2017.

Lamilami, Lazarus. *Lamilami Speaks: The Cry Went Up: A Story of the People of Goulburn Islands, North Australia*. Sydney: Ure Smith, 1974.

Lamshed, Max. 'Native's odyssey: Remarkable record of year's travel: 400 places named'. *The Advertiser* (Adelaide), 26 August 1932, p. 19.

——'Monty': *The Biography of CP Mountford*. Adelaide: Rigby, 1972.

Langton, Marcia. *Burning Questions: Emerging Environmental Issues for Indigenous Peoples in Northern Australia*. Darwin: Northern Territory University, 1998.

——*An Aboriginal Ontology of Being and Place: The Performance of Aboriginal Property Relations in the Princess Charlotte Bay Area of Eastern Cape York Peninsula, Australia*. PhD thesis, Macquarie University, 2005.

——'Earth, wind, fire, water: The social and spiritual construction of water in Aboriginal societies'. In B David, B Barker & IJ McNiven (eds), *The Social*

Archaeology of Australian Indigenous Societies, Canberra: Aboriginal Studies Press, 2006, pp. 139–60.

——'Prologue'. In Rachel Perkins & Marcia Langton (eds), *First Australians: An Illustrated History*, Melbourne: Melbourne University Press at The Miegunyah Press, 2008, pp. xxiv–ix.

——'Botanists, Aborigines and native plants on the Queensland frontier'. In J-C Verstraete & D Hafner (eds), *Land and Language in Cape York Peninsula and the Gulf Country*, Amsterdam: John Benjamins, 2016, pp. 221–40.

Latz, Peter. *Bushfires & Bushtucker: Aboriginal Plant Use in Central Australia*. Illustrated by Jenny Green. Alice Springs: IAD Press, 1995.

Latz, Peter & Griffin, GF. 'Changes in Aboriginal land management in relation to fire and to food plants in Central Australia'. In BS Hetzel & HJ Frith (eds), *The Nutrition of Aborigines in Relation to the Ecosystem of Central Australia*, Melbourne: CSIRO, 1978, pp. 77–85.

Lawrence, Roger. *Aboriginal Habitat and Economy*. Occasional Paper No. 6. Canberra: Department of Geography, Australian National University, 1968.

Layton, Robert. *Uluru: An Aboriginal History of Ayers Rock*. Canberra: AIAS, 1986.

Layton, Robert, Foley, Robert & Williams, Elizabeth. 'The transition between hunting and gathering and specialized husbandry of resources'. *Current Anthropology* 32, 1991, pp. 255–63.

Leacock, Eleanor & Lee, Richard. *Politics and History in Band Societies*. Cambridge: Cambridge University Press, 1982.

Lee, Jennifer R. *Ngawurranungurumagi Nginingawila Ngapangiraga: Tiwi–English Dictionary*. Nguiu, NT: Nguiu Nginingawila Literature Production Centre, 1993.

Lee, Richard B & DeVore, Irven. *Man the Hunter*. Chicago: Aldine, 1968.

Levitt, Dulcie. *Plants and People: Aboriginal Uses of Plants on Groote Eylandt*. Canberra: AIAS, 1981.

Littleton, Judith, Walshe, Keryn & Hodges, John. 'Burials and time at Gillman mound, Northern Adelaide, South Australia'. *Australian Archaeology* 77, 2013, pp. 38–51.

Long, Andrew. *Aboriginal Scarred Trees in New South Wales: A Field Manual*. Hurstville: NSW Department of Conservation, 2005.

Lourandos, Harry. 'Aboriginal settlement and land use in south-western Victoria: A report on current field work'. *Artefact* 1, 1976, pp. 174–93.

——'Aboriginal spatial organization and population: South western Victoria reconsidered'. *Archaeology and Physical Anthropology in Oceania* 12, 1977, pp. 202–25.

——'Change or stability? Hydraulics, hunter-gatherers and population in temperate Australia'. *World Archaeology* 11, 1980, pp. 245–66.

——'Intensification: A late Pleistocene-Holocene archaeological sequence from southwestern Victoria'. *Archaeology in Oceania* 18(2), 1983, pp. 81–94.

——*Continent of Hunter-Gatherers: New Perspectives in Australian Prehistory*. Cambridge: Cambridge University Press, 1997.

——'Review of *Australia and the Origins of Agriculture* by Rupert Gerritsen'. Australian Archaeological Association, 1 June 2010. https://australian archaeologicalassociation.com.au/journal/review-of-australia-and-the-origins-of-agriculture/ (accessed 27 February 2020).

Love, JRB. *The Grammatical Structure of the Worora Language of North-western Australia*. Munich: Lincom Europa, 2000.

Love, JRB (comp. & ed. by David M Welch). *Kimberley People: Stone Age Bushmen of Today*. Virginia, NT: David M Welch, 2009.

Lucas, Diane & Searle, Ken. *Walking with the Seasons in Kakadu*. Sydney: Allen & Unwin, 2005.

McCarthy, Frederick D. 'The grooved-conical stones of New South Wales'. *Memoirs of the Australian Museum (Mankind)* II, 1939, pp. 161–9.

——'Some unusual cylindro-conical stones from New South Wales and Java'. *Records of the Australian Museum* 21(5), 1944, pp. 257–60.

——*Aboriginal Tribes and Customs*. Petersham, NSW: Sanitarium Health Food Co., 1950.

——'Ecology, equipment, economy and trade'. In Helen Sheils (ed.), *Australian Aboriginal Studies: A Symposium of Papers Presented at the 1961 Research Conference*, Melbourne: Oxford University Press, 1963, pp. 171–91.

——*Australian Aboriginal Stone Implements*. 2nd edn. Sydney: Australian Museum, 1967.

——*Australian Aboriginal Stone Implements*. 2nd edn (revised). Sydney: Australian Museum Trust, 1976.

McCarthy, Frederick D, Bramwell, Elsie & Noone, HVV. 'The stone implements of Australia'. *Australian Museum Memoir* 9, 1946, pp. 1–94.

McConnel, Ursula H. 'The Wik-Munkan tribe of Cape York Peninsula, Part 1'. *Oceania* 1, 1930a, pp. 97–104.

——'The Wik-Munkan tribe, Part 2: Totemism'. *Oceania* 1, 1930b, pp. 181–295.

——'Science—but not from an armchair: Adventures in anthropology'. *Sydney Morning Herald Women's Supplement*, 8 March 1934, p. 17.

——'Native arts and industries on the Archer, Kendall and Holroyd rivers, Cape York Peninsula, north Queensland'. *Records of the South Australian Museum* 11, 1953, pp. 1–42, plates I–XVII.

——*Myths of the Munkan*. Melbourne: Melbourne University Press, 1957.

McCourt, Tom. *Aboriginal Artefacts*. Adelaide: Rigby, 1975.

McKelson, KR. *Studies in Karajarri*. Unpublished manuscript, AIATSIS, Canberra, 1989.

McKinlay, John. *McKinlay's Journal of Exploration in the Interior of Australia (Burke Relief Expedition)*. Melbourne: FF Bailliere, 1861.

Macknight, CC. *The Voyage to Marege': Macassan Trepangers in Northern Australia*. Melbourne: Melbourne University Press, 1976.

McNiven, Ian J et al. 'Dating Aboriginal stone-walled fishtraps at Lake Condah, southeast Australia'. *Journal of Archaeological Science* 39, 2012, pp. 268–86.

——'Phased redevelopment of an ancient Gunditjmara fish trap over the past 800 years: Muldoons trap complex, Lake Condah, southwestern Victoria'. *Australian Archaeology* 81, 2015, pp. 44–58.

——'The Moyjil site, south-west Victoria, Australia: Excavation of a last interglacial charcoal and burnt stone feature: Is it a hearth?' *Royal Society of Victoria* 130, 2018, pp. 94–116.

McNiven, Ian & Bell, IJ. 'Fishers and farmers: Historicising the Gunditjmara freshwater fishery, western Victoria'. *La Trobe Journal* 85, 2010, pp. 83–105.

McNiven, Ian J, Dunn, E, Crouch, J & Gunditj Mirring Traditional Owners Aboriginal Corporation. 'Kurtonitj stone house: Excavation of a mid-nineteenth century Aboriginal frontier site from Gunditjmara country, south east Victoria'. *Archaeology in Oceania* 52, 2017, pp. 171–97.

Maddock, Kenneth. *The Australian Aborigines: A Portrait of Their Society*. London: Allen Lane / The Penguin Press, 1972.

Maiden, JH. *The Useful Plants of Australia (including Tasmania)*. Sydney: Turner & Henderson, 1889.

Malinowski, Bronislaw. *Coral Gardens and Their Magic: A Study of the Methods of Tilling the Soil and of Agricultural Rites in the Trobriand Islands*. Vol. 1: *The Description of Gardening*. Vol. 2: *The Language of Magic and Gardening*. London: Allen & Unwin, 1935.

Martin, Sarah. *Eyre Peninsula and West Coast: Aboriginal Fish Trap Survey*. Unpublished report for Department of Environment and Planning, South Australia, 1988.

——*Inscribing the Plains: Constructed, Conceptualised and Socialized Landscapes of the Hay Plain, South Eastern Australia*. PhD thesis, Department of Archaeology and Anthropology, University of New England, 2007.

Massola, Aldo. 'The native fish traps at Toolondo, in the Wimmera'. *Victorian Naturalist* 79, 1962, pp. 162–6.

——'A history of Lake Condah Reserve: An address to the Society on Tuesday evening, 19th June, 1962', *Victorian Historical Magazine* 34(1), 1963, pp. 29–47.

——*Journey to Aboriginal Victoria*. Adelaide: Rigby, 1969.

——*Aboriginal Mission Stations in Victoria*. Melbourne: Hawthorn Press, 1970.

——*The Aborigines of South East Australia as They Were*. Melbourne: Heinemann, 1971.

Meehan, Betty. *Shell Bed to Shell Midden*. Canberra: AIAS, 1982.

Meehan, Betty & Jones, Rhys (eds). *Archaeology with Ethnography: An Australian Perspective*. Canberra: Department of Prehistory, Research School of Pacific Studies, Australian National University, 1988.

Megaw, JVS (ed.). *Hunters, Gatherers and First Farmers Beyond Europe: An Archaeological Survey*. Leicester: Leicester University Press, 1977.

Meggitt, Mervyn. *Desert People: A Study of the Walbiri Aborigines of Central Australia*. Sydney: Angus & Robertson, 1962.

Memmott, Paul. *Gunyah, Goondie + Wurley: The Aboriginal Architecture of Australia*. Brisbane: University of Queensland Press, 2007.

Memmott, Paul & Fantin, Shaneen. 'The study of indigenous ethno-architecture in Australia'. In Bruce Rigsby & Nicolas Peterson (eds), *Donald Thomson, the Man and Scholar*, Canberra: Academy of the Social Sciences in Australia, 2005, pp. 185–210.

Memmott, Paul & Horsman, Robyn. *A Changing Culture: The Lardil Aborigines of Mornington Island*. Student text. Wentworth Falls, NSW: Social Science Press, 1991.

Memmott, Paul, Round, Erich, Rosendahl, Daniel & Ulm, Sean. 'Fission, fusion and syncretism: Linguistic and environmental changes amongst the Tangkic people of the southern Gulf of Carpentaria, northern Australia'. In J-C Verstraete & D Hafner (eds), *Land and Language in Cape York Peninsula and the Gulf Country*, Amsterdam: John Benjamins, 2016, pp. 105–36.

Merlan, Francesca. *Caging the Rainbow: Places, Politics, and Aborigines in a North Australian Town*. Honolulu: University of Hawai'i Press, 1998.

Mitchell, Thomas L. *Three Expeditions into the Interior of Eastern Australia; with Descriptions of the Recently Explored Region of Australia Felix, and of the Present Colony of New South Wales*. 2 vols. London: T & W Boone, 1839.

——*Journal of an Expedition into the Interior of Tropical Australia in Search of a Route from Sydney to the Gulf of Carpentaria*. London: Longman, Brown, Green, & Longmans, 1848.

Monaghan, Paul. *Laying Down the Country: Norman B Tindale and the Linguistic Construction of the North-west of South Australia*. PhD thesis, University of Adelaide, 2003.

Moore, AMT. 'The transition from foraging to farming in Southwest Asia: Present problems and future directions'. In DR Harris & GC Hillman (eds), *Foraging and Farming: The Evolution of Plant Exploitation*. London: Unwin Hyman, 1989, pp. 620–31.

Moore, David R. 'Cape York Aborigines and Islanders of western Torres Strait'. In D Walker (ed.), *Bridge and Barrier: The Natural and Cultural History of Torres Strait*, Canberra: Australian National University, 1972, pp. 327–43.

——*Islanders and Aborigines at Cape York*. Canberra: AIAS, 1979.

Morgan, John. *The Life and Adventures of William Buckley: Thirty-two years a Wanderer Amongst the Aborigines of the then Unexplored Country around Port Phillip, now the Province of Victoria*. Hobart: Archibald MacDougall, 1852 / London: William Heinemann, 1967.

Mortimer, Lorraine. *Roger Sandall's Films and Contemporary Anthropology: Explorations in the Aesthetic, the Existential, and the Possible*. Bloomington: Indiana University Press, 2019.

Morton, John. 'The effectiveness of totemism: "Increase ritual" and resource control in Central Australia'. *Man* (New Series) 22, 1987, pp. 453–74.

Mountford, Charles P. *The Aborigines and Their Country*. Adelaide: Rigby, 1969.

Mulvaney, DJ. *The Prehistory of Australia*. London: Thames & Hudson, 1969.

Mulvaney, John & Kamminga, Johan. *Prehistory of Australia*. Sydney: Allen & Unwin, 1999.

Munday, Bruce. *Those Dry Stone Walls: Stories from South Australia's Stone Age*. Adelaide: Wakefield Press, 2012.

Myers, Fred. *Pintupi Country, Pintupi Self: Sentiment, Place, and Politics among Western Desert Aborigines*. Washington, DC: Smithsonian Institution Press, 1986.

Neidjie, Bill, Davis, Stephen & Fox, Allan. *Kakadu Man … Bill Neidjie*. Queanbeyan, NSW: Mybrood, 1985.

Nekes, Hermann & Worms, Ernest A. *Australian Languages (Micro-Bibliotheca Anthropos*, 10). Fribourg: Anthropos Institut, 1953. (2006 edn ed. William B McGregor, Berlin: Mouton de Gruyter.)

Nugent, Suzanne. *Sticks and Stones: A Functional Analysis of Aboriginal Spears from Northern Australia.* PhD thesis, University of Queensland, 2015.

O'Brien, Peter. *Bitter Harvest: The Illusion of Aboriginal Agriculture in Bruce Pascoe's Dark Emu.* 2nd edn. Sydney: Quadrant Books, 2020.

O'Connell, James F et al. 'When did *Homo sapiens* first reach Southeast Asia and Sahul?' *Proceedings of the National Academy of Sciences of the United States of America*, 115(34), 2018, pp. 8482–90.

O'Connor, Sue. 'The stone house structures of High Cliffy Island, north-west Kimberley, WA'. *Australian Archaeology* 25, 1987, pp. 30–9.

——'30,000 years of Aboriginal occupation: Kimberley, north-west Australia'. *Terra Australis* 14. Canberra: ANH Publications and Centre for Archaeological Research, Australian National University, 1999.

O'Keefe, Susan. *Over and Under: Geography and Archaeology of the Palm Islands and Adjacent Continental Shelf of North Queensland.* Master of Arts thesis, John Curtin University, 1991.

Orme, Bryony. 'The advantages of agriculture'. In JVS Megaw (ed.), *Hunters, Gatherers and First Farmers beyond Europe: An Archaeological Survey*, Leicester: Leicester University Press, 1977, pp. 41–9.

Palmer, Edward. 'On plants used by the natives of north Queensland, Flinders and Mitchell Rivers, for food, medicine, &c., &c.' *Journal and Proceedings of the Royal Society of New South Wales* 17, 1883, pp. 93–113.

Pardoe, Colin & Hutton, Dan. 'Aboriginal heritage as ecological proxy in south-eastern Australia: A Barapa wetland case study'. Preprint, *Australasian Journal of Environmental Management*, 2020. https://www.researchgate.net/publication/338688722_Aboriginal_heritage_as_ecological_proxy_in_south-eastern_Australia_A_Barapa_wetland_case_study (accessed 8 July 2020).

Pascoe, Bruce. *Dark Emu: Black Seeds: Agriculture or Accident?* Broome: Magabala Books, 2014.

——*Dark Emu: Aboriginal Australia and the Birth of Agriculture.* 2nd edn. Broome: Magabala Books, 2018.

——*Young Dark Emu: A Truer History.* Broome: Magabala Books, 2019a.

——*Salt: Selected Essays and Stories.* Melbourne: Black Inc., 2019b.

Peirce, Augustus Baker. *Knocking About: Being some Adventures of Augustus Baker Peirce in Australia.* Edited by Mrs A. Leatherbee, illustrated by the writer. New Haven, Connecticut: Yale University Press, 1924.

Pensalfini, Rob. *Jingulu Texts and Dictionary.* Canberra: Pacific Linguistics, 2011.

Perkins, Rachel & Langton, Marcia (eds). *First Australians: An Illustrated History.* Melbourne: Melbourne University Press at The Miegunyah Press, 2008.

Peterson, Jane. 'Book review: *Changing Natures: Hunter-Gatherers, First Farmers and the Modern World*, by Bill Finlayson & Graeme M Warren (Duckworth Debates in Archaeology)'. *AJA Online*, January 2012. https://www.ajaonline.org/book-review/1042 (accessed 13 February 2020).

Peterson, Nicolas. 'Demand sharing: Reciprocity and the pressure for generosity among foragers'. *American Anthropologist* 95, 1993, pp. 860–74.

——'The use of Spencer's photographic imagery'. In P Batty, L Allen & J Morton (eds), *The Photographs of Baldwin Spencer*, Melbourne: Melbourne University Press at The Miegunyah Press, 2005, pp. 154–89.

Peterson, Nicolas with Long, Jeremy. *Australian Territorial Organization: A Band Perspective*. Sydney: Oceania Monographs, 1986.

Piddington, Ralph. 'Totemic system of the Karadjeri tribe'. *Oceania* 4, 1932, pp. 373–400.

Poignant, Roslyn & Poignant, Axel. *Encounter at Nagalarramba*. Canberra: National Library of Australia, 1996.

Povinelli, Elizabeth. *Labor's Lot: The Power, History, and Culture of Aboriginal Action*. Chicago: Chicago University Press, 1993.

Prescott, JR & Sherwood, JE. 'Thermoluminescence ages for an unusual shell deposit at Point Ritchie, Warrnambool, Australia'. In JR Prescott (ed.), *Archaeometry: Australasian Studies*, Adelaide: Department of Physics and Mathematical Physics, University of Adelaide, 1988, pp. 61–9.

Presland, Gary (ed.). 'Journals of George Augustus Robinson January–March 1840'. *Records of the Victorian Archaeological Survey* 5, 1977a.

——'Journals of George Augustus Robinson March–May 1841'. *Records of the Victorian Archaeological Survey* 6, 1977b.

[Radcliffe-]Brown, AR. 'Three tribes of Western Australia'. *Journal of the Royal Anthropological Institute* 43, 1913, pp. 143–94.

Radcliffe-Brown, AR. 'Notes on totemism in eastern Australia'. *Journal of the Royal Anthropological Institute* 59, 1929, pp. 399–415.

Ray, Sidney H. *Reports of the Cambridge Anthropological Expedition to Torres Straits. Vol. III: Linguistics*. Cambridge: Cambridge University Press, 1907.

Reed, AW. *An Illustrated Encyclopedia of Aboriginal Life*. Sydney: AH & AW Reed, 1969.

Richards, Thomas. 'A late nineteenth-century map of an Australian Aboriginal fishery at Lake Condah'. *Australian Aboriginal Studies* 2, 2011, pp. 64–87.

Roberts, Rhys. *The Peramangk and Culturally Modified Trees: Significant Heritage Sites*. Honours thesis, Department of Archaeology, Flinders University of South Australia, 2000.

Rose, Frederick GG. *The Traditional Mode of Production of the Australian Aborigines*. Sydney: Angus & Robertson, 1987.

Rosengren, Neville. 'Lake Condah area: Lava surface features'. In Anne Clarke, *Lake Condah Project Aboriginal Archaeology*. Occasional Report No. 36, Victoria Archaeological Survey, 1991, pp. 90–103.

Roth, Walter E. 'North Queensland Ethnography Bulletin no. 16: Huts and shelters'. *Records of the Australian Museum* 8(1), 1910, pp. 55–66.

Sahlins, Marshall. *Stone Age Economics*. Chicago: Aldine, Atherton Inc., 1972.

Satterthwait, Leonn D. 'Aboriginal Australian net hunting'. *Mankind* 16, 1986, pp. 31–48.

Sharp, R Lauriston. 'The social organization of the Yir-Yoront tribe, Cape York Peninsula'. *Oceania* 4, 1934a, pp. 404–31.

——'Ritual life and economics of the Yir-Yoront tribe of Cape York Peninsula'. *Oceania* 5, 1934b, pp. 19–42.

——*The Social Anthropology of a Totemic System in North Queensland, Australia*. PhD dissertation. Harvard University, 1937.

——'People without politics'. In Verne F Ray (ed.), *Systems of Political Control and Bureaucracy in Human Societies*, Seattle: University of Washington Press, 1959, pp. 1–8.

——'Steel axes for stone-age Australians'. In TG Harding & BJ Wallace (eds), *Cultures of the Pacific: Selected Readings*, New York: The Free Press, 1970, pp. 385–96.

Shepherdson, IG (Ella). *Half a Century in Arnhem Land*. One Tree Hill, SA: Ella & Harold Shepherdson, 1981.

Sherwood, JE. 'The Moyjil site, south-west Victoria, Australia: Prologue: Of people, birds, shell and fire'. *Royal Society of Victoria* 130, 2018, pp. 7–13.

Sherwood, JE et al. 'The Moyjil site, south-west Victoria, Australia: Chronology'. *Royal Society of Victoria* 130, 2018, pp. 32–49.

Sherwood, JE, McNiven, IJ & Laurenson, Laurie. 'The Moyjil site, south-west Victoria, Australia: Shells as evidence of the deposit's origin'. *Royal Society of Victoria* 130, 2018, pp. 50–70.

Shnukal, Anna. *Broken: An Introduction to the Creole Language of Torres Strait*. Canberra: Pacific Linguistics, 1988.

Silcock, JL. 'Aboriginal translocations: The intentional propagation and dispersal of plants in Aboriginal Australia'. *Journal of Ethnobiology* 38(3), 2018, pp. 390–405.

Smith, Mike. *The Archaeology of Australia's Deserts*. Cambridge: Cambridge University Press, 2013.

Smith, MA, Ward, I, Moffat, I. 'How do we distinguish termite stone lines from artefact horizons? A challenge for geoarchaeology in tropical Australia'. *Geoarchaeology*, 35(2), 2020, pp. 232–42.

Smyth, LR. *The Aboriginal Population of Australia*. Aborigines in Australian Society no. 14. Canberra: ANU Press, 1980.

Smyth, R Brough. *The Aborigines of Victoria, with Notes Relating to the Habits of the Natives of Other Parts of Australia and Tasmania*. 2 vols. Melbourne: John Ferres, Government Printer, 1878.

Spencer, Baldwin. *Native Tribes of the Northern Territory of Australia*. London: Macmillan, 1914.

——'Aborigines'. In AW Jose & HJ Carter (eds), *The Australian Encyclopaedia, Vol. 1: A to LYS*, Sydney: Angus & Robertson, 1927, pp. 15–16.

Spencer, Baldwin & Gillen, FJ. *The Native Tribes of Central Australia*. London: Macmillan, 1899.

Stanner, WEH. 'The Daly River tribes: A report on field work in north Australia'. Part 1: *Oceania* 3, 1933, pp. 377–405; Part 2: *Oceania* 4, 1933, pp. 10–29.

——*On Aboriginal Religion*. Sydney: Oceania Monograph No. 11, 1963.

——*After the Dreaming: The 1968 Boyer Lectures*. Sydney: ABC, 1969.

——'Caliban discovered'. In WEH Stanner, *White Man Got No Dreaming: Essays 1938–1973*, Canberra: ANU Press, 1979 (1962), pp. 144–64.

Strahan, Ronald (ed.). *Mammals of Australia*. Washington, DC: Smithsonian Institution Press, 1995.

Strehlow, TGH. *The Sustaining Ideals of Aboriginal Societies*. Adelaide: Aborigines Advancement League Inc. of South Australia, 1956.

——'Culture, social structure, and environment in Aboriginal Central Australia'. In RM Berndt & CH Berndt (eds), *Aboriginal Man in Australia: Essays in Honour of Emeritus Professor AP Elkin*, Sydney: Angus & Robertson, 1965, pp. 121–45.

Sturt, Charles. *Narrative of an Expedition into Central Australia*. 2 vols. London: T & W Boone, 1849.

Sutton, Peter. *Wik: Aboriginal Society, Territory and Language at Cape Keerweer, Cape York Peninsula, Australia*. PhD thesis, University of Queensland, 1978.

——'Linguistic aspects of ethnobotanical research'. In B Rigsby & P Sutton (eds), *Contributions to Australian Linguistics*, Canberra: Pacific Linguistics, 1980, pp. 303–14.

——'Aboriginal ceremonial sites of New South Wales'. Unpublished report for NSW National Parks and Wildlife Service, 1985.

——'Material culture traditions of the Wik people, Cape York Peninsula'. *Records of the South Australian Museum* 27, 1994, pp. 31–52.

——*Wik-Ngathan Dictionary*. Adelaide: Caitlin Press, 1995.

——*Native Title in Australia: An Ethnographic Perspective*. Port Melbourne: Cambridge University Press, 2003.

——'Australian anthropologists and political action 1925–1960'. *Oceania* 79, 2009, pp. 202–17.

——'The logic of Wik camping, north Australia'. In Karen Hardy (ed.), *Archaeological Invisibility and Forgotten Knowledge. Conference Proceedings, Łódź, Poland, 5–7 September 2007*, Oxford: Archaeopress (British Archaeological Reports International Series 2183), 2010a, pp. 91–107.

——'Ursula McConnel's tin trunk: A remarkable recovery'. *Transactions of the Royal Society of South Australia* 134, 2010b, pp. 101–14.

——'Comment on Denham's *Beyond Fictions of Closure in Australian Aboriginal Kinship*'. *Mathematical Anthropology and Cultural Theory* 5(5), 2013a, pp. 1–5. http://mathematicalanthropology.org/Pdf/Sutton_MACT0513.pdf (accessed 20 January 2021).

——'Cross-comment on Denham's *Beyond Fictions of Closure in Australian Aboriginal Kinship*'. *Mathematical Anthropology and Cultural Theory* 5(6), 2013b, pp. 1–6. http://mathematicalanthropology.org/Pdf/Sutton2_MACT0513.pdf (accessed 20 January 2021).

——'Small language survival and large language expansion on a hunter-gatherer continent'. In Tom Güldemann, Patrick McConvell & Richard A Rhodes (eds), *The Language of Hunter-Gatherers*, Cambridge: Cambridge University Press, 2020, pp. 356–91.

Sutton, Peter (ed.). *Dreamings: The Art of Aboriginal Australia*. New York: Asia Society Galleries & George Braziller; Melbourne: Viking/Penguin; London: Viking, 1988.

Sutton, Peter et al. *Aak: Aboriginal Estates and Clans between the Embley and Edward Rivers, Cape York Peninsula*. Unpublished report (1000pp.). Adelaide: South Australian Museum, 1990.

Sutton, Peter & Hale, Ken. *Linguistic Organisation and Native Title: The Wik Case, Australia*. Canberra: Asia-Pacific Linguistics, 2021 (in press).

Sutton, Peter & Palmer, Arthur B. *Daly River (Malak Malak) Land Claim*. Darwin: Northern Land Council, 1980.

Sutton, Peter, Martin, David & von Sturmer, John. 'Supplementary site report'. Appendix 3 of *The Wik Peoples Native Title Determination Application QC94/3*. Unpublished report. Cairns: Cape York Land Council, 1997.

Sutton, Peter & Smyth, Dermot. 'Ethnobotanical data from Aurukun Shire, Queensland'. Mainframe computer printout, 1980, 149pp.

Taylor, Rebe. *Unearthed: The Aboriginal Tasmanians of Kangaroo Island*. Adelaide: Wakefield Press, 2000.

Thieberger, Nicholas & McGregor, William. *Macquarie Aboriginal Words: A Dictionary of Words from Australian Aboriginal and Torres Strait Islander Languages*. Macquarie University: The Macquarie Library, 1994.

Thomas, William. 'Brief account of the Aborigines of Australia Felix'. In TF Bride (ed.), *Letters from Victorian Pioneers: Being a Series of Papers on the Early Occupation of the Colony, the Aborigines, etc.* Melbourne: Trustees of the Public Library, 1898, pp. 65–100.

Thomson, Donald F. 'The hero cult, initiation and totemism on Cape York'. *Journal of the Royal Anthropological Institute* 63, 1933, pp. 453–537, plates XXVII–XXXVI.

——'A new type of fish trap from Arnhem Land, Northern Territory of Australia'. *Man* 38, 1938, pp. 193–8.

——'The seasonal factor in human culture illustrated from the life of a contemporary nomadic group'. *Proceedings of the Prehistoric Society* 5, 1939, pp. 209–21.

——*Economic Structure and the Ceremonial Exchange Cycle in Arnhem Land*. Melbourne: Macmillan, 1949.

——'The fishermen and dugong hunters of Princess Charlotte Bay'. *Walkabout* 22(11), 1956a, pp. 33–6.

——'The Aborigines of Australia'. In *Australian Junior Encyclopaedia, Vol. 1*. 2nd edn. Sydney: Australian Education Foundation, 1956b, pp. 70–97.

——*Kinship and Behaviour in North Queensland: A Preliminary Account of Kinship and Social Organisation on Cape York Peninsula*. Canberra: AIAS, 1972.

Thomson, Donald F (comp. Nicolas Peterson). *Donald Thomson in Arnhem Land*. Melbourne: Currey O'Neil, 1983.

Thorpe, WW. 'Ethnological notes, no. 1'. *Records of the Australian Museum* 16(5), 1928, pp. 241–53.

——'Ethnological notes, no. 4'. *Records of the Australian Museum* 18(6), 1932, pp. 302–11.

Tibby, J et al. 'Environmental change and variability in southwestern Victoria: Changing constraints and opportunities for occupation and land use'. In Bruno David, Bryce Barker & Ian J McNiven (eds), *The Social Archaeology of Australian Indigenous Societies*, Canberra: Aboriginal Studies Press, 2006, pp. 254–69.

Tindale, Norman B. 'Culture succession in south eastern Australia from late Pleistocene to the present'. *Records of the South Australian Museum* 13(1), 1957, pp. 1–49.

——'Ecology of primitive aboriginal man in Australia'. In A Keast, RL Crocker & CS Christian (eds), *Biogeography and Ecology in Australia*, Den Haag: Junk, 1959, pp. 37–51.

——'The Pitjandjara'. In MG Bicchieri (ed.), *Hunters and Gatherers Today: A Socioeconomic Study of Eleven Such Cultures in the Twentieth Century*, New York: Holt, Rinehart & Winston, 1972, pp. 217–68.

——*Aboriginal Tribes of Australia: Their Terrain, Environmental Controls, Distribution, Limits, and Proper Names*. Berkeley: University of California Press, 1974.

——'Adaptive significance of the Panara or grass seed culture of Australia'. In RVS Wright (ed.), *Stone Tools as Cultural Markers*, Canberra: AIAS, 1977, pp. 345–7.

Tindale, Norman B & Lindsay, HA. *Aboriginal Australians*. Brisbane: Jacaranda Press, 1963.

Tobler, R et al. 'Aboriginal mitogenomes reveal 50,000 years of regionalism in Australia'. *Nature* 544, 2017, pp. 180–4.

Tonkinson, Robert. *The Mardu Aborigines: Living the Dream in Australia's Desert*. Fort Worth, TX: Holt, Rinehart & Winston, 1991.

Turpin, Myfany & Ross, Alison. *Kaytetye to English Dictionary*. Alice Springs: IAD Press, 2012.

Vaarzon-Morel, Petronella (ed.). *Warlpiri Women's Voices (Warlpiri Karnta Karnta-kurlangu Yimi): Our Lives, Our History*. Alice Springs: IAD Press, 1995.

Vaarzon-Morel, Petronella & Gabrys, Kasia. 'Fire on the horizon: Contemporary Aboriginal burning issues in the Tanami Desert, Central Australia'. *GeoJournal* 74, 2009, pp. 465–76.

Veth, Peter, Myers, Cecilia, Heaney, Pauline & Ouzman, Sven. 'Plants before farming: The deep history of plant-use and representation in the rock art of Australia's Kimberley region'. *Quaternary International* 30, 2016, pp. 1–20.

Waddy, Julie. *Classification of Plants & Animals from a Groote Eylandt Aboriginal Point of View*. 2 vols. Darwin: ANU North Australia Research Unit, 1988.

Walmbeng, Rex. 'Mythological affinities of shell mounds'. Appendix B in Roger Cribb, Rex Walmbeng, Raymond Wolmby & Charles Taisman, 'Landscape as cultural artefact: Shell mounds and plants in Aurukun, Cape York Peninsula'. *Australian Aboriginal Studies* 2, 1988, pp. 72–3.

Walsh, Fiona Jane. 'Review of R Gerritsen, *Australia and the Origins of Agriculture* (2008)'. *GeoJournal* 74, 2009, pp. 499–501.

Walshe, Keryn. 'Investigator Isles Expedition 2006: Two stone implements from Flinders Island, South Australia'. *Transactions of the Royal Society of South Australia* 132(2), 2008, pp. 45–50.

——'Archaeological evidence for a sealer's and wallaby hunter's skinning site on Kangaroo Island, South Australia'. *Journal of Island and Coastal Archaeology* 9(1), 2014, pp. 130–43.

——'Echidna to wolf's head: A nineteenth-century sealer's ornament from Kangaroo Island, South Australia'. *The Artefact* 39, 2018, pp. 5–8.

Warner, W Lloyd. *A Black Civilization: A Social Study of an Australian Tribe*. New York: Harper & Brothers, 1937 (2nd edn. 1958).

Webb, Leonard J. *Guide to the Medicinal and Poisonous Plants of Queensland*. Commonwealth of Australia: Council for Scientific and Industrial Research Bulletin No. 232. Melbourne: JJ Gourley, Government Printer, 1948.

Wells, Ann E. *Milingimbi: Ten Years in the Crocodile Islands of Arnhem Land*. Sydney: Angus & Robertson, 1963.

Wesson, Jill. *Excavations of Stone Structures in the Condah area, Western Victoria*. Masters preliminary thesis, La Trobe University, Melbourne, 1981.

Westell, Craig & Wood, Vivienne. 'An introduction to earthen mound sites of South Australia'. *Journal of the Anthropological Society South Australia* 38, 2014, pp. 30–65.

Wettenhall, Gib, with the Gunditjmara people. *The People of Budj Bim: Engineers of Aquaculture, Builders of Stone House Settlements and Warriors Defending Country*. Heywood, Vic.: em PRESS Publishing, 2010.

White, Peter. 'New Guinea and Australian prehistory: The "Neolithic" problem'. In DJ Mulvaney & J Golson (eds), *Aboriginal Man and Environment in Australia*. Canberra: ANU Press, 1971, pp. 182–95.

——'Revisiting the "Neolithic problem" in Australia'. *Records of the Western Australian Museum* 79, 2011, pp. 86–92.

Whitehurst, Rose. *Noongar Dictionary: Noongar to English and English to Noongar*. Bunbury, WA: Noongar Language and Culture Centre, 1992.

Williams, AN et al. 'Sea-level change and demography during the last glacial termination and early Holocene across the Australian continent'. *Quaternary Science Reviews* 182, 2018, pp. 144–54.

Williams, Elizabeth. 'Documentation and archaeological investigation of an Aboriginal "village" site in south western Victoria'. *Aboriginal History* 8, 1984, pp. 173–88.

——*Wet Underfoot? Earth Mound Sites and the Recent Prehistory of South West Victoria*. PhD thesis, Australian National University, 1985.

——'Complex hunter-gatherers: A view from Australia'. *Antiquity* 61(232), 1987, pp. 310–21.

——*Complex Hunter-Gatherers: A Late Holocene Example from Temperate Australia*. Oxford: British Archaeological Reports, 1988.

Williams, MAJ, Spooner, NA, McDonnell, K, O'Connell, JF. 'Identifying disturbance in archaeological sites in tropical northern Australia: Implications for previously proposed 65,000-year continental occupation date'. *Geoarchaeology*, 36, 2021, pp. 92–108.

Williams, Nancy M & Hunn, Eugene S. *Resource Managers: North American and Australian Hunter-Gatherers*. Boulder, CO: Westview Press, 1982.

Williams, RM. *Song in the Desert*. Sydney: Angus & Robertson, 1998.

Winterbotham, Lindsey Page. 'The Gaiarbau story: Some native customs and beliefs of the Jinibara tribe as well as those of some of their neighbours in south-east Queensland'. In G Langevad (ed.), *Queensland Ethnohistorical Transcripts* 1(1), 1982, pp. 20–134. Brisbane: Archaeology Branch, Queensland.

Wiseman, Judith. *Thomson Time: Arnhem Land in the 1930s: A Photographic Essay*. Melbourne: Museum of Victoria, 1996.

Wolfe, Patrick. 'Robert Manne, the apology, and genocide'. *The Monthly* 94, 2008, pp. 31–3.

Wood, Ray. '*Wangga*: The linguistic and typological evidence for the sources of the outrigger canoes of Torres Strait and Cape York Peninsula'. *Oceania* 88, 2018, pp. 202–31.

Wood, R et al. 'Towards an accurate and precise chronology for the colonization of Australia: The example of Riwi, Kimberley, Western Australia'. *PLOS One* 11(9), 2016.

Worsnop, Thomas. *The Prehistoric Arts, Manufactures, Works, Weapons, etc., of the Aborigines of Australia*. Adelaide: CE Bristow, Government Printer, 1897.

Wright, Richard VS (ed.). *Stone Tools as Cultural Markers: Change, Evolution and Complexity*. Canberra: AIAS, 1977.

Yen, DE. 'The domestication of environment'. In DR Harris & GC Hillman (eds), *Foraging and Farming: The Evolution of Plant Exploitation*, London: Unwin Hyman, 1989, pp. 55–75.

Yibarbuk, Dean. 'Introductory essay: Notes on traditional use of fire on upper Cadell River'. In Marcia Langton, *Burning Questions: Emerging Environmental Issues for Indigenous Peoples in Northern Australia*, Darwin: Northern Territory University, 1998, pp. 1–6.

Index

Note: Illustrations are indicated by an *i* following the page number